KU-379-301

Cross-examination
in Criminal Trials

To Anthony

# Cross-examination in Criminal Trials

**Marcus Stone,** MA, LLB
Advocate, Sheriff of Lothian and Borders at
Linlithgow and formerly Sheriff of Glasgow
and Strathkelvin at Glasgow

**Butterworths**
London
1988

| United Kingdom | Butterworth & Co (Publishers) Ltd, 88 Kingsway, LONDON WC2B 6AB and 61A North Castle Street, EDINBURGH EH2 3LJ |
| --- | --- |
| Australia | Butterworths Pty Ltd, SYDNEY, MELBOURNE, BRISBANE, ADELAIDE, PERTH, CANBERRA and HOBART |
| Canada | Butterworths Canada Ltd, TORONTO and VANCOUVER |
| Ireland | Butterworth (Ireland) Ltd, DUBLIN |
| Malaysia | Malayan Law Journal Sdn Bhd, KUALA LUMPUR |
| New Zealand | Butterworths of New Zealand Ltd, WELLINGTON and AUCKLAND |
| Singapore | Butterworth & Co (Asia) Pte Ltd, SINGAPORE |
| USA | Butterworths Legal Publishers, ST PAUL, Minnesota, SEATTLE, Washington, BOSTON, Massachusetts, AUSTIN, Texas and D & S Publishers, CLEARWATER, Florida |

All rights reserved, No part of this publication may be reproduced or transmitted in any form or by any means (including photocopying and recording) without the written permission of the copyright holder except in accordance with the provisions of the Copyright Act 1956 (as amended) or under the terms of a licence issued by the Copyright Licensing Agency Ltd, 33–34 Alfred Place, London, England WC1E 7DP. The written permission of the copyright holder must also be obtained before any part of this publication is stored in a retrieval system of any nature. Applications for the copyright holder's written permission to reproduce, transmit or store in a retrieval system any part of this publication should be addressed to the publisher.

Warning: The doing of an unauthorised act in relation to a copyright work may result in both a civil claim for damages and criminal prosecution.

© Butterworth & Co (Publishing) Ltd 1988

A CIP Catalogue record for this book is available from the British Library.

ISBN 0 406 10505 7

Typeset by Cotswold Typesetting Ltd, Gloucester
Printed in Great Britain by Billing & Sons Ltd, Worcester

# Foreword

Even in these days of undemonstrative advocacy, there are some great cross-examiners whose every word and movement command attention and frequently create tension. There are some pretty awful ones as well. Not all the latter are to be found amongst the young and inexperienced, just as not all the former are senior and supposedly leading advocates. The worst cross-examination I have ever heard was by a silk who manfully, almost single-handed, managed to secure the conviction of his client in the teeth of no evidence by getting him to stand up in the dock whilst he asked the frightened eyewitness, who had hardly lifted his eyes from the floor since he had come into court, 'That's not the man who pointed the gun at you, is it?'—with the inevitable result.

That which distinguishes the best cross-examiners from the rest is the confidence which they inspire in their knowledgeable audience that they obviously know what they are doing and why and have thought about how to achieve their objective. They do not cross-examine on a wish and a prayer; they are not pursuing the merely desirable at the expense of the necessary; they have decided what is attainable; they understand how witnesses work and the fallibility of human recollection and accuracy under stress and they have that inexplicable sixth sense which enables them to 'feel' the witness long before the tribunal can recognise what is happening.

It is unlikely that anyone has ever taught them their skills. They have learnt by observation of their elders and their contemporaries, and those skills upon which they so greatly depend have been long in coming.

It is incredible that it has taken so long for the legal professions, here and abroad, to acknowledge that it is possible—and, even, desirable—to teach the skills of advocacy; and regrettable that, even now, so much of the teaching is unstructured, frequently idiosyncratic and, in many cases, an uncomfortable reflection of the blind leading the blind.

So far as I am aware, Marcus Stone is the first person in the United Kingdom to essay a comprehensive study of cross-examination, to identify the skills that are involved and to explain them and, above all, to place them in the context of the whole trial process. The latter is so important: cross-examination, particularly a successfully destructive cross-examination, can too frequently become an end in itself, with the triumphant advocate forgetting the purpose of the whole operation.

The most crucial lesson which this book teaches, in various ways but all the way through, is encapsulated at the beginning of chapter 8: "a cross-examiner must know what he can do, how he can do it, and the probable effects of doing it . . . ." With cross-examination as with every other element of his tasks, the advocate must be master of his field, not a mere wandering, semi-informed hopeful, striking here, striking there, wishing but seldom achieving. And his field includes understanding and compassion for human weaknesses. There is more than an echo of Birkett's exposition of the good advocate in this book. In his Presidential Address to the Holdsworth Club in 1945, Birkett said:

It is well if the advocate is possessed of a quick mind, alert to seize the unexpected opportunity, to adapt himself to the sudden changes which occur in the conduct of a case . . . But more important than the quick mind is the understanding heart, the insight into human nature, the natural sympathy with all sorts and conditions of men, the intuitive recognition of what the particular situation demands.

The lesson that understanding witnesses and why they may depart from total accuracy and recall is needed, is vitally important to the cross-examiner. Even genuine human recollection is fallible. Marcus Stone sets out to teach that lesson to the aspiring advocate: a cynical old hand would wish that some judges and even more magistrates would learn that lesson as well.

As he takes us through cross-examination, its purpose(s), its place in the trial process, the material upon which it works, the rules by which it must be conducted, its relationship with examination-in-chief, its different techniques and its problems, Marcus Stone does more than instruct the beginner. He has made at least one senior think again about what he is doing and why—and how he can do it better. Almost every page is illuminated by his long and varied experience, by his learning, by his insight and by his love of his profession. The only pity (for an English barrister) is that it has taken a Scot to do this—even if he is a friend.

The Temple                                      Michael Hill, QC
September 1988

# Preface

It is remarkable that on the crucial subject of cross-examination pen has not been put to paper, whereas impressive-looking volumes flaunt dubious knowledge, or even ignorance, of less important human affairs.

Everyone sees advocacy, the art of persuasion in court, as a profession. Nearly all criminal trials turn on issues of fact, where cross-examination is the essence of adversarial confrontation. Yet although advocates may not know the elements of the art, they are turned out as qualified for professional practice. University courses in criminal law, procedure and evidence ignore the central fact-finding process and do not develop the skill which is required, especially in cross-examination. Post-graduate training in advocacy is still elementary and unsystematic.

Fact-finding depends on whether evidence is held to be truthful, untruthful, accurate or mistaken. This field and the techniques of presenting, testing or challenging evidence, require study. Practitioners deal with it every day, but it is alien to the academic teaching of law. If advocacy is a profession, and not just an activity for amateurs or born geniuses, it should be an integral part of legal training, and qualification.

So far as skill in cross-examination is concerned, a barrier is the lack of any specialized, systematic and comprehensive textbook on the subject in British legal literature. Isolated and anecdotal chapters on the topic in a few books on advocacy do not meet the need. It is the aim of this work to do so.

Its objective is to provide a foundation for developing practical skill in cross-examination. Like so many skills, this one depends on natural aptitude, learning the techniques, practical experience in applying them and noting the results.

In anticipation of objections, it is stressed that this book is not in competition with either natural ability nor experience in the courts, both of which are essential. It offers a basis for maximizing them.

The view that ability in cross-examination is just a natural gift, and that there is nothing to learn, is untenable. Of course innate talent may settle whether a pianist, pilot or advocate will surpass ordinary proficiency and attain levels of virtuosity—but not straight from school without training or experience! Moreover, if advocacy is just a matter of aptitude, how does a professional differ from a gifted amateur? Often, what counts is not what is inherited, but how it is used—a matter of motivation and effort.

Of course, personal qualities affect style but all styles are found in successful advocates.

Would even a genius in cross-examination agree that he was as good at the start as at the end of a long and successful career? If not, what did he learn in between? This book sets out to provide some of the answers. Most advocates absorb such information naturally over a long period. The present material is the result of studying many thousands of witnesses under cross-examination, throughout 40 years at the bar and on the bench.

But court experience is not enough per se. Some advocates never seem to learn. Experience just reinforces their poor methods. Even for able advocates, experience is enhanced if it is based on clear insight into what goes on, not just intuitive leaps at witnesses. If advocacy is not calculating, what is?

If cross-examination is a mystique, beyond explanation or learning, this is odd. Other complex intellectual processes can be analysed, e g, logic, semantics, psychotherapy, the art of negotiation, and so on. Also, advocates and courts analyse the significance of cross-examination constantly. But the best answer to such mysticism is the validity of the present analysis.

Cross-examination is seen here not in isolation, but as an integral part of advocacy and of the whole trial process, distinguishing its constructive and destructive functions. Challenging the witness or the evidence are considered separately, in detail. Emphasis is placed on the importance of contradicting evidence by other evidence in support of destructive cross-examination.

The context of the trial is explained, including the nature of the real issues of fact, how errors arise in testimony, and the various forms of deception which play a major role in criminal trials. A full account is given of examination-in-chief and re-examination, with recommendations for speeches in relation to cross-examination.

Questions of law, including the rules of evidence, being outwith the subject, are omitted. There are many excellent books on the law of evidence which may be consulted for full statements of the law where required.

Simply by reading a book one cannot learn to become a good cross-examiner any more than one can learn to swim. Practice and experience are required. But a sound analysis is a basis for intelligent and directed development of skill by practice. Various techniques and tactics may be tried out, and maximum benefit can be derived from experience, by reflecting on the results.

Efficiency is the immediate goal for a cross-examiner. In the vast majority of trials, especially in summary trials, virtuosity in cross-examination would offer little or no advantage over the professional competence which is attainable by any advocate of reasonable aptitude.

The development of skill would including a growing understanding of witnesses, increasing familiarity with recurrent problems and patterns of evidence and their weaknesses, a better grasp of typical court situations, more insight into the probable views taken by courts of different kinds of evidence, and practice in using a variety of techniques in different circumstances.

The text covers cross-examination by either the prosecution or defence counsel or solicitors in both jury trials and summary trials. Obviously, it also applies, substantially, to civil courts, although no reference is made to this.

Cross-examination is based on processes in human nature which are not confined to any jurisdiction. The present material applies to any adversarial system of criminal procedure, i e, all criminal courts conducted in the English language.

This book is intended mainly but not exclusively for those who are preparing for or are engaged in criminal advocacy. At the outset, guidance is essential, but even experienced advocates should benefit from a systematic analysis of the whole field of cross-examination.

Lay magistrates rarely have court experience on appointment and gain it only slowly by intermittent service on the bench. This book should increase their insight into the trial process and assist them in fact-finding.

For police officers who are regularly subjected to vigorous cross-examination, the analysis should add to their grasp of the process. It will also enable them to foresee challenges to evidence which they are assembling, and when reinforcement is desirable.

Mysteries should be removed by the text for many persons connected with the courts, other than lawyers, e g, expert witnesses, doctors, psychiatrists, forensic scientists, psychologists, social workers or journalists. Their roles should become more meaningful by a better appreciation of the context.

Since technicalities, especially of the law, are avoided, the book is suitable for general readers who are interested in the subject of the criminal process for its own sake. They may also develop a personal interest in it if they become involved as jurors, witnesses or otherwise.

Edinburgh
August 1988

Marcus Stone

# Acknowledgments

In a book like this, where the text, but not the subject, is innovative, the opinions of distinguished readers are invaluable. Even a lack of comment may suggest that some hazard has been avoided. But when encouragement and detailed advice, are added, gratitude must be even greater.

I have to thank Michael Hill, QC for his Foreword, as well as His Honour Judge McLean and Peter G B McNeil, QC, PhD both for their most valuable comments and for what they omitted. However, the responsibility for any inadequacies is mine alone.

# Contents

# CHAPTER 1

# Cross-examination: preliminary

I The rules of evidence
II Ethics
III The role of cross-examination

Cross-examination must be understood in its context, which includes the rules of evidence, ethics and other trial processes.

## I THE RULES OF EVIDENCE

An advocate on his feet, should know, instantly, which way he can go. This is no time to consult law books. The rules of admissibility should be second nature. Mastery of the law of evidence is essential.

But cross-examination, as a persuasive art, starts where the law of evidence stops. The techniques and tactics of cross-examination presented here are based on human nature, not on the law of evidence. They are valid in any English-speaking court, whatever the legal framework.

For the rules of evidence relating to cross-examination in any given country, reference should be made to standard texts. Some rules which apply in English courts are mentioned here, but only to explain points of practice in cross-examining—not to state the law. No case decisions are cited.

## II ETHICS

An advocate's conduct is regulated by explicit professional codes, judicial dicta, tradition and practice. A few principles are stated here.

The ethics of advocacy impose limits on cross-examination; victory at all costs is unacceptable. Improper conduct noted in court may lead to objection, criticism, reprimand, exclusion of evidence, or worse. Impropriety discovered after the trial may also have repercussions.

1

Essentially, the ethics of advocacy maintain personal integrity in an adversarial conflict.

An advocate's duty is to present his case. He should do this as forcefully as he can, without becoming personally identified with it. He should neither form, nor express in court, any opinion on it, even if an impression of belief is conveyed.

A cardinal principle, from which others flow, is that an advocate must not knowingly mislead or deceive the court. By the nature of things, one side of the case will normally be based on inaccurate or false evidence. But the advocate is not accountable for this, provided that his presentation is sincere. This means that he must only assert facts responsibly on the basis of information, not invention, and he must not challenge, or try to disprove, facts which he knows to be accurate.

All advocates have the above duties, but a prosecutor, as a public official, has additional obligations, e g to disclose any material evidence which may help the defence. He should present his case with the aim of assisting the court to reach a true verdict, and not just to win.

His cross-examination, especially of the accused, should be fair and reasonable, and should be based on his information both for and against guilt. It should not be exaggerated or distorted to secure a conviction. Where he can competently attack an accused's character, he should only do this if it is necessary, and not just to create prejudice.

The defence have more latitude. They need not disclose adverse evidence in order to assist the Crown.

In cross-examination, the defence advocate must not suggest facts without grounds, e g that someone else was the offender. He may test, but must not attack, Crown evidence for inaccuracy, e g by denying the crime, unless this is based on his information. He must not devise a defence.

Normally, a defence advocate has no incriminating information and is free to contest anything which differs from what he was told. Otherwise, ethical problems may arise. He could still conduct a legal type of defence independently of the facts, e g by objections to the admissibility of crucial evidence or by a no case submission.

# III    THE ROLE OF CROSS-EXAMINATION

A cross-examiner's practical decisions should be based on a realistic grasp of what he can hope to achieve. Exaggerated or mistaken views of the role of cross-examination can be a handicap.

## A The adversarial system

The adversarial system of court procedure consists of a conflict between the prosecution and the defence, unlike a state-directed enquiry into facts. The parties decide what evidence to collect, present, agree or dispute. The court's role is limited to judgment. The advocate's partiality contributes to impartial justice. The Bar and Bench co-operate to this end.

Less dynamic procedure could be imagined, where the evidence of witnesses is not challenged directly, but is simply compared and assessed by the court—rather like the Eurovision Song Contest. This would be less effective. Mere competition between contradictory assertions would not be enough. Sound judgment is helped by contentious advocacy, which directly tests evidence for accuracy, and exposes errors or lies. The opposing points of view must actually meet head-on in confrontation, as occurs in cross-examination.

## B Misconceptions

A whole spectrum of views on the role and value of cross-examination can be found in fragments of legal literature; quotations may be found to support any position. Typically, they are unsystematic personal impressions, not based on analysis. They are vitiated by their variety and disagreement. The following antithesis of idealistic and cynical views, will suffice to show the range.

Wigmore was enthusiastic:

> . . . it is beyond any doubt the greatest legal engine ever invented for the discovery of truth . . . The fact of this unique and irresistible power remains, and is the reason for our faith in its merits . . . cross-examination, not trial by jury, is the great and permanent contribution of the Anglo-American system of law to improved methods of trial procedure.
>
> [John Henry Wigmore, *Evidence* (3rd edn) para 1367]

Archbishop Whately was less impressed:

> I think that the kind of skill by which the cross-examiner succeeds in alarming, misleading or bewildering an honest witness may be characterized as the most, or one of the most, base and depraved of all possible employments of intellectual power.
>
> [Archbishop Whately, *Elements of Rhetoric*, p 165]

These, and many less extreme views, err in describing cross-examination in isolation, rather than as an integral part of a complex process. When it is so seen, its role in the criminal trial emerges.

## C   Cross-examination in context

The context in which cross-examination occurs consists of the real situation under enquiry, and the trial process as a whole.

The reality underlying the trial is the paramount consideration. The aim of the system of justice is to discover this, not to provide a forum for intellectual combat, where winning is all. Cross-examination is intended to contribute to fact-finding, not concealment of facts. The truth ought to determine success. In practice, truth, in the mouths of most witnesses, is fairly robust under attack, as one would hope. Cross-examination is not designed to destroy true and accurate evidence. Many would contend that it rarely does so. Others focus on miscarriages of justice which are known to have occurred. Vigilance is necessary to prevent them, but their frequency should not be exaggerated.

However significant cross-examination may be, its effect depends on its complex interaction with a number of other factors, which are mentioned here briefly. The subject will be developed in relation to the use of various techniques and tactics, in different situations. Cross-examination is usually important, and often crucial, but it rarely determines the verdict by itself. Its role must be understood as part of the whole trial process.

Cross-examination has an important constructive function. Here the advocate seeks positive and favourable evidence to build up his case, from the opponent's witness. The techniques for doing this will be studied in detail. Such concessions from an opponent's witness can have a strong impact. Yet they are not usually a substitute for the evidence-in-chief led by the cross-examiner. The positive evidence obtained in cross-examination, normally supplements and emphasizes the main body of positive evidence which a party leads himself; the constructive effect of cross-examination depends on good evidence-in-chief. An exception is where a defence advocate is able to elicit such helpful evidence from a Crown witness, that he need not lead any evidence himself.

The destructive function of cross-examination is to weaken or destroy the evidence of the opponent's witness. Where this succeeds, it is normally the result of a combination of factors. Few cases are won by cross-examining one witness or by one devastating blow, to the exclusion of everything else in the trial. Daily experience in criminal courts—especially in summary trials— shows that, apart from exceptional cases, an advocate should not normally expect to win by one brilliant coup in cross-examination.

An exaggerated view of what can be achieved may induce an advocate to cross-examine, or to go on with it for too long, where this is unnecessary, dangerous, or actually harmful to his case. A realistic view will enhance his performance.

The key to destroying evidence is to contradict it in some way. All forms of contradiction flow from the axiom that something cannot both be and not be at the same time; the existence of one fact excludes the existence of the other.

In criminal trials contradiction is found in inconsistency in a witness's evidence, conflict in evidence given by two or more witnesses, inconsistency of oral with real or documentary evidence, and contradiction of testimony by common experience of reality, viz impossibility or improbability.

Cross-examination, unaided, can usually show inconsistency or improbability in the evidence of a witness, which may be enough to weaken confidence in it, but perhaps not enough to destroy it. Destruction or, where appropriate, the creation of reasonable doubt, may require more effective contradiction by confrontation or comparison with other positive and acceptable evidence.

To destroy evidence may not prove a desired positive fact, e g to negate an alibi does not put the accused at the scene of the crime. But positive evidence may both prove a fact and negate whatever contradicts it.

A realistic aim for a cross-examiner is to weaken the evidence challenged, so that it is defeated by his own positive and contradictory evidence, which is accepted by the court, after surviving cross-examination itself.

The context includes the effect of final argument in organizing, giving meaning to, and emphasizing the evidence, and enhancing the effect of cross-examination.

Above all, the effect of cross-examination depends on the court's judgment, which is not to be regarded as just the passive product of advocacy. It is an active and independent process, applied holistically to the evidence at the final stage.

The contribution to justice made by unsuccessful cross-examination should be noted. Able cross-examination, instead of destroying evidence, may actually strengthen it. Many innocent persons owe their acquittals to the way in which they withstood forceful cross-examination by the Crown.

On the view stated, if Whately's depraved advocate managed to shake an honest witness, in order to win his case, he would still need the support of perjured evidence which survived cross-examination and defeated his opponent's evidence. But one would hope that the opponent, in cross-examining, was not as inept as the first advocate was depraved.

Whately's scenario is hardly the norm. It is rather a stereotyped reflection of popular mythology. The complex process of a criminal trial has many built-in checks to offset the kind of situation which he describes. The truth is not so fragile as he claims.

On the other hand, Wigmore idealizes and oversimplifies the picture; he appears to overvalue cross-examination, as if it were the only thing which counted. Cross-examination is important and may often be crucial, but generally this will be in the context of other factors in the trial.

A cross-examiner should present his case as forcefully as he can, without forming a judgment. He should expect the party to win, whose case is based on reality, and properly presented in all respects, in which cross-examination is a vital element.

He cannot alter the reality, but he can certainly maximize his own presentation and seek to impair the case put forward by his opponent. That is the approach taken here. This having been done, with integrity and vigour, the verdict is a matter for the court.

# CHAPTER 2

# The anatomy of a criminal trial

I  Introduction
II  Alternative defences
III  Commission of crime
IV  Identity

## I  INTRODUCTION

In nearly all criminal trials, the essential question is one of fact, not law. Despite the wide variety of criminal situations, issues of fact often fall into recognizable patterns. An analysis of these is given here, as a guide to the areas where cross-examiners may expect to find material errors or lies, viz in relation to disputed facts.

## II  ALTERNATIVE DEFENCES

By law, for conviction, the prosecutor has the burden of proving what he states in the Indictment or Information, viz. (i) that the crime was committed (including any necessary knowledge or intent), and (ii) that it was the accused who committed it. But the burden is less in practice. The real issue is generally restricted to whichever one of these two Crown requirements the defence choose to dispute. This is, of course, not a matter of law. For convenience, it may be called the 'rule of alternative defences'.

Irrespective of innocence or guilt, the logical and practical implications of denying one of the two foundations of the Crown case, have the effect of limiting the defence to that one issue. This is explained below.

The defence, who create the issue, know what it is when they make their selection. But for tactical reasons, usually of little importance, they rarely admit undisputed facts formally, as they could do, to make evidence unnecessary. But assuming that the supporting evidence is sufficient, these uncontested facts are easily proved, as a rule. This is seen in one trial after another.

The prosecutor usually discovers the real issues from pre-trial disclosure of the defence case in committal proceedings, depositions, statements, interviewing witnesses, exchange of information or discussion. Otherwise, the issues soon become obvious in the trial, from opening speeches, when made, or defence cross-examination of Crown witnesses. Later, the defence may also lead evidence and present arguments to the same effect.

The 'rule of alternative defences' follows from the fact that few defences take the purely legal form of simply testing Crown evidence, objecting to admissibility of evidence, or contending that there is no case to answer. The defence usually put forward some version of the facts contradicting one or other of the two assertions in the Crown case.

Although a defendant need not testify and, if he refrains from doing so, comment is restricted, it may be assumed that he will give evidence to support a positive version of the disputed facts, which contradicts the Crown version. Any other defence evidence may then be expected to coincide with the accused's testimony, in whole or in part.

Most crimes, whether serious or not, occur at specific times and places. For simplicity, this may be taken as typical, although some crimes consist of a course of conduct over a period, e g fraud or child neglect.

An accused who testifies that he was not at the scene of the crime, whether or not he pleads alibi, cannot personally deny that the crime was committed, and it is not to be expected that he would call other defence witnesses to do so. Without such information, a defence advocate could not dispute the crime either (although he could of course test the evidence). Thus, the only real issue would be that of the accused's identity as the offender.

An accused who, in evidence, denies that the crime was committed, places himself at the locus, and thereby concedes the issue of his identification so far as presence is concerned; often this will be conclusive in establishing that he was the offender—especially if no others are involved. Then, only the crime will be in issue.

If other persons were there, an accused who admits that he was at the scene of the crime, may claim that one or more of them, committed the crime, and that he was not involved. This would then raise a special kind of question of relating his admitted identity to observed actions. This would be the only issue.

In all these examples, which cover nearly every situation, the 'rule of alternative defences' is found to apply; i e the defence is either that the crime was not committed, or that it was not committed by the accused, but both contentions cannot be put forward, for the reasons given.

The 'rule' is not absolute of course. Exceptions may be encountered in unusual circumstances. One illustration of this would be where an accused admitted his presence at the locus, while denying that he was involved in the incident under enquiry, which, in any event, he claims, did not constitute a crime, e g if he was a non-participating member of a crowd of football fans charged with disorderly conduct. Here, both the crime and identity are in dispute, but this rarely occurs.

Cross-examiners should know that in almost every trial, either party's evidence may be mistaken or untruthful but only on one question, viz whether the crime was committed, or whether the accused was the offender, but not on both issues. However, even closer guidance may be given.

## III  COMMISSION OF CRIME

Though absolute rules cannot be stated, pointers can be given to the kinds of crimes most likely to be disputed, viz those involving transient facts, because proof depends on eyewitness evidence, unsupported by evidence of enduring facts. Thus, an intangible crime, or one containing an essential but intangible element, is likely to be contested.

On the basis of tangibility, crimes may be analysed into result-crimes, conduct-crimes, and object-crimes.

### A  Result-crimes

An act which must have a specific physical result to be criminal is a result-crime, e g murder requires death caused by the attack. Most serious crimes come within this class, e g crimes of violence causing injury; sexual crimes involving intercourse; dishonest transfer of property; criminal damage to property; and road traffic offences causing death, injury or accident.

The physical results of such crimes are usually lasting and indisputable, e g the victim's fractured skull, or the vandalized police van.

Such facts, even if they no longer exist at the time of the trial, would have endured for long enough to provide abundant and cogent evidence.

Even an audacious liar might shrink from denying that a headless body riddled with bullets was the result of a murder, or that medical evidence of sexual violation was unsound. Cross-examiners are unlikely to find that evidence about such physical consequences requires challenge. Lies or errors, involving the denial of a real fact, or the assertion of a non-existent fact, are not normally found in this area.

A result-crime may include an essential but intangible element, where the Crown must prove that the act was done with a certain quality of knowledge or intention. Sometimes, this may be inferred from the act or the result, e g where the owner of a starved dog is charged with cruelty. At other times, the act or the result may give no clue to the mental state, e g in a question of whether taking the wrong coat from a cloakroom was theft or absent-mindedness.

So no dispute is likely if the crime can be proved by the act and the result, but disputes about some intangible quality, viz a mental state, are likely to give rise to lies or errors, for which cross-examiners should be ready.

## B   Conduct-crimes

A conduct-crime is one committed by a forbidden act alone. It needs no physical result, and may be wholly intangible, e g menacing someone with a knife, disorderly conduct in public, driving while disqualified, intimidating witnesses, or some forms of indecency based on *mens rea* alone.

Attempts to commit result-crimes, e g murder, assault, theft, or arson, which stop before they cause the forbidden effect, may be regarded as conduct-crimes for present purposes.

Here, proof must depend on eyewitness evidence, which is usually in sharp conflict; no traces remain after the event to point one way or another.

Evidence of ambiguous acts or of impressions based on suspicion, if admitted, is open to error arising from bias, e g misinterpreting neutral conduct.

Evidence of conduct-crimes is vulnerable to errors and lies, because it often consists of assertion and counter-assertion by eyewitnesses. Here, there is ample scope for cross-examination.

Whether conduct-crimes were committed is commonly the real issue. As they are proved by eyewitnesses, who must have seen the offender, the issue of identity is often eliminated, e g if the witnesses knew the accused personally, or if he is arrested at the time. In any event, if an accused contests such a crime, he almost always places himself at the locus.

## C   Object-crimes

Object-crimes are committed by virtue of the offender's forbidden relationship to some object. They differ from result-crimes in producing no result, and from conduct-crimes, because more than an act, i e the object, is required.

Examples are possessing prohibited drugs, a weapon in a public place, a firearm without a certificate, obscene publications for sale, or stolen property.

Such crimes may involve both tangible and intangible facts in various combinations. The intangible facts are those most likely to be in issue, and to give rise to mistakes or lies, with opportunity for cross-examination. Examples may be an accused's state of knowledge about an object, or the circumstances of possession.

The relevant objects would be produced as exhibits in the trial. Sometimes their nature is not in doubt, e g a piece of cannabis resin. In other cases, the nature of the exhibit could be the issue, e g whether a magazine was obscene, or whether an article was an offensive weapon.

Because of the wide variety of object-crimes, it cannot be said, generally, whether the commission of the crime or the implication of the accused is likely to be the real issue, but for both to be issues would be exceptional.

# IV IDENTITY

Identification evidence for the Crown may be, and for the defence, usually is, direct. Crown circumstantial evidence is considered in the next chapter.

For the reasons given, the issue of identity is common where a result-crime is charged, and uncommon in a charge of a conduct-crime. In object-crimes, the issue will vary according to circumstances.

Three types of defence based on identity are possible, according to whether the accused claims that he was not at the locus of the crime, whether he pleads alibi, or whether he admits that he was at the locus, but did not commit the crime.

## A Accused not at locus

The defence may simply deny that the accused was at the locus when the crime was committed. He need not give or lead evidence, or say where he was at that time, i e plead alibi. If he did testify, he might claim, not unreasonably, that he had forgotten, or was unsure of, where he was, although he certainly was not at the locus of the crime.

The target of defence cross-examination would be the reliability or credibility of the prosecution evidence. But since the defendant may be expected to know the truth, the prosecutor would cross-examine him on the basis that he was lying.

## B   Alibi

The defence that the accused was absent from the locus at the time of the crime, may be supported by proof that he was at a specified place, with other defence witnesses, i e an alibi.

Crown witnesses, especially if they are independent, and unconnected with each other, are likely to be cross-examined on the basis that their visual identifications are mistaken. Less commonly, malicious lying about the accused's implication may be imputed to those who are alleged to be motivated, e g police witnesses or accomplices.

Since defence witnesses supporting the alibi usually know the accused, mistaken identification may be unlikely, unless conditions were difficult. They, and the accused, are likely to be cross-examined as untruthful, on the assumption that the real situation must be known to them.

Alibi witnesses may of course be correct in identifying the accused, as being where they say, but they could be mistaken or untruthful about when that happened. False alibis are sometimes planned by falsifying the date of a real event. A prosecutor might cross-examine them to the effect that the accused could have been with them—but not when the crime was committed.

Challenging alibi evidence as false is common. Destroying it does not per se prove the opposite case, viz presence at the locus, or that the accused committed the crime, e g a false alibi may be intended to boost a weak, but genuine, defence.

## C   Accused at locus: uninvolved

An accused may admit that he was at the locus of a crime, having been recognized or arrested there, yet he may deny any part in a crime which another committed. A conflict of direct evidence is typical. The responsibility of one person for another's acts is a different question, i e one of substantive law. Here, the alternatives are mere presence, which is not a crime, unless, per se, it contributes to the criminal situation, or criminal acts carried out personally. In this rather special issue of relating admitted identity to criminal acts, errors in observing facts rather than of visual identification may occur. In confusing events involving several persons, generalized evidence may not discriminate sufficiently between individuals, or discussion may influence the evidence of observers.

Many opportunities arise for cross-examination concerning eye-witness errors or lies, or false denials by the accused.

This guide to where a cross-examiner may look for mistakes or lies, is followed in the next two chapters by an analysis of such inaccurate evidence.

# CHAPTER 3

# The reliability of evidence

I    Introduction
II   Errors in evidence
III  Evidence of identity

## I  INTRODUCTION

The subject of this chapter is the reliability of evidence, i e the extent to which it is acceptable as being free from mistake. In the next chapter, the credibility of evidence will be considered, i e the extent to which it is acceptable as truthful.

The reliability of evidence is a question of great importance in courts. The law cannot stop errors in evidence from occurring altogether, but it tries to minimize them so far as rules and procedures can do this. However, mistakes are involuntary. No offence is committed by making a genuine mistake, however serious its consequences.

The oath, and penalties for offences relating to testimony, may make witnesses more careful and more responsible in marginal situations, e g if they are giving doubtful evidence, or are accused of bias, but these provisions cannot guarantee accuracy.

Pre-trial police procedure governing confessions or the identification of suspects, is regulated by the Police and Criminal Evidence Act 1984 and related Codes of Practice.

These rules are designed to minimize errors as well as impropriety. But success depends very much on the integrity and conduct of police officers in informal situations which are hard to control.

The law also tries to prevent mistakes by means of rules of evidence which exclude unreliable forms of testimony, and by requiring corroboration, or warnings to be given to juries, in circumstances where evidence may be unreliable.

Despite these, and other measures, the possibility that evidence is mistaken always exists. As Bentham said, 'Witnesses are the eyes and ears of justice'. Trust in honest witnesses is the foundation of any system of justice, but it is necessary to reckon with the universal fallibility of observation or memory. The risks are either that mistaken evidence may be accepted, or that accurate evidence may be rejected as mistaken or unreliable. Moreover, even accurate evidence may be incomplete, and the omissions may distort the picture. Almost anyone's report of any incident, is likely to fall short of total recall, and to contain some element of error, although it is usually minor.

In showing the limitations of testimony, and in exposing errors, cross-examination can be crucial. As the witness's sincerity is accepted and the evidence itself is usually reasonable, it is important to demonstrate how the errors arose.

To expose the origins of mistakes in evidence, a cross-examiner who is truly a professional, should have a mastery of this subject. It is clearly one of vital importance, and the material would lend itself to systematic exposition and instruction.

However, this type of practical psychology is omitted from both professional legal training and texts on the law of evidence. It forms no part of the qualification of advocates although such insight is necessary in conducting a criminal trial.

Even more surprising is the fact that it is not to be found in any usable or practical form in texts on psychology, although psychologists have investigated testimony experimentally for almost a century. Their research has been almost entirely confined to laboratories or artificial situations, so that they lack insight into the probative meaning of errors in real life situations, and in the courts. This subject has been expounded fully elsewhere.

Advocates have had to rely on their common sense, in the hope that they will pick up this essential knowledge with experience. But this takes time, and may be incomplete when it is needed. An advocate may be faced at any time with evidence of a kind which he must challenge, but on grounds of which he has no previous experience.

To meet this obvious gap in the advocate's training, the following account is given of how errors arise in evidence.

## II  ERRORS IN EVIDENCE

The subject of how errors in evidence are caused belongs to psychology. The approach here is a common-sense one, with a view to application in court, rather than that of theoretical psychology.

Two types of errors in evidence are considered: those which arise in the course of observation, and those which develop in memory in the interval between observation and the trial.

## A   Errors of observation

Errors of observation may arise from features of the event, the conditions under which it is seen, the state of the witness, or any combination of these. To conform to the topic, the negative aspects of relevant factors are stated, as possible sources of errors of observation, e g poor lighting. If these factors were inverted, they would contribute to accuracy of observation, e g good lighting.

### 1   The event

In regard to features of the event, the focus is on problems created by what is seen, e g the driver's face in a car driven at high speed—not the circumstances in which it is seen, e g from far away.

*(a)   Degree of exposure.*   The duration, repetition, or frequency of occurrence of an incident, fix the maximum time for watching it. How long it need last for accuracy varies with the kind of event and the attention given to it. The time and degree of attention need only be enough and no more, e g staring at skid marks adds nothing, but to grasp some facts needs time, e g suspicious conduct in a store. More time may increase the confidence of the witness, or the court, in his account.

Except where the facts fix the degree of exposure, e g seeing a runner's face as he looks back, estimates of time are notoriously subjective and unreliable. Time may seem longer under stress.

Cross-examination can rarely show that accuracy is impossible because of the brevity of exposure; the lapse of time is usually unsettled, and witnesses who give positive evidence insist that it was sufficient. But the evidence may be deemed to be too unreliable to accept if enough doubt is cast on it, e g if too much detail is reported on the basis of a rapid glance, or the testimony is dogmatic, where some uncertainty would be expected.

Psychologists disagree on whether the time spent on looking at a face affects later recognition. One view is that active attention to the face is a more favourable factor than seeing it for a long time.

*(b)   Movement.*   Movement of objects or persons can create difficulties for observers. Other factors are often also involved, e g where one motor car obstructs the view of another. The degree of exposure is usually a part of the problem and much of what was said above is applicable.

*(c)   Number of persons.*   To watch more than one person at a time is confusing, especially if they are separated or moving in different directions, or if one blocks the view of another.

Cross-examiners often probe police evidence about offences committed by a disorderly group. In an unexpected and confusing situation, it is unlikely that one officer would have the visual and attention span to watch everyone, or that, by chance or design, each police officer would watch a different suspect. The risk is that rough and ready impression evidence may be given, e g 'They were all in it'. Mere presence which does not contribute to the criminal situation is no crime. If the whole group were acting together with a common criminal aim, exactly what individuals did might not matter. But this is not designed to replace accurate observation of individuals where that is necessary. It is essential that such evidence be scrutinized and tested carefully in cross-examination, to avoid possible implication of innocent persons in the criminal acts of others.

*(d) Violence.* Eyewitnesses, as well as victims of violence, may experience stress. Cross-examiners may suggest that this hindered their observations.

If it can be shown that the witness became disorientated or hysterical, or that his attention was distracted from what he describes, this form of challenge may have some value. Otherwise, it may not have much success. People regularly report violent incidents with accuracy.

*(e) Ambiguity.* Observed facts themselves, or what they mean in relation to each other, may be ambiguous. Some conduct-crimes are open to ambiguity, e g whether touching a child in a swimming pool was accidental or indecent. Ambiguity about identification may arise if resemblance is confused with recognition. This could be a crucial defect. If evidence is admitted which contains an element of impression or interpretation based on observed facts, that basis should be probed. Another view may then be suggested, e g that a driver's slow speech was due to a defect, not drink.

*(f) Salient facts.* Commonplace facts may not be noticed, whereas novel, unusual, urgent or important facts may stand out, command attention, or even dominate the situation, e g a person may focus on the knife presented to him. Salient facts may rob other facts of attention.

It is claimed that facts on the periphery of attention may be absorbed, although the witness does not know this at the time or later. This is supported by reports of recall of details under hypnosis. But for the practical purposes of cross-examination, even if such unconscious retention of information occurs, it is inaccessible in court. It can be a valuable approach to show that a witness is likely to have attended to pressing or salient facts, without noticing secondary facts as fully and as precisely as he claims. If so, his evidence would then be vulnerable to suggestions that he had filled in the gaps by imagination or by discussion with other witnesses.

*(g)* *Sounds.* Sounds other than speech, e g bangs, breaking glass, screams, or screeching brakes, usually colour an event, but are not the main facts. Possible errors about the nature and location of sounds may be worth probing in cross-examination.

*(h)* *Speech.* Evidence about spoken words raises questions of admissibility, for which reference should be made to texts on the rules of evidence. Various situations, where evidence is admitted, involve typical event factors related to the accuracy of hearing and memory of statements.

Evidence is admissible to prove that a statement was made, not that it is true, if the making of the statement, regardless of its truth, is relevant to the issue, e g as evidence of the state of mind or conduct of persons present.

Evidence of a statement led in order to prove its truth, is inadmissible under the general exclusion of hearsay, subject to exceptions.

The main exception, governed by the Police and Criminal Evidence Act 1984 concerns informal admissions and confessions made out of court.

A noteworthy common law exception covers statements which are part of the *res gestae*, e g which accompany and explain an act, reveal a person's physical condition or state of mind, or are spontaneous exclamations of a victim of an offence, or an observer.

Despite legal limitations therefore, a good deal of evidence refers to spoken words.

Attention to what is heard, and memory for what is attended to, are both selective. Much is ignored or rapidly forgotten. Months later, unless the words were noted at the time, or made a special impact, only the sense will probably be recalled, not the words verbatim. Generally, only police note spoken words, but in some situations, e g the locus of a crime, perhaps they cannot do this, and must await return to the police station, or other opportunity. In uncontrolled situations, as at the locus of a crime, it is quite easy for a witness to mishear what is said, because of various factors, e g poor articulation, background noise, people speaking or shouting at the same time, or distraction by what is happening. Evidence given from memory can seldom claim successfully, to repeat the exact words. A cross-examiner could easily cast doubt on the evidence or suggest that the words were different.

But even where only the gist of what was said is reported from memory, it is liable to attack. A cross-examiner might contend that the witness has misunderstood the words, or go on to suggest an alternative meaning for them. Such evidence involves interpretation or impression, but is usually admissible, as the only way in which the witness can inform the court of what he heard. Apart from the lack of a verbatim account, what the words were intended to convey would involve facts such as tone, volume or emphasis, all in the context of what was said to or by the speaker earlier or later.

At a certain level, admissible impression evidence about the gist of what a person said may shade into an inadmissible inference by a witness. Inferences are for the court alone to draw. Arguments, but not cross-examination, on the point, would be allowed.

Statements taken by police include admissions and confessions by suspects, and statements from witnesses which may be admitted if they testify differently and deny previous inconsistent statements—irrespective of their truth.

Where police witness are challenged about statements written in their notebooks, the circumstances usually exclude mistake, although lying may be possible.

Such statements are usually noted in controlled settings, commonly, in police stations, where there would be no background noise or distractions. This reduces the chance of mishearing.

If the statement was read over to the person making it, and he signed it, the possibility of mishearing should be eliminated altogether.

Two or more police officers may speak to the making of a statement in identical terms. If it was incorrect, each must have made the same mistake.

In such situations, it is absurd for a cross-examiner to suggest that no statement of any kind was made, and to attribute the entry in the notebook and the testimony to mistake; but such inept cross-examination is, in fact, encountered. If no statement was made, the attack on the witness can only be that he is lying.

If the cross-examiner accepts that a statement was made, but claims that it was in different terms from those noted and spoken to, the position, while less extreme than outright denial, is close to it. Unless the suggested divergence from accuracy refers to only a word or two, with an ambiguous sound, which might have been misheard by one or more officers, mistake is usually out of the question, and the allegation again should be one of lying.

If the advocate accepts the terms of the statement, but contends that they have a particular meaning, cross-examination about that is likely to be excluded, although it may be allowed about the context and related circumstances. Here, the court has an exact record of the words spoken on which it can place its own interpretation.

Evidence of identification by voice is exceptional. It is admissible, and there are special rules for identity parades held for this purpose. Such evidence is generally thought to have little weight per se. To weaken it further, a cross-examiner might, where appropriate, explore the witness's degree of familiarity with the voice or otherwise, and the circumstances in which he heard it at the time of the crime. The possibility of suggestive influence should be probed if necessary.

The effect of the gradual introduction of tape-recording in police stations remains to be seen.

*(i) Touch, smell, taste.* Evidence of touch, smell or taste is not common. It is subjective, and its reliability may be uncertain.

Witnesses may speak to sensations of touch to supplement visual evidence of the same facts, e g in indecency charges, or where blows left no injury. Evidence of touch may be given on secondary points, e g the heat of a car engine.

Evidence of odours is rare, apart from smelling alcohol from a driver's breath, or prohibited drugs.

Evidence of tracking suspects, by police dog handlers, depends on smell, but as the dogs are not available for cross-examination, it may have more value for narrative than for proof.

Evidence of taste arises sometimes, e g in charges of poisoning or contraventions of the Food and Drug Acts.

When evidence of touch, smell or taste is given, it is impossible, in cross-examination, to test the accuracy of the actual sensations which witnesses report, but the surrounding circumstances may be probed as a guide to reliability. If a specially trained police officer says that he smelled cannabis resin in a bedroom, this may be unverifiable or beyond contradiction, but he may not be relied on if he seems to be biased. After cross-examination, the court's view of such evidence is likely to depend on the witness's self-assessment if he is trusted.

*(j) Abstract qualities.* Even the most concrete physical situations have abstract qualities, which may give rise to disputes.

Questions often arise about distances, e g in road traffic offences. Dates, times or intervals may be in issue in any kind of trial. The order of events may be crucial in many incidents. Physical layout, dimensions, and the relationship of things to each other, are often important. Features such as weights, quantities, colours, or speed may be of significance.

Accuracy can rarely be expected in evidence of such facts, even from conscientious witnesses. They will offer subjective estimates, which, notoriously, will be likely to support the general tenor of their evidence. If courts must decide such facts with precision, they should do so with caution.

A cross-examiner, to whom such evidence is important, should try to support his contentions by confronting the witness with something objective, which is contained in evidence of his own witnesses, or real or documentary evidence, which the court is likely to accept. Visual aids are often available, but too little effort is made to obtain them. He might then avoid the unconvincing process of assertion and counter-assertion, which is only too common, by establishing something which is exact.

## 2   Conditions of observation

The surrounding circumstances in which a witness sees an event, differ from the event itself, and may encourage or interfere with the completeness or accuracy of observations.

Often such facts, not being those in issue, are brought out for the first time in cross-examination.

It is generally to be expected that witnesses will support any positive evidence which they give, by claiming that the conditions of observation were adequate for this purpose. Such evidence may be subjective and difficult to challenge. A cross-examiner may have to rely on contrary evidence about the conditions of observation which he leads himself.

*(a)   Lighting*. Offences often happen, and wrongdoers are often seen, in relative darkness. The quality of the light may then become vital. Apart from moonlight, issues often arise about artificial lighting. It would be exceptional to lead objective evidence of such facts as its strength or location, shadows, or how street lighting affected colours.

Few witnesses will admit in cross-examination that the light was too poor for them to see what they assert. Contrary evidence may be needed to support such a criticism.

Where the Crown case is based on visual identification in bad lighting, the defence should emphasize this in relation to the Turnbull Guidelines, which will be discussed later.

*(b)   Distance*. If the witness was not close enough for clear observation, he may have completed his evidence by discussion or imagination.

Frequently, evidence about distance as an aspect of the conditions of observation, is inadequate. It only tends to be satisfactory when it is part of the issues, as in road traffic offences, where measurements are provided.

In giving estimates of how far they were from what they saw, adjacent witnesses usually differ significantly. Sometimes distances may be calculated from other facts, e g a number of car lengths.

Without objective evidence, the question of the viewing distance may not be settled.

Witnesses will again insist that they were near enough to see what they claim to have seen. The reliability of their evidence is unlikely to be decided by the matter of viewing distance alone.

*(c)* *Weather*. Visibility may be reduced by weather conditions of various kinds, e g rain or snow as obstacles in themselves, or by obscuring windows, windscreens or spectacles. Difficulty may also be caused by mist, fog, or dazzling sunshine. Witnesses who give affirmative evidence are unlikely to accept any suggestion in cross-examination that the weather created difficulties of observation.

*(d)* *Obstructions*. Natural or artificial obstacles, people or ve-hicles, may block observation of an incident, totally or in part. If this is to be the basis of cross-examination, it is desirable to fortify it by objective evidence of the layout and the location of any obstructions, as shown by plans or photographs, or by leading evidence in support. Otherwise, if something was not seen properly because of obstructions, evidence which depends on filling in the gaps by speculation, may escape exposure.

*(e)* *Distractions*. Observation may be impeded by something which diverts a witness's attention away from what is important. This might be something on which he is concentrating when an incident occurs unexpectedly, e g if he is driving a car or serving a customer. If something happens in front of him, he may be distracted by trying to find a way to escape from the situation. If he is under threat, or being attacked, the witness will not be watching another person who is being threatened or attacked. If the main facts are observed, peripheral facts may not be noticed. A cross-examiner should use his imagination to project himself into the situation.

### 3   State of witness

The completeness and accuracy of observation may be affected to some extent by the state of the witness, viz his permanent eyewitness abilities, or temporary physical or psychological condi-tion.

*(a)* *Permanent features*. People vary in permanent eyewitness abilities, e g acuteness or defects of vision or hearing, or good or

poor memory for faces, words or numbers, and so on. But psychological research has not provided any usable data for use in court in this respect. A witness cannot be said to be more or less trustworthy as an observer, by virtue of membership of any class, e g age, sex, or occupation.

There is no universal agreement about the abilities of children as witnesses, nor has it been proved that police are any better than lay observers, or that training improves ability to identify. A cross-examiner can only exploit any defects which come to his notice, e g whether the witness was wearing his hearing aid when the conversation took place.

Personal tendencies are difficult to pin down or to demonstrate, in an unknown witness, e g a tendency to exaggerate. Generally, permanent eyewitness qualities offer few openings for cross-examination.

*(b)   Physical condition.*   Common physical conditions of a temporary kind which can impair observation include drink, drugs, illness or fatigue, and injury. Alcohol interferes with perception, but to what extent cannot be decided precisely, so far as witnesses are concerned. The degree of impairment depends on too many factors, e g amount and type of drink, when taken, food, physique, individual metabolism, and sometimes the sobering effect of what occurred. Unless there is ground for suggesting that a witness was almost in a stupor, a cross-examiner cannot destroy, although he may weaken, his evidence, because he had been drinking. The higher mental functions, e g understanding or memory, are those most affected, rather than the senses of vision or hearing. Since there is an element of interpretation in all perception, drink may produce some errors in reporting a complicated incident. But witnesses who give firm evidence will not accept that they were too drunk to observe what they claim to have seen. Usually it is only reluctant witnesses who agree that they were too drunk to report anything. In cross-examination, to elicit that a witness had been drinking is worthwhile as it can weaken confidence in his evidence. But often, this line of enquiry is overdone to no effect, by probing every detail of what he drank, as if this were conclusive.

How particular medical or prohibited drugs may affect observation is a technical matter beyond the present enquiry. A cross-examiner who intends to challenge evidence on this basis, should take steps to acquire the necessary information.

In daily life, illness or fatigue may reduce alertness to what is going on. Some specific effect of the condition, would require to be shown, as a ground for a significant attack on evidence.

Injuries of various kinds could interfere with observation, either directly or by distracting the witness. If evidence is to be attacked on this ground, medical advice may be desirable. But in most cases, the question is one of common sense. An injury, and accompanying pain and anxiety, could have absorbed attention to the exclusion of other matters. On the other hand, perception could have been affected directly, e g as result of blows to the eyes. Unpredictable consequences may follow from heavy bleeding which diminishes cerebral blood flow, or traumatic head injuries. Victims of serious attacks or traffic accidents may be intermittently unconscious or dazed. The kind of injury, where it was sustained, and how it was caused, may suggest limited observation. An attacker may have been unseen, if the wound is on the back of the head. If a victim who was kicked on the ground has multiple bruises, he would probably be protecting his face and head, and might be challenged about his identification of the assailants. Injuries may show that a witness was attacked severely, so that he would not be watching a similar attack on his friend at the same time.

*(c)  Psychological state.*  Some errors in evidence have psychological causes. Currently, psychologists have little to offer for practical use in court. They claim that the selectivity of attention, the effect of expectations, and the effect of stress, are significant, and also suggest that there are other relevant factors. This subject will be treated only briefly, for practical reasons. One, is doubt about whether the interfering process exists—which is usually controversial. Another reason is that such processes are unknown to the witness. Honest witnesses are under consideration here. A final reason is that such data are private, and a witness who knew them would not normally reveal them.

An acquaintance with controversial psychological processes of a subtle kind, which are unknown to the witness, or in any event private, cannot really help a cross-examiner. These matters are inaccessible.

Interfering elements may sometimes be shown by inference from objective circumstances.

Attention is certainly selective, but psychology cannot specify what will or will not receive attention, nor is there agreement about whether or not peripheral facts are registered.

Common experience shows that attention has a limited span, is not continuous, and moves from one thing to another, in a voluntary or involuntary sequence. We cannot focus on every element in a situation at the same moment; something may be missed. An urgent fact, e g a fire in the basement, may dominate a whole complex situation.

Attention to salient facts may rob other facts of attention. If so, it may be natural that some facts are recalled vaguely, and dogmatic evidence may be an unreliable blend of observation, imagination, and inference.

Witnesses who testify firmly about some fact will not normally concede that their attention was elsewhere at the time. However, it is not impossible for this to be shown in cross-examination, although it is difficult. The key is to approach the matter from the point of view of the objective circumstances. In many cases, they make it obvious what received the witnesses' exclusive attention, e g if youths are showering police with bricks, their identification of ten assailants from observation at that very time, may be reasonably challenged as doubtful.

When we perceive something, our higher mental functions weave sensations of sight or sound into meaningful patterns, which are partly based on experience, and our expectations may then colour our observations. Thus, psychologists say that we may sometimes tend to see what we expect to see. Hunters in America often shoot each other, thinking that they are shooting deer.

While the influence of expectations on observation may be accepted, it is to be supposed that they would operate where the facts are inherently obscure or ambiguous. It is not recommended that a cross-examiner should try to show that a witness suffered from a hallucination, or even an optical illusion.

Inherently ambiguous facts include some conduct-crimes, in which the absence of physical results contributes to uncertainty about the action, e g young girls conditioned to expect indecency, may see it in an innocent contact. Expectations may colour acts charged as attempted crimes, e g store detectives may see a shoplifter in every customer who takes an article from the counter.

Perhaps visual identification evidence is the most vulnerable to the influence of expectations, e g identification of a suspect who only resembles the offender, because he is expected to be in the identity parade.

In suitable circumstances, a cross-examiner may usefully explore the possibility that evidence in some way reflects what a witness expected to see, as well as what he did actually see. This could take the form of colouring the evidence in one direction or another, even to the extent of creating total misinterpretation of the situation, or misidentifying an innocent person.

As a foundation for this, emphasis should be placed on the ambiguity, obscurity and doubtful nature of the facts, or the difficult conditions of observation. Even though the witness does not co-operate, it is often possible to show the nature of his expectations or preconceived ideas, and that they played a part in his report.

The psychologist's view that stress sometimes enhances and sometimes impedes observation is of no help in cross-examination. A common-sense view would be that incompleteness of evidence might depend on the extent to which the witness was distracted from his observations, by features which created the stress. If he was disorientated, this could weaken his testimony, though he might still recall the central incident. Again, some special stressful element, e g a revolver pointing at him, might have dominated his attention, to the exclusion of other facts. Beyond that it would be hard to show any specific effect of stress on evidence.

## B Errors of memory

Oral evidence is given from memory although it may sometimes be aided by writings, plans or photographs. Although memory is fallible, it is reasonably reliable for essential facts, and courts rely on the memories of honest witnesses for this.

If the witness's recollection is imperfect, his report may be incomplete or inaccurate; also he may testify less confidently, which may create doubt.

### 1 Forgetting

Memory fades with time, even if the original observation was strong. Inevitably, long periods elapse between the dates of most crimes and trials, while suspects are traced and caught, and cases prepared. The increasing volume of court business also causes delays.

Psychologists, in their classical curve of forgetting, say that it occurs more rapidly soon after the event, and then slows down. But whether this applies to recall of a face is controversial.

It cannot be said who will forget what after which interval. Not only the period of time, but also the degree of attention given to the facts, their significance for the witness, and his individual ability to remember, all enter into it.

The extent of forgetting may range from a mild dimming of a recalled image, and reduced confidence in it, to complete amnesia for a fact, event or face. It has been shown that secondary details are more quickly and more easily forgotten than the central facts of an incident. Recall of the nature and meaning of a crime as a whole, is likely to endure. The essential facts, which are the subject of direct eyewitness testimony, are resistant to forgetting. Details, which have no significance for the witness, are the facts which tend to slip away. They may, of course, form part of circumstantial or indirect evidence, and their loss could be important. Minor discrepancies between witnesses to the same facts, which arise from universal fallibility of observation or memory, are commonplace. Inexperienced advocates, on the basis of a list of such discrepancies, contend that the evidence which these witnesses gave about the main facts, must be held to be unreliable. This is usually an exaggerated and unimpressive argument.

The most critical danger of mistaken recollection after a long delay, is that of misidentifying a person with whom the witness was not familiar. But if, on the other hand, he did know the suspect, the risk of mistake is less, even after a delay; what he recalls then is personal identity with its associations, rather than a face.

What weight to give to a gap between the event and the trial is always a matter for the court's practical judgment in the particular circumstances.

Cross-examination on this would generally be based on probabilities, i e the aim would be to weaken the evidence. The hope that a firm report by the witness will be destroyed because of the passage of time alone, is not realistic.

After a long delay, if too much detail is put forward, or if the witness is dogmatic about some facts, and unsure about collateral facts, his evidence may be suspect.

A jury will not be impressed by an unfair attack on a witness of obvious sincerity, who claims to remember something. It may be best to suggest, in a moderate and reasonable way, that he may be mistaken, because of faded memory, without undue elaboration. This would be a foundation for establishing contrary facts by other evidence.

## 2   Suggestion

Suggestion occurs when an idea is accepted simply because it is presented, regardless of other reasons. The weaker the memory, the more vulnerable it will be to distortion by suggestion. Such errors are likely to increase with the extension of the interval after the crime.

If another person merely says something or conveys information to a witness, he may still influence him, without intending this. Media comment is restricted by law. The most likely suggestive influences are those of discussion between witnesses, and the effect of pre-trial enquiries and taking statements. There is considerable scope for evidence to be so affected.

Suggestion can alter the recollection of the event in various ways. In the witness's recollection it can add facts which did not exist or exclude those which did, to the extent of changing the meaning of the incident. An image of the event may be formed which is a compromise between the true memory and the additional material. The witness, unaware of this, may believe that his memory is authentic and unimpaired. He would give his evidence persuasively with the same assurance as if it were unaffected.

As occurs in forgetting, the essential facts are the most resistant to such distortion.

*(a)  Discussion of evidence.*  It is natural for witnesses associated with each other, as members of a family, friends, neighbours, or fellow employees, to discuss an unusual event which they saw, and the evidence which they will give. Such discussion is usually undetectable and is forbidden only if it is done in order to give false testimony. However, there is a real risk that evidence will be affected by discussion and it should be discouraged by those involved in conducting a trial.

Witnesses obviously feel guilty about discussing their evidence. They admit it only reluctantly, and then, invariably, they deny that it influenced them.

To deny discussion is sometimes so unlikely as to be absurd, e g between members of a family who were involved in a dramatic event. At times, one witness admits that he discussed his evidence with another, who denies it. Such an improbable denial, or such inconsistency between witnesses, may be adverse to trust in these witnesses, and can give a cross-examiner the opening he seeks.

It is surprising how often witnesses who appear to be otherwise honest, can be faulted in this respect.

Police have to discuss cases as part of their duties, in pursuing enquiries and preparing for trial. In good faith, and unintentionally, they may influence each other by exchanging information. In practice, cross-examiners do not seem to make use of this opportunity as much as they could. One reason may be defence concern lest an accused's previous convictions were to be disclosed.

Police knowledge of a defendant's previous convictions, communicated by one officer to another, may tend to reinforce identifications.

Some police communications may be confidential.

*(b)  Taking statements.*  Initial police enquiries in order to trace and apprehend suspects are often made in informal settings even if notes were taken. Verbal exchanges at this stage, perhaps enhanced by the authority attaching to police officers, may, by unintended suggestion, introduce new elements to witnesses' eventual evidence. Police know that they should interview eyewitnesses separately, and should not ask leading questions, but realistically, these precautions may not always be observed if the matter is

urgent. Hearsay, opinions and guesses, may all be useful initially, and may be communicated freely between police and witnesses, both in making enquiries and in taking statements. The risk of influencing evidence by suggestion here would be difficult to eliminate. But this can be a fertile area for probing by a well-prepared cross-examiner.

Pre-trial enquiries by, and statements given to, solicitors involve similar risks of unintended suggestion. Cross-examination on the matter would be defeated by the objection of confidentiality. Professional integrity is the protection.

*(c)   Self-induced errors.*  It is a matter of common experience, confirmed by psychology, that over a period internal processes alone may affect a witness's memory of an event.

On a conscious and intellectual level, a witness may plan, streamline and rehearse his evidence, picturing and pondering on the event, completing gaps by speculation, settling inconsistencies and doubts by inference, and adjusting and modifying his evidence in various ways. He would know that he is doing this.

However, he would be unaware of the working of emotional influences on his memory at an unconscious level. His motives, fears and wishes, could incline his memory in some direction. He might forget unpleasant aspects of the event, or prefer one verdict or another, or want to please the police, or play a worthwhile role as a citizen. Vanity, embarrassment or bias may enter into it. Much testimony given by truthful witnesses is probably tainted by such common processes, but probably not to the extent of affecting the outcome. The common-sense view is that if the essential facts were clear initially, they are less likely to be affected by autosuggestion than minor facts.

Such psychological processes are inaccessible in court, even if they are accessible to the witness. Witnesses would deny a cross-examiner's contentions that they had consciously tailored their evidence, or that it was modified by autosuggestion. With no objective basis to put forward, such cross-examination is unlikely to have an impact.

## III   EVIDENCE OF IDENTITY

Whether or not the accused was the offender, is perhaps the most common question in criminal trials. In exposing errors in visual or circumstantial evidence of identity, cross-examination can play a crucial role.

The sources of error described in section II apply to evidence of identity as well as to evidence of the crime. But there are additional or specific causes of error in evidence of identity, which require further discussion. In particular, the fallibility of eyewitness identification is generally accepted; special care is always needed, to avoid a possible miscarriage of justice.

Convictions have been quashed and Royal Pardons granted for this reason. Public concern led to the appointment of the Devlin Committee, which reported in 1976 in these terms:

> We are satisfied that in cases which depend wholly or mainly on eye-witness evidence of identification there is a special risk of wrong conviction. It arises because the value of such evidence is exceptionally difficult to assess; the witness who has sincerely convinced himself and whose sincerity carries conviction is not infrequently mistaken.
> [*Report on Evidence of Identification in Criminal Cases* (HC, 26 April 1976) para 338]

Thereafter, guidelines were laid down in *Turnbull* ([1977] QB 224), which advocates must know.

The guidelines cover cases which depend wholly or substantially on the accuracy of visual identification, which the defence claim is mistaken. To meet special risks of error, listed there, of the kind considered in section II, various warnings and explanations are required about the circumstances of the identification.

The guidelines apply to both trials on indictment and to summary trials. A conviction may be quashed if they are not followed where they should be.

On a submission of no case to answer, if the quality of identification is good, even if there is no supporting evidence, the decision should be left to the jury. But if the quality of the identifying evidence is poor, and there is no other evidence to support it, the judge should withdraw the case from the jury.

This leading judgment extends the application of law to dubious identification, so that in cases to which *Turnbull* applies—primarily 'fleeting encounters' cases—this is a question of law as well as of fact. *Turnbull* does not apply to every issue of identification. Reference should be made to appropriate texts for a fuller account. As the law is not the direct subject of this book, issues of identification will be treated as questions of fact in the rest of this section.

## A  Visual identification

The Devlin Report distinguished three forms of visual identification: recognition; resemblance; and noting a distinctive characteristic. Discussions usually concentrate on the face, but, of course, a general impression may include other aspects, e g physique, posture, or movement. Thus recognition or resemblance, may be combined with recalling distinctive characteristics.

## 1   Recognition

Recognition is the strongest form of visual identification. When a witness recognizes a suspect, he recalls the offender's face and matches it with the suspect's face. This is accompanied by a subjective feeling of familiarity. If recognition is accepted by the court, identity is proved.

As objects of perception, many human faces are similar, unlike the difference between the face of a dog and that of a cat. Mistakes of recognition are not surprising. Psychologists continue to study the question intensively, but nothing significant for application in court has yet emerged.

Cases have occurred where a genuine feeling of familiarity with the suspect's face arose from seeing him previously in a context other than that of the crime. To suggest this in cross-examination may have value where the witness's sincerity is accepted and scope for previous contact can be shown, e g if the witness and the accused live near each other. Even if the suggestion is denied, the possibility would at least be conveyed to a jury.

A witness can only convey his feeling of familiarity with a face in terms of degrees of confidence. This is difficult for a cross-examiner to test or destroy, or for a court to assess.

The identification may be strongest, if the suspect was already familiar to the witness before the crime. But even here, and in cases where the offender was unknown to the witness, the circumstances of the identification may have been liable to the difficulties discussed in the previous section and be open to challenge.

In appropriate cases, difficulties with regard to the witness's memory may be the subject of cross-examination, e g forgetting in relation to the lapse of time, or the suggestive influence of discussions between witnesses.

In any case, where a defence advocate cannot destroy evidence of recognition, he may so weaken it, that it will be defeated if he leads acceptable contradictory evidence. Even if he cannot achieve this, he may still succeed by raising a reasonable doubt about the evidence.

## 2   Resemblance

Evidence of resemblance is only evidence that the suspect's appearance is similar to that of the offender. This may be true although the suspect had nothing to do with the crime. Such evidence may support proof of identity, but it cannot prove it per se. Its weight would depend on the circumstances of observation and the context of all the evidence.

A cross-examiner should pay the closest attention to the actual words and nuances, and be ready to expose any ambiguity between recognition and resemblance, and to object to any leading.

Such evidence is inherently uncertain; it has a built-in element of doubt. The witness saw the offender but cannot say that the suspect is the same person. He only looks like him. This favours the defence as well as the Crown and should be stressed.

Evidence of resemblance involves similar risks to those affecting recognition, viz perceptual similarity of the two faces, a feeling of familiarity from seeing the suspect in an innocent context, and typical sources of error arising from the circumstances of observation, or in memory.

A defence advocate need not attack the witness's sincerity. He may probe the alleged resemblance for details to shake it, or accept it. He may intensify the uncertainty so that contrary defence evidence is accepted, or leaves a reasonable doubt.

## 3 Distinctive characteristics

A witness may identify some special characteristic of the suspect which he also saw on the offender, e g a scar or tattoo.

Whether the characteristic was unusual or distinctive, or whether it was common, would be likely to determine the weight of such evidence.

Ordinary features like blue eyes or brown hair might have little value. On the other hand a unique birthmark might be convincing. In between, there may be a range of frequency of such features. To show that it is not uncommon might be a line of defence evidence, or cross-examination, in suitable cases.

In this type of evidence, what the witness perceives is also there for the court to see, and is beyond challenge. But, in suitable circumstances, the accuracy of his observation of the feature on the offender may be open to the usual objections.

## 4 Descriptions

Risks of mistaken identification can arise from giving descriptions of the offender to the police, for circulation, viz sex, age, height, build, hair, eyes, complexion, physical defects, facial blemishes, clothing, mode of speech, gait and so on. Such descriptions assist police enquiries, but are generally regarded as poor forms of identification.

A witness, not on oath, may describe an offender in informal but urgent circumstances, e g massive enquiries into abduction of a child, where thousands of people are interviewed. One witness might be questioned in another's presence, although this is not approved practice. They co-operate. Even a guess may help to trace the offender. Police may ask leading or suggestive questions to which helpful witnesses reply by stretching their image of the offender beyond the bounds of accuracy.

The danger is that unsound or incorrect verbal descriptions may be given in such circumstances, and may persist into later procedure, and the trial. As studies have shown, verbal labels included in a description may affect later visual identifications. Also, a witness may feel that he is committed to an identification matching his original description.

All this is valuable material for a cross-examiner who understands such processes and how they may lead to mistaken identifications or at least weaken their reliability. If material discrepancies come to the notice of the prosecution, or in any event on defence request, they should supply the defence with copies of the initial descriptions given to the police. They can then be compared with the defendant's appearance in the dock.

## 5   Facial Likeness Systems

Other initial forms of identification are artists' impressions, or Facial Likeness Systems, e g Identikit or Photofit, where a witness directs the creation of an offender's image for circulation.

This type of technology is likely to develop using computers and holography to produce coloured three-dimensional images. Images can already be distributed by telephone line.

These images are not normally produced as exhibits in the trial, as they are superseded by physical identification in a parade, or in the dock. Also questions of admissibility, as yet not clarified, may arise, and which are affected by which party seeks to produce them, and for what reason.

If these initial images were consistent with physical identifications, there would seem to be no reason for the Crown to produce them.

But the defence may seek their production, or comment on their absence, if they challenge the reliability of physical identification, e g on the ground of a material discrepancy between the image and the defendant, or because creating the image, with another person, may have affected the accuracy of identification.

## 6   Photographs

To identify a suspect at an early stage, e g to trace an offender at large, it may be essential for police to ask witnesses to select the offender's photograph from those of persons with criminal records. But photographs should not be shown to witnesses after a suspect has been arrested, and physical identification in a parade is possible.

It is accepted that showing photographs is inherently suggestive and that where it is necessary, it must be done fairly. Risks include the inferior quality of reproduction compared with the reality, physical identification always being better, or that the situation itself, or something said by a police officer, might influence the witness by suggesting that the offender's photograph is among those shown.

The Code of Practice for the Identification of Persons governs the procedure. The judge has a discretion to exclude evidence of identification if there has been non-compliance or irregularity in showing photographs.

Essential rules are that photographs should not be shown if an identification parade is possible; that they should be shown in a series; and that they should not be shown to witnesses before a parade.

Perhaps the greatest danger is that a witness may identify a suspect physically, because he is comparing him with a photograph, not the offender. Even if initial use of photographs cannot be shown to have caused mistaken physical identification later, it may reduce its reliability.

These matters could be a basis for destructive cross-examination, but for a defence dilemma.

The prosecution should not produce the photographs or refer to their use for identification purposes, as this would inform the jury that the defendant had a criminal record. The prosecution should advise the defence of the existence and use of the photographs, and the defence should always ensure that they are told about this.

It is then for the defence to weigh up the advantages or disadvantages of disclosure. In this situation, due weight should be given to the occurrence of such gross irregularity or such an opportunity for destructive cross-examination, that any identification would be vitiated.

## 7   Identification out of court

Identification of a suspect out of court may occur informally; in a confrontation with a single suspect; in a group identification; or in an identification parade.

In urgent and informal circumstances, a witness, accompanied by police, may identify a suspect, e g by going round an area in a police car soon after an assault or watching a pub where the suspect may go.

Confrontations between a witness and a single suspect, perhaps in a police station, are discouraged by The Code of Practice for the Identification of Persons. An identification parade is the preferred method. If it cannot be held, then the suspect should be identified in a group of people, in a non-suggestive setting, e g a railway station, and no leading questions should be asked. If this is impracticable, confrontation with a single suspect is a last resort, and the suspect's solicitor should normally be there.

Identifications out of court may be essential for police purposes, but they can create problems for proof since the informal, uncontrolled, situation lacks desirable precautions. The witness may be influenced by things said or done, or unintended hints from police, or other witnesses if they are not excluded.

One advantage, however, is that an identification out of court is often made at an early stage, before memory has dimmed. It is also a basis for, and reinforces, dock identification which follows it.

In preparing the defence case, close enquiry should be made into the circumstances of any identification out of court, as a ground for possible cross-examination.

The danger is that of suggestion. Any suggestive elements in the situation which could have influenced the identification should be probed. Much may depend on the integrity and fairness of individual police officers both at the time of the identification, and in giving evidence. A mistaken identification out of court may persist, without correction, to the stage of dock identification.

The defence are assisted here by the Crown's obligation to prove guilt beyond reasonable doubt. It may be impossible to show, conclusively, how subtle factors inclined the witness to make a wrong identification. It may even appear that the identification is possibly correct. But it could be enough, for the purpose of acquittal, to establish that, in the circumstances, the identification should be regarded as unreliable, thus creating a reasonable doubt about this crucial question.

## 8   *Identification parades*

The Code of Practice for the Identification of Persons governs the conduct of identification parades.

Although the accused is not compelled to take part, evidence of his refusal may be given in the trial, and he would then become liable to identification in a confrontation or in the dock. He should be informed of this.

The rules are designed to ensure that parades are conducted

fairly, without any suggestive elements to influence the witness. The main rules include the following. Before a parade, no information about the suspect's identity or description may be given to a witness and no photograph should be shown to him. The composition of the parade should be fair. Witnesses at a parade must be separated. Proper instructions and warnings should be given, including the fact that the offender may not be on the parade. Witnesses should be told not to make a positive identification if they cannot do so.

Cross-examiners should be familiar with the rules. Any breach may have consequences in law, as well as in evaluation of the facts. If flaws in the procedure emerge, there may be a question of whether the identification is inadmissible or whether the objections are matters of weight.

To prepare himself for challenging an identification at a parade, a cross-examiner should be in possession of the relevant information. The defendant's solicitors should have attended the parade, to note, and to object to, any irregularities, whether adjustments were made at the time or not.

A cross-examiner would try to bring out any breach of the rules, including the omission of necessary warnings, or any unfairness. Anything would be objectionable which directed a witness's attention specially to the suspect, instead of to everyone on the parade equally.

Again, destructive cross-examination might succeed if it were simply to show that the identification has been rendered unreliable by irregularities, or words used by identifying witnesses which implied doubt, although it could not be proved that it was necessarily incorrect. To raise a reasonable doubt about this, would mean that the Crown had failed to discharge their burden of proof, and acquittal would follow.

## 9 Dock identification

The general rule is that a witness should not be asked to identify the accused for the first time in dock at the trial, unless in exceptional circumstances. The concern is that seeing the accused in the dock may influence a witness, so that he is more likely to identify him in error.

It is thought that dock identification is more reliable when it confirms an earlier identification. As an exception, a witness may make a dock identification for the first time, where the defendant refused to participate in an identification parade.

The aim of defence cross-examination would be related to the crucial nature of the issue of visual identification, the real possibilities of mistake, and the burden of proof beyond reasonable doubt on the Crown for conviction. The cross-examiner may try, at least, to show that the evidence is unreliable, even if he cannot prove that it is inaccurate.

The identification out of court may be attacked on the grounds referred to above. Provided that the cross-examiner has a mastery of what occurred, the informality of the circumstances often provides an opening for criticisms. That the witness was not on oath when he reached his critical decision, may be stressed.

Although the dock identification may be challenged on the basis that the witness is influenced by the suggestive situation of the defendant, no witness is likely to admit such highly irresponsible conduct. Yet some witnesses reveal their uncertainty.

It may be better to persist in the challenge to the earlier identification, and to suggest that the witness may feel that he must conform to it, even if it was dubious, and he is no longer sure of it.

Other opportunities for cross-examination may arise from any inconsistency between the dock identification and the earlier identification, e g if the witness denies or cannot remember the earlier one, or claims to have identified someone else, or says that the accused is not the offender.

The Crown might then call other witnesses to repair the damage, by speaking to the previous identifications. The admissibility of such evidence for that purpose, has been doubted by some legal writers. Reference should be made to the cases.

## B  Circumstantial evidence

In any trial, visual identification evidence incriminating the accused may be supplemented by circumstantial evidence of identity, or the Crown evidence may be wholly circumstantial.

Circumstantial evidence of identity is evidence of circumstances from which the accused's identity as the offender may be inferred. The questions of fact which arise concern (i) the facts, and (ii) what the facts mean. It is the inferences made from the facts which may incriminate the accused.

Each element may be insufficient in itself to implicate the accused, but cumulatively, they may lead inevitably to that conclusion. Single facts may seem trivial, but linked with others, they may make a meaningful pattern pointing to the accused's guilt.

The facts and circumstances covered by this kind of evidence may be of any kind. The accused may be implicated by evidence of his motives, conduct before and after the crime, personal traces which he left on a victim or at the locus, or traces of the victim or the locus which he carried away on his person, forensic evidence of many types, possession of incriminating articles, real evidence, or admissions made to the police.

Circumstantial evidence often includes fragmentary and neutral facts here and there, spoken to by honest and unconnected witnesses, which are unlikely to be exposed as mistaken by cross-examination. Evidence about a variety and number of minor facts, and particularly about exhibits, may not be very prone to error. But any such allegation should follow the lines suggested in the earlier discussion of the sources of error in evidence.

When police witnesses testify to admissions and confessions made to them by the accused, they are not giving direct evidence of his commission of the crime. Such evidence is regarded here as being a special form of circumstantial evidence. The scope for cross-examination to show errors in admissions and confessions has already been discussed.

Once the facts constituting circumstantial evidence have been established, the remaining question is what they mean.

Obviously, the Crown contention is that an inference should be drawn from the circumstantial evidence, beyond reasonable doubt, to the effect that the accused is the offender. Whether to draw that inference or not is a question for the court, not a Crown witness. However, direct evidence contradicting any incriminating inferences may be given by the defendant and other defence witnesses. They would then be liable to cross-examination by the prosecutor, generally on the basis that they are lying.

CHAPTER 4

# The credibility of evidence

I   Introduction
II  Analysis of lying

## I   INTRODUCTION

In this book, and in courts generally, the term 'credibility' means the extent to which evidence is accepted as truthful. It excludes unintentional inaccuracy, i e errors, and refers to lies, i e intentional and motivated attempts to deceive. It is a matter of degree, but unquantifiable.

Credibility is treated here as a quality of evidence, not of witnesses. Statements are the object of belief; witnesses are the objects of trust. To impute credibility to a witness, implies a fixed quantum of veracity which settles the question. It stems from a bygone division of people into truthful and untruthful classes. Modern views are more complex, i e whether or not the witness will tell the truth depends, not on a specific trait, but rather on the whole individual, his motivations, and the particular situation to which he reacts.

Lying is rife in criminal trials. It is a more serious problem than crucial errors in evidence. This is seen every day in conflicting testimony, where some witnesses must know the truth.

The trial process depends on belief in the testimony of these witnesses who are trusted. Issues of credibility involve risks: a lie may be believed; the truth may be disbelieved; or doubt may remain, which also affects the outcome. Credibility must be decided correctly to avoid miscarriages of justice.

Cross-examination by each party, whether or not it succeeds, can contribute powerfully to a proper decision. The value of destroying an opponent's evidence is obvious; but intensive cross-examination which makes no impact on evidence, may enhance its credibility, and is equally valuable to the court, although not to the cross-examiner. An advocate is bound to put his case to some witnesses, but apart from this it is tactically better not to cross-examine at all, than to do so badly.

Since an advocate assists the court whether he succeeds or fails, he can cross-examine as forcefully as he wishes, unrestrained by ethical doubts, provided that he challenges credibility responsibly, on the basis of his information, which is not for him to judge.

The law cannot eliminate lying evidence, but tries to discourage it by setting up an adversarial system, with appropriate rules of procedure, evidence, and penalties, as a context for evidence to be led, tested, contradicted, and evaluated.

Daily conflicts of sworn testimony signify that the oath or affirmation are mere formalities for many witnesses. Except for witnesses who take them seriously, they are feeble as deterrents to lying, and of no help in cross-examination or assessing evidence. Some witnesses may tell the truth because of the religious sanction, and others from a sense of duty or fear of penalties. The oath is unlikely to deter witnesses with strong motives for lying.

Penalties for contempt of court or perjury may have an unwanted effect in reinforcing falsehood. Witnesses must have strong motives to risk committing perjury. Once they have lied, these motives are reinforced by fear of the penalties which may follow from exposure. This double motivation may discourage retraction of lies, even under forceful cross-examination.

Open misconduct in testifying, e g evasiveness or fencing with questions, can be dealt with at once, by warnings or penalties, but most lying evidence is more covert. Perjury may only become apparent in a later trial. Some forms of false testimony do not constitute perjury in law, or else are undetectable, e g omitting material facts, or giving evidence a twist in a false direction. Perjury is hard to prove. Most trials would be duplicated by later trials for perjury. Only a small fraction of false evidence becomes the subject of prosecution.

The law also tries to deter interference with witnesses, but often in vain. Intimidation by threats to witnesses or their families or fear of reprisals, is a substantial cause of lying. Threats may be verbal, and undetectable, even if witnesses are not too afraid to report them. The protection available to threatened persons is often inadequate.

The intimidated witness, usually called by the prosecution, is not an uncommon figure in criminal courts. Typically anxious and subdued, the witness gives evasive, inconsistent or improbable evidence in barely audible tones, caught in a dilemma between fear of the threats, and fear of the law. Under pressure depending on the person and circumstances, such a witness may persist in his falsehoods. Fabricated 'amnesia', or inability to identify are two major positions which are very hard to demolish.

Intimidated witnesses often reverse their true evidence. A useful provision allows a cross-examiner to refer the witness to any previous inconsistent statement which he made on a specified occasion. If he denies it, the statement may be proved by other witnesses. If admitted or proved, it can be compared with and used to discredit his present evidence. The previous statement is only admissible for this purpose, not as evidence on the issues. It will prove neither that the contrary of his evidence in court nor that the statement itself are true.

All aspects of the rules of evidence, procedure, or proof, related to credibility, cannot be reviewed here. The oath, penalties for testifying falsely, or interfering with witnesses, and the admissibility of previous inconsistent statements, were mentioned above because of their direct relevance. Among other matters, cross-examiners must, of course, be thoroughly familiar with the following two major areas of the law.

The Police and Criminal Evidence Act 1984, and related Codes of Practice, in regard to evidence of confessions and admissions are designed to minimize possible lying by witnesses on either side. The various discretions conferred on judges to exclude evidence which was improperly obtained, or which is unfair or prejudicial, should be known. The rules relating to pre-trial identification procedures were discussed in the previous chapter.

The requirements for proof include safeguards against the acceptance of lies, in the form of judicial warnings to juries, or magistrates' self-direction, about the risks of convicting on the basis of some kind of evidence, and in a few cases, the need for corroboration. Above all, placing the burden of proof on the prosecution and requiring a standard of proof beyond reasonable doubt for guilt, is the overall protection against wrongly giving effect to lies, by conviction. Lying and its exposure, are psychological processes. However, psychology as a formal subject can offer no help to the cross-examiner at the present time.

Since early this century, psychologists have carried out research into the reliability of perception and memory. They claim that their findings can contribute to court processes. As has been shown elsewhere, this claim is unfounded. The methodology of psychological research, is experimental and statistical, and is confined to the laboratory or to artificial situations. The findings add nothing material to common sense, yet many are still controversial.

This methodology cannot cope with the motivational processes, the real life events, and the court situation in which lying occurs; hence, psychologists have ignored lying. No current body of psychological knowledge has any practical value for application to the problem of credibility in courts. If it were otherwise, the legal profession would have seized on it long ago.

No psychological technique or test is known which can penetrate the mind of an individual in isolation, to ascertain if he is lying. Moreover, even if this were possible, it would not reveal the truth—which is not necessarily just the contrary of a lie. By psychological criteria alone, it is not possible to detect lies or discover the truth.

The best way of attaining the truth, which has been developed so far, is the holistic comparison of various reports about a common reality, after they have been tested or challenged adversarially, i e a criminal trial. This underlines the function and importance of cross-examination. On comparing the experience and insight of the two professions, it is clear that, at the present time, it is the psychologist who can learn about lying from the cross-examiner, and not the converse.

A decision to lie must, of course, be the culmination of a complex motivational process, but it is unnecessary, and in the present state of psychology impossible, to go into that.

Thus, an understanding of lying must be practical, based on common sense, experience of life and the courts, and free from psychological jargon or theorizing.

## II ANALYSIS OF LYING

The practical questions, 'Who lies?'; 'What do they lie about?'; 'How do they lie?'; and 'How can lying be detected?', divide the subject naturally into lying witnesses; subjects of lying; forms of lying; and detection of lying.

### A  Lying witnesses

The first question, 'Who lies?' cannot be answered by suggesting that any class of witnesses is more likely to lie than another. Witnesses cannot be classified in this way.

To expect any category of witnesses to be either wholly honest or liars, irrespective of the circumstances, would now be regarded as naive and simplistic. As a result of many factors, including cultural changes, the spread of popular psychology, the development of the media, and the experience of the courts, people are more aware of the variety and reality of human nature, than they used to be.

It is now less surprising when persons deemed to have integrity, are found to have lied, including presidents threatened with impeachment, millionaires who resort to prohibited company practices, or clergymen, protesting innocence, who are convicted of unpleasant sexual offences.

It is a common experience in court to see 'respectable' persons trying to bend the truth. Experience in summary criminal courts shows that the 'respectable' image of motorists, has been somewhat impaired by the lengths to which many offenders, previously of good character, will go to retain their driving licences.

These are examples of persons accused of some offence, in whom lying may be explained by strong motivation. But witnesses other than the accused, may be highly motivated also, e g relatives or friends of an accused, or prosecution witnesses such as accomplices diverting guilt away from themselves, or who are malicious.

Every day, in courts throughout the land, police witnesses from whom impeccable standards of conduct are demanded, face attacks on their truthfulness. Even where they are unfounded, this is a live issue.

For practical purposes, courts and advocates must assume that any type of witness may lie in some circumstances. Whether or not that will happen will be determined by the interaction of the individual, his motives, and the situation.

Lying is always the result of a complex process of this kind. People of the highest character will lie if the situation requires it. In deciding this, they will give expression to their own values, whether or not they coincide with social values. Any other view is unrealistic.

The variety and complexity of individual responses to particular situations must be stressed. A court should never entertain fixed views about the truthfulness or otherwise of any class of witnesses. To do so would be a prejudgment or a prejudice. The following are merely illustrations.

## 1   Prosecution witnesses

Police are the most common prosecution witnesses and testify in most criminal trials, but without special status. Nowadays, police evidence is attacked constantly, but the attacks are usually directed against the truthfulness of the police witness as an individual, not the policy, traditions or integrity of police as a body.

The mildest charge may be that the witness, convinced of the accused's guilt, and misconceiving the public interest, has wilfully coloured the facts to secure a conviction. The defence may hope that this charge of perjury may derive support from the partiality implied by the police duty to trace and apprehend suspects, and assemble incriminating evidence—although that is radically different.

Again, it may be suggested that false police evidence is given irresponsibly or maliciously, e g where an accused is identified as one of a group of wrongdoers or as having resisted arrest, without foundation.

A common accusation is that a confession or admission has been falsely imputed to the defendant, perhaps by two officers, and entered in their notebooks. Such evidence, if accepted, though false, could overcome any weakness in the Crown case.

The worst allegation would be that of a criminal conspiracy by a number of officers, to convict a person known to be innocent, perhaps aggravated by 'planting' false exhibits, or intimidating civilian witnesses.

A common weakness of such challenges is that the defence often cannot suggest, let alone prove, sufficient motivation for such illegal conduct, despite the risks of detection, loss of career and pension, and imprisonment.

Sometimes the ranks, numbers of officers, and activities involved, create such a danger of exposure, that falsehood seems unlikely. Moreover, even if lying in court seems safe, unforeseen evidence, e g a genuine confession, might emerge later, or a public inquiry might be held, which would expose the perjury. Police officers know that such things happen.

However disturbing allegations of false police evidence may be, courts must consider them impartially. Sometimes they are only desperate inventions of an accused. Yet, false police testimony is in fact proved to occur at times. Every case must be investigated on its merits.

It is a defence advocate's duty to take such a line on the basis of responsible information and instructions. However, unless extreme attacks are supported by positive defence evidence, he may be liable to criticism.

The defence may contend that the evidence of accomplices who are Crown witnesses is untruthful. This may derive support from the witness's admitted bad character, and potential motives for lying. Accomplices may minimize their own blame and add to the blame of others, to gain immunity or a lighter sentence. Such evidence has always been regarded with caution and a judge must warn a jury about the danger of convicting on such evidence unless it is corroborated.

Complainants in sexual offences may be accused of lying. It may be suggested that a female consented to sexual intercourse, and now denies it for personal reasons, or that the charge is the result of hysterical fantasy or malice.

In charges of sexual offences, a jury must be warned of the danger of convicting on the uncorroborated testimony of the complainant. Thus the issue of credibility is often acute.

The rules relating to the evidence of children, sworn or unsworn, and the requirements as to warnings and corroboration, show that cross-examination to the effect that the witness is lying, will usually raise a very live issue.

A crime of violence may have involved a struggle, between several persons, and perhaps issues of self-defence. Complainants and their associates may continue this battle in the courtroom, implicating persons falsely out of animosity.

## 2 Defence witnesses

Defendants under cross-examination are generally treated as lying, since, presumably, they know the truth of the prosecutor's assertion which they deny. It would be highly exceptional, although possible, for an accused to be mistaken in his evidence when he denies guilt, e g if he was unaware that the car which struck the injured child was the one which he was driving. Defendants are accused of lying more than any other class of witnesses and are probably the most motivated. However, a defendant would be seeking acquittal, whether or not he was guilty, so that motive alone cannot determine the truth or falsity of his evidence. The defendant's denials of guilt may be truthful.

Friends, relatives, workmates or other associates of an accused, who speak to the main facts, or to an alibi, are generally challenged as lying, for similar reasons. They too are likely to know the truth.

If the evidence of independent defence witnesses is challenged, the criticism will normally be that it is mistaken or unreliable. Alibi evidence of this kind may be given, e g if the manager of a bar confirms that the defendant was there with other alibi witnesses, but cannot recall the exact date and time.

## 3 Independent witnesses

Irrespective of whether they are called by the prosecution or the defence, some witnesses may be described in court as independent. By this is meant that they are witnesses with no apparent interest in, or connection with, the case, or the parties, e g persons passing by when a bank was robbed.

As such witnesses are believed to have no other motivation than to tell the truth, courts often accept that they are likely to have done so, although their evidence could, of course, be incomplete, mistaken, or biased.

Deliberate lying by such witnesses is not usually expected, on the view that no normal person would wish to contribute to an unjust conviction or acquittal, and risk severe penalties, for no reason.

Naturally, this is not a matter where rules can be applied, but apart from challenging the reliability of the evidence, it is usually difficult to attack it as untruthful without any foundation in other evidence.

Witnesses who may fall into this category include eyewitnesses to an incident in which they were not involved or persons speaking to separate items of circumstantial evidence. Expert witnesses may sometimes be so regarded, because of their professional status.

### 4   Specially motivated witnesses

Any witness, including an independent witness, may have some unsuspected and special reason for lying.

Examples are a sense of loyalty to the party who called them, hidden partisanship in the form of hostility to criminals or to the police, inflating the list of stolen goods to exaggerate an insurance claim, avoiding adverse publicity, vanity, embarrassment, fear and so on.

But to lie in any serious way, for such reasons, especially in any way which might contribute to an unjust conviction, is not usually to be expected—unless an apparently neutral witness is really a pathological liar with the ability to conceal his falsehood.

Such tendencies may not be obvious but they may be perceived by a cross-examiner who is alert for them and who listens to the evidence-in-chief with some imagination.

## B   Subjects of lying

What witnesses may lie about are the real issues of fact, which were examined in chapter 2. The 'rule of alternative defences' explained there means that if lying occurs, it will normally relate to either the commission of the crime or the identity of the offender, but rarely to both issues.

Exceptions can occur, of course. A neat example is where a disqualified accused is charged with driving a motor car, and claims that it was his passenger who was driving, this being a lie. The issue is primarily one of identification, the two men having been seen by police to change their seats. However, if the passenger was driving, no offence was committed as he is a qualified driver. Here the issue of identity and of the commission of the crime are inextricably bound up with each other, but such situations are rare.

Where the commission of a result-crime is the issue, questions of credibility may be expected to refer to the intangible elements, e g whether the alleged victim of rape consented to sexual intercourse, or whether the accused's state of fear justified his attack in self-defence.

Similarly, lying is common in conduct-crimes, because proof rests solely on verbal assertions unconfirmed in the tangible world.

No general statement can be made about the incidence of lying in object-crimes, because of their variation.

Where identity is the real issue, lies, if told, will refer either to the accused's presence at the locus or to his alibi defence, but the question will seldom arise in circumstantial evidence or in expert evidence.

## C Forms of lying

### 1 Affirmative and negative lies

To assert a fact, which did not happen, or to deny one which did, is the most stark form of lying—the type which could constitute perjury. To lie like this, a witness must be highly motivated. When he has done so, he has an additional motive for not admitting his falsehood and disclosing the truth, viz the risk of penalties in the trial, or in a later prosecution for perjury.

So, because of this double motivation, such a witness will rarely retract such false evidence and substitute the truth. However, destructive cross-examination may succeed in weakening lying evidence of this gross type, so that it succumbs to the more credible evidence led by the cross-examiner.

This pattern would be typical. Cross-examination would have performed its valuable function in gnawing away at the supports, but the final blow would be given by contradictory evidence which was preferred as a result. This is closer to the daily reality of criminal courts, especially in summary trials which constitute the overwhelming majority, than the dramatic coup de grâce of popular mythology, in the course of the cross-examination.

### 2 Reluctance and evasiveness

In witnesses who are not sufficiently motivated to commit outright perjury, unwillingness to tell the truth is often expressed as reluctance to testify rather than by specific lies.

Testimony which is obviously reluctant would damage the impression which a perjurer would wish to make, viz that of a plausible story, told confidently.

Such witnesses rarely fail to answer at all, as they would incur penalties. However, they may answer evasively. Their dilemma is that of a wish to hide the truth, and fear of the consequences of being seen to do so. This conflict may be aggravated if they made previous inconsistent statements, from which they fear to deviate too much.

Typically, this occurs when Crown witnesses depart from the incriminating evidence expected from them, and give evidence which is harmful to the prosecutor's case. The prosecutor may then, with the court's leave, cross-examine his own witness.

The cause may be intimidation or spontaneous fear of reprisals. Even an imprisoned accused, acting through others, may be a danger. Only limited protection can be given by police. Some witnesses ask for their addresses to be concealed, or move to another area.

It is common for reluctant and evasive evidence to be given by victims of domestic violence, or members of the family, after a reconciliation has occurred.

When evidence of this kind is given, in any situation, a cross-examiner can exploit the witness's conflict by reinforcing his fear of non-compliance with his oath. If the witness has not gone beyond the point of no return, he may, by firmness, warnings, and perhaps by reference to previous inconsistent statements, be led to testify properly. Otherwise, the court may have to intervene—which may have a persuasive effect on later witnesses who testify similarly.

## 3  Omissions

The oath to tell 'the whole truth', is an obligation on the witness to answer questions, not to volunteer relevant information, and report all that he knows about the issue. Advocates prefer strictly controlled interrogation, without the risks of unexpected adverse evidence. Judges, being impartial, do not ask open-ended questions. It is not the practice, after a witness has been questioned, to invite him to add anything further which he thinks may be helpful. As a result, vital facts may slip through the net.

Taking advantage of this, motivated witnesses who are unwilling to commit perjury by outright lying, may try to omit important facts if they can. This involves less guilt and fear than lying; it is simpler, since nothing need be prepared or recalled; if detected it is not liable to penalties for perjury and might be excused as ignorance or forgetting.

However, omissions become lies and perjury, if the concealed facts are not disclosed in answer to a direct question about them, or even an indirect question, which brings the facts reasonably within its scope.

The remedy consists of thoroughness of cross-examination. Questions should be formulated carefully to eliminate possible omissions, by preventing the witness from avoiding the real point. Specific leading questions, e g 'Did the accused pick up a brick?' should be combined with general ones, e g, 'What was the accused doing?', to bar any escape.

The aim is either to make the witness disclose what he is concealing, or else commit perjury—which this class of witness wishes to avoid.

If a witness has not omitted any facts to which a direct question referred, he would not incur any risk by revealing them. The prognosis for cross-examination is therefore good.

## 4 False qualifications

A witness may state facts more or less truthfully, while giving them a bias intentionally in some way which can range from minor colouring to major distortion. Such subtle forms of deceit may be described as 'false qualifications'.

One way of doing this is to adjust the facts or their interpretation in the desired direction. It is easier to do this in admissible impression evidence of a somewhat ambiguous incident, e g a manner of driving, suspicious conduct in a shop, acting as look out, or ambiguous contact which may or may not have been sexually motivated. The same facts can always be stated in very varied ways, and witnesses should describe them in their own language.

Another form of false qualification consists of the way knowledge of facts is expressed. Witnesses can give their evidence, truthfully enough, but in a way which suggests doubt when, really, they are sure. For support in this, they may refer to barriers to observation or memory.

Conversely, witnesses may express certainty about facts of which they are unsure, e g if police witnesses after discussing the case, make much firmer identification of the accused, than observation would justify.

If the evidence creates a false impression intentionally to some extent, its factual foundations should be probed, which may have the effect of undermining the unwanted conclusion. Any unjustified gloss on the facts actually seen, can be met by suggesting a contradictory alternative.

Close attention should be given by advocates to the precise language used by a witness to describe his state of knowledge of the facts, to see if it may contain false innuendos or implications. But it is objectionable to repeat an answer with a different gloss.

However, it is the fact that the suggestions of doubt or certainty are false which is objectionable, not these qualifications of the state of knowledge in themselves. Although definite evidence is preferable, the qualified evidence of an honest witness may be quite acceptable.

Cross-examination often succeeds in moving false qualifications in a more favourable direction. The witness was insufficiently motivated to commit perjury, and may not have gone too far in a false direction, so that he is not at great risk if he is induced to rectify his earlier evidence.

Other innominate forms of deception exist which would be recognized when they are met, e g telling the truth in a humorous, sarcastic or exaggerated manner which induces disbelief.

## D   Detection of lying

A cross-examiner's ability to expose lying is aided by knowing how the court decides whether or not testimony is truthful, or why the court is unable to reach a decision. Primarily, this must be seen from the point of view of the court, not of the advocate. The desired judgment is the advocate's target. He can then apply this insight in cross-examination.

The evaluation of credibility can only be analysed in terms of practical courtroom psychology, based on general judicial and professional experience of what happens in criminal trials, and, ultimately, on common sense. No other basis exists. Psychology, as a formal discipline, offers no explanation of lying and no help in its detection.

It is emphasized that the judgment of credibility is holistic. Single elements which enter into it may be unimpressive in themselves. However, when everything is compared and integrated, the conclusion may be compelling. This must be kept in mind during the discussion of the separate elements.

The two main questions which arise for a court are 'Can the witness be trusted?' and 'Is the evidence itself acceptable?'. For belief, affirmative answers must be given to both questions. A negative answer to either, would cause the testimony to be rejected.

If a witness is trusted, but is talking nonsense, his testimony will be rejected on the view that he must be mistaken. On the other hand, even the most plausible story may be disbelieved, if the court has no confidence in the witness. Within these extremes, various combinations may arise, but the important point is that belief depends on both the witness and the evidence, not on either one alone.

### 1   The witness

A witness begins as a cipher. Trust has to be created. Whether or not he is truthful, has to emerge. There are substantial difficulties in making a rapid assessment of a disputed quality in a total stranger, under restricted conditions—especially when others conduct the enquiry. This makes demands on a court's understanding of human nature, experience of life, intuition and common sense.

Four aspects of human nature enter into evaluating a witness, viz personality, character, motivation and demeanour. Personality refers to the witness's individuality; character refers to the moral aspect of his personality; motivation refers to the directions in which he is impelled by specific feelings; and demeanour refers to his non-verbal expression of feelings while testifying.

*(a) Personality.* Personality refers to the distinctive features of a person which make him an individual. Relevant questions are: 'What kind of person is this?' and 'Does this help in deciding whether he is telling the truth or lying?'.

Psychology, today, gives no guidance. The *Penguin Dictionary of Psychology* defines personality as:

> . . . a term so resistant to definition and so broad in usage that no coherent simple statement about it can be made.
> Arthur S Reber (ed) *Penguin Dictionary of Psychology* (1987)

Less wary psychologists have produced countless definitions of personality, and attempted classifications of people into types, which has resulted in a sea of unhelpful controversy. Courts must assess the relevance of a witness's personality on the basis of a common-sense view of human nature, although this too has its limitations.

Obviously a court cannot be expected to attain deep insight into a witness's personality. The information is not available. A trial is no place for autobiography or for a psychodynamic analysis of a witness, while he speaks of matters other than himself, i e the issues.

These limitations also apply to a defendant as a witness, even where his personality may also be part of the issues of fact.

Inevitably, a court's impression of a witness as a person, will contribute to its view of whether or not he is truthful. The witness may be weighed up as an individual, e g a courageous bystander who stopped the robbery, or his membership of a class of persons may dominate, e g the hospital surgeon who operated on the injured victim.

The view taken of the witness's personality is certainly part of the assessment process. The kind of person he is, would be likely to have a bearing on whether he is telling the truth or lying, but it is impossible to state the nature of this relationship specifically and explicitly. In this field, the intuitions of the tribunal of fact play a large part.

But it can be said confidently that per se, an impression of a witness's personality is an unreliable basis for deciding on his veracity. At best, it has limited value, and at worst, it can be misleading. Personality only acquires value as a guide to veracity in the context of the total equation, the holistic assessment of credibility.

Cross-examiners are recommended simply to treat witnesses as individuals, not types, using their personal insight into human nature, and their experience of life. Whatever its limitations, this common-sense approach, is better than a theoretical classification which gives no practical guidance.

*(b)   Character.* 'Character' as a general term, has many meanings. They need not be explained and any attempt to define the word comprehensively would be unsatisfactory.

As applied to a witness, in the context of assessing evidence, character usually refers to the moral aspect of personality. It is not a separate compartment of human nature; it simply consists of a number of personality traits which are normally valued, e g kindness, courage or sincerity.

It may be contended that a 'good' person is likely to tell the truth, or conversely, that a 'bad' person is likely to lie, or even that this depends on a single disposition to be truthful or to lie.

Some persons are indeed more trustworthy than others as a rule, but this is too imprecise for general application. By itself, it omits the complexity of human nature and the reality of how a person is motivated in a particular situation. Character and truthfulness are abstractions. An abstract statement of their relationship has no practical value. The underlying human reality would be lost in generalizations.

Neither psychology nor common sense would divide witnesses into those of good character who are normally truthful, and those of bad character who are normally liars. No fixed quantum of veracity is inherent in anyone.

On a practical level, the neutral facts, showing the witness's role in society, are normally elicited in evidence-in-chief e g age, occupation, marital status, or children. Character may be assumed to be good unless it is attacked. However, whether or not advocates try to set up good character or to attack it deliberately, a court is forming an impression about this in the course of the evidence.

Other texts should be consulted for the rules of evidence which limit attacks on character, including that of the accused, where the rules are complex and statutory. The prosecutor can, of course, cross-examine other defence witnesses as to bad character and previous convictions. It may imperil the defence to call witnesses with extensive records.

If the defence cross-examination of a Crown witness makes an imputation against character, or if the accused puts his character in issue, or in certain other circumstances, the accused will be exposed to cross-examination as to his bad character and previous convictions. Thus, a defence advocate is likely to be careful if the accused has a significant criminal record.

Evidence of character designed to discredit a witness, tends to be limited to his criminal record, although in certain circumstances other evidence may be called to attack his credibility.

Whether or not a witness will tell the truth, depends more on his motives in that situation, than on his general character, or some fixed trait of truthfulness. To apply the word 'credible' to a witness, wrongly suggests such a uniform quality.

Good general character, alone, does not ensure that a witness is truthful. It is only one factor and may be overcome by strong motives for lying in a particular situation. Following their own values, people of seemingly good character may take the risk of lying to help a friend or relative, e g in supporting a false alibi.

Countless defendants lie, to avoid conviction. The media are full of reports of the false protests of innocence of many who would be described as respectable. Such cases include sexual abuse of children by schoolmasters, fraud or embezzlement by trusted executives or local government councillors, drink-driving offences by public figures or shoplifting by mature ladies. It is often said in excuse that such offences were out of character.

The veracity of police witnesses, who are supposed to be persons of integrity, is attacked regularly. The imputation is that their normal good character is overcome by their specific motives in the particular situation, which lead them to lie.

The conclusion must be that character counts, but that alone it is an inadequate guide to truthfulness.

*(c) Motives.* As was seen, the view which a court is able to form of a witness's personality and character is of limited value in detecting lies.

Personality and character are hidden and complex; a court only gets a surface impression of them which is not clarified by psychological explanation.

The witness always has these dispositions. They are general qualities, without specific aims, not a response to his situation in the trial. A simpler notion of human nature is needed for court purposes.

The concept of motive, is simpler, and more useful in lie detection. A motive is taken here to be a transient state of arousal which impels a person towards a definite goal (although many psychologists would disagree). Above all, it is directional, i e it has a specific aim. It is a witness's response to his situation, expressed in purposive action.

Naturally, a single motive cannot explain behaviour, which results from the interaction of many variables, including conflicting or unconscious tendencies—a kaleidoscopic process best left to psychologists.

'Motive' here means more than just wanting something to happen; that is just a feeling. If a feeling is expressed in action, by doing something to achieve the desired end, that is a motive. What a witness may do to achieve his end, is to lie. Then his testimony is motivated, i e dictated by his aim, not his knowledge of the facts.

Whether a witness's feelings are involved, and if so, in what direction, is often clear to advocates and to the court. They may be conceded, but if not, they can be inferred from personal links with and interest in the situation, and various objective circumstances. This does not depend on deep insight into the witness's personality or character.

In other than genuinely neutral witnesses, feelings, which could develop into motives to falsify evidence, may be classified on a simple directional basis, viz. towards conviction or acquittal, or satisfaction of some personal purpose regardless of the verdict.

The relevance of feelings and motives to lie detection may be illustrated as follows.

A mother testifies in support of her son's alibi. Obviously, from her evidence and her relationship to the accused, she hopes for his acquittal. Her feelings are consistent with either the truth or falsity of her evidence. Assuming, for illustrative purposes, the absence of any other information or guidance, what inference about the truthfulness of her evidence should be drawn from her feelings?

It would be unsound, illogical and unfair to conclude that the only explanation for her evidence is the motive to have her son acquitted, so that she must be lying. She may be telling the truth, although her feelings impel her in that direction.

But her feelings are still relevant material for consideration and may enter into the question of credibility, which would not have happened with an independent witness. Although this does not settle the question, it may weaken her evidence and reduce the weight of the alibi. The view, 'She would say that to save her son, wouldn't she?' may have some effect. The answer to the above question, which was confined strictly to the role of motivation, is that the credibility of her evidence is left in doubt.

If the doubt is accepted as a reasonable one, it would, of course lead to acquittal. But the present enquiry is into the importance of motivation in lie detection, i e in a question of fact.

A prosecutor, in cross-examining the mother, would not be restricted to the matter of her motivation, e g he could test her evidence and show that it was self-contradictory, or that it conflicted with alibi evidence from other witnesses. In the context of such probative defects, her motive might become a dominant and sinister explanation for her evidence, so that it is rejected.

In order to expose evidence as false, and as arising from motivation directed towards a desired verdict, a foundation should be laid by firmly establishing the witness's personal involvement in the issue.

If the witness's connection with the trial is obvious, e g if he is a close relative of the defendant, there is no need to belabour the point. But if the link is not apparent, it should be brought out clearly and specifically, e g if he has business dealings with the accused.

Animosity towards a party, as well as favourable feelings, should be taken into account.

If the witness admits his interest, the point is made. If he resists it unreasonably, his credit will suffer.

Any non-disclosure of material facts in evidence-in-chief, which link the witness to the issue, is likely to be damaging to the opponent. It may seem as if they were deliberately concealed. Such omissions should be exposed, stressed and exploited.

As was seen in the discussion of lying witnesses, some, who are indifferent to the verdict, may lie for personal reasons. Advocates should be alert to such possibilities, and they may need to probe the evidence imaginatively to reveal such motives.

Once a possible motive for lying has emerged, it may be suggested explicitly to the witness that he is in fact lying for that reason. Naturally, he will deny this. But the cross-examiner has then shown the court where he stands, has put his case to the witness, and has perhaps gained from the persuasive effect of suggestion.

Feelings and possible motives which could lead witnesses to lie, are factors to consider in assessing evidence, but alone they are inconclusive. Like other mental processes, extrinsic confirmation is needed to establish their presence and effect on testimony. Again, it is stressed that any sound evaluation of evidence is holistic, and must take everything into account. Lie detection based on a single clue would be unsound and unsafe.

Realising this, a cross-examiner should try to expose inconsistency, improbability and lack of realism in the evidence itself, to suggest that it is to be explained by motivation, rather than regard for the truth. This, combined with evidence showing that the witness has feelings which could motivate him to lie, is a powerful form of challenge.

*(d)   Demeanour.*   The traditional view is that a witness's 'demeanour' gives some guidance to his veracity. The higher appeal courts, where evidence is not led, are reluctant to evaluate the accuracy of evidence, because they have not seen the demeanour of witnesses in the lower court.

Dictionary definitions of 'demeanour' are not informative, e g 'bearing or mien'; 'outward behaviour'; or 'the way a person behaves towards others'.

The subject of demeanour raises a question of human nature, i e of psychology, viz 'Can one tell, just by looking at a witness, whether he is speaking the truth or lying?'. The psychologists' approach will be considered below.

A common-sense view of what demeanour means in court is that it consists of visible and audible facts about a witness, other than the content of his evidence. This includes both fixed and variable characteristics, and all forms of self-expression, whether simple or complex, voluntary or involuntary.

Fixed characteristics include age, sex, physique, appearance, hairstyle, clothing or ornaments. They fall into this category, as they may mean something about a person, and are static in court.

Variable and voluntary aspects include posture, gestures, movements, or facial expressions which can be controlled; audible features include the rate, emphasis, pitch or fluency of speech.

Variable and involuntary signs include uncontrolled facial expressions, e g blushing, blanching, perspiring, and other physical signs, e g tremors and the like.

Variable and complex conduct includes fainting, having to go to the toilet, crying, asking for water, loss of temper, hysteria, illness, or distress.

These examples are far from exhaustive.

What help can psychology offer here? Is a witness's demeanour a reliable guide to whether or not he is lying? What signs of lying should a court look for?

The term 'demeanour' is absent from psychological dictionaries. But the divisions of psychology include the study of non-verbal communication (NVC), i e forms of communication other than language—the popular term is body language. Paralinguistics, another branch, studies forms of vocal communication other than semantic, viz how the voice is used, rather than what is said. The adoption of physiology by psychology, to create the subject of physiological psychology, should also be noted.

These disciplines cover the whole field, i e non-verbal or vocal signs, and physiological manifestations. If there is any merit in basing lie detection on demeanour, it should have been supported by psychological research. Is this so?

Starting with the last topic, no psychologist or physiologist can claim, scientifically, that any special physiological processes occur in the brain, during the complex cognitive act of lying, nor that there are any specific physical or vocal signs of lying, which express that process. The physiological psychology of emotion, itself controversial, is a different question. Clearly, any scientific findings about the relationship between demeanour and lying, are not based on physiology.

Apart from this, has any link between demeanour and lying emerged from psychological research?

The typical methodology of such research consists of experiments in controlled but artificial settings, combined with statistical analysis to extract correlations between the variables studied.

Dominated by behaviourist views, until recently psychologists, with few exceptions, concentrated on experimental study of behaviour ignoring inner mental experience. The problem of lying with its cognitive and motivational complexities, especially in real life situations, was beyond its scope.

Ever since some psychologists began to study lying they have approached it in this experimental way, and on behaviouristic assumptions. The results to date have been negative, as one researcher states:

> A major problem lies in the researcher's present inability to specify the cues that signal deception or prevarication on the part of the witness.
> [Gerald R Miller & F Joseph Boster 'Three Images of the Trial: Their Implications for Psychological Research', in Bruce Dennis Sales (ed) *Psychology in the Legal Process* (1977) p 31]

The most impressive view is that of Professor Paul Ekman, in the USA, perhaps the world leader in the field, summarizing his findings after intensive research into bodily signs of lying for about 25 years [Paul Ekman, *Telling Lies* (New York, 1986)]:

> People would lie less if they thought there was any such certain sign of lying, but there isn't. There is no sign of deceit itself—no gesture, facial expression or muscle twitch that in and of itself means that person is lying.

He confirms this again:

> No clue to deceit, in face, body, voice, or words, is foolproof, not even the autonomic nervous system activity . . .

Ekman's research counters claims by 'judges of men' that they can tell whether or not someone is lying, just by looking at him. He finds that few persons achieve better than chance accuracy:

> Most people believe they can detect false expressions: our research has shown most cannot.

Ekman's overall view is that most liars can deceive most people most of the time. Of course, his approach is concerned with deciding truthfulness on the basis of demeanour alone, and shows its inadequacy. Judgment of testimony by a court is not confined to demeanour; it depends on many other factors.

Ekman found that bodily signs of anxiety sometimes go with lying, but sees them only as clues, never as sure indications. He agrees that truthfulness is not shown by lack of such signs; some liars show none.

Ekman's valuable contribution in the form of negative findings after intensive research, shows that while there are physical signs of emotion or anxiety, there are no specific signs of lying. Psychology does not support the view that from a witness's demeanour alone, it is possible to know whether or not he is lying. Obviously, in court, no final conclusion, and certainly no conviction, should ever be based on physical signs alone.

The caution engendered by psychology, finds its parallel in the views of a distinguished judge, Lord Devlin, who questions the traditional view of the significance of demeanour in lie detection:

> The great virtue of the English trial is usually said to be the opportunity it gives to the judge to tell from the demeanour of the witness whether or not he is telling the truth. I think that this is overrated.

He adopts the following views of Mr Justice McKenna:

> . . . I doubt my own ability . . . to discern from a witness's demeanour, or the tone of his voice, whether he is telling the truth . . . For my part I rely on these considerations as little as I can help.

Lord Devlin states a holistic approach:

> It is the tableau that constitutes the big advantage, the text with illustrations, rather than the demeanour of a particular witness.
> [The Rt Hon Lord Patrick Devlin, *The Judge* (1979) p 63]

Experience in court confirms the limited role of a witness's demeanour in judgment. Mostly, no significant signs are shown at all. Occasionally, some recognizable signs of anxiety may be noted, but they could be due to many things other than lying, as the following illustrations show.

The witness may just be a nervous person. Individuals vary. How can a court know that anxiety is not an everyday state of this witness?

A witness may merely be anxious about the court situation. Many find it an ordeal to testify in public, or fear that they may be made to look foolish in cross-examination.

Some people may fear the responsibility for the consequences of their evidence, e g the verdict or the sentence, or other consequences.

Intimidated witnesses may fear reprisals or the penalties of the law.

A truthful witness may be concerned about the possible verdict.

An honest and conscientious witness may be worried about being disbelieved though he is telling the truth.

Other feelings may complicate the picture, e g anger, surprise, or defiance.

Whatever the witness's overall response to the situation may be, it might persist throughout his testimony. How can this be related to particular statements?

On the other hand, for many reasons, a lying witness may show no signs of anxiety.

Although he is in fact anxious, he may not be a person in whom this manifests itself physically.

He may be a relaxed person by nature, keeping or seeming calm in situations where others would show signs of stress.

He may be a natural or experienced liar, with good self-control or acting ability.

He may be indifferent to the outcome. It may not be important to him. An accused may already be serving a sentence of imprisonment. The charge may be minor or one where a severe penalty would be incompetent, or where he has grounds for leniency of sentence. A remote associate of the accused may be willing to lie, but unworried about success or failure.

The witness may be confident that his lie will be believed, and, in any event he may know that it is undetectable so far as penalties are concerned.

Scepticism must be maintained in the face of any view that such states of mind can be distinguished just by looking at a witness. Even if there were reliable signs of deceit, contrary to psychological findings, who could be trusted to interpret them correctly, and on what basis? Preconceived notions, e g that liars always avert their gaze, could create real mischief. Such powers to 'judge men' exceed those claimed by Lord Devlin.

The complexity of responses and the differences between individuals are such that, in isolation, so far as lying is concerned, anything about a particular witness's behaviour, may mean anything.

The conclusion must be that it is only proper for observation of a witness's demeanour to play a minor role in lie detection. Alone, it is an unsound basis for deciding whether or not he is lying, and it should never be the ground of conviction.

Does demeanour have any value at all? It must be accepted that people do communicate meanings and feelings to each other in non-verbal ways. To transmit and to receive such signals is an innate biological process. It plays some part in forming trust in people. But much of this is unconscious, very variable in form of expression, or ability to detect, and it lacks precision. For practical reasons, and in the interests of justice, it is submitted that the status of non-verbal communication in court should be limited to colouring evidence which is assessed on some other reliable basis.

The role of cross-examination in relation to demeanour now arises.

Witnesses are rarely asked about their demeanour directly, e g by questions like 'Why are you blushing now?'. At critical points in the testimony, to ask about significant changes might sometimes have value, e g 'Why did you get angry when I asked you if you knew that he had taken the car?'.

But there may be good reasons for not asking a witness about his demeanour. The court may be expected to note it without the mediation of advocacy. Such questions could only be suggestive; a physical sign cannot be linked significantly with the quality of a statement. The question may seem to be meaningless or trivial. Insistent questioning on the issue may be more productive, and may deprive the witness of a chance to think. Close questioning of a captive witness about his or her personal reactions may create distress, or seem to be unnecessary, offensive, inhuman or unfair. This may be tactically unwise, and could antagonize a jury. A judge would, of course, disallow improper treatment.

But cross-examination in other ways is facilitated by the opacity of demeanour. Cross-examination about the matter would be pointless, if courts could tell that witnesses were lying, just by looking at them.

But since lying is protected by a more or less impervious shield, it can only be exposed indirectly, by cross-examination on the issues, followed by holistic judgment in which what the witness says is compared with what others say, and various tests are applied. In this way, the enigma of lying is circumvented and overcome.

## 2    The evidence

There are two barriers to belief in testimony, viz distrust of the witness, and implausible evidence. Possible sources of distrust in witnesses arising from personality, character, motives and demeanour, have been discussed; they matter, but usually the main indication that evidence is untruthful is given by its defective features.

While defects in evidence are discussed here, in themselves, it is again emphasized that the most forceful way to expose falsehood is to combine an attack on defects in evidence with challenging the witness, on the grounds discussed, and to overcome the false evidence, thus weakened, with one's own credible and forceful evidence.

Evidence should be treated as defective and implausible if, on any material point, it is shown to be inconsistent, impossible, improbable, unrealistic, or contradicted by other accepted evidence. If the witness must know the facts, the inference would then be that he is lying. If so, after putting this to the witness explicitly at the proper stage, perhaps at the end of cross-examination, repeated accusations and denials would be unproductive. Lying will be inferred, not admitted.

The focus of cross-examination here is objective. It refers directly to the evidence about the issues.

*(a)   Inconsistency.*   The term 'inconsistency' here, refers to self-contradiction by a single witness, or by a party, where the evidence of two or more of his witnesses is in conflict. The term 'contradiction' refers to the usual adversarial conflict between witnesses on opposite sides.

Inconsistency is a logical flaw, irrespective of the underlying facts. It means that two statements cannot both be true together, e g that the accused was, and was not at home at a given time. At least one statement must be, and sometimes both may be, untrue. It is for logicians to work out the possible combinations and implications. The main point is that inconsistency shows that something is wrong with the evidence, but it does not prove any facts.

What is the effect of inconsistency in showing that evidence is untruthful? This depends on the type of inconsistency, where it is found, and how it is exploited.

Minor inconsistencies, wherever they are found, may mean very little. They are common as a result of the normal fallibility of observation and memory. Two eyewitnesses seldom give absolutely identical accounts. Inexperienced advocates often exaggerate the importance of such discrepancies.

But details sometimes give important guidance to credibility. Where evidence of collateral facts and circumstances is being elicited to test the truth of a central fact, e g an alibi, even small variations between a party's witnesses may cast doubt on the main fact in issue. Also, disagreement about details of circumstantial evidence, may have a crucial effect on the resulting inference. In either of these contexts, inconsistencies in a party's evidence may point to lying.

Material inconsistencies require explanation and at least one alternative must be rejected. If found in the evidence of a single witness, who must know the facts, this points to lying on his part. But if the inconsistencies only emerge on comparing the evidence of two or more witnesses for a party, it may be difficult to say which one may be accurate, mistaken, or lying.

Because the Crown must prove guilt beyond reasonable doubt for conviction, any material inconsistency in their evidence is likely to imperil their case, especially if it refers to any question of identification of the offender.

Even material inconsistency in defence evidence may not be so critical, since nothing need be proved and reasonable doubt is enough for acquittal.

Experienced advocates are constantly alert for evidence-in-chief which does not fit together, and for inconsistencies of any kind, which they can attack and exploit in cross-examination. But even where inconsistency emerges, a cross-examiner should not suggest that a witness is lying, when a mistake is reasonably possible, or more likely. To do otherwise may offend the witness and antagonize a jury. On the other hand an advocate should not shrink from putting to a witness that he is lying, where that is appropriate. It is weak and unimpressive to suggest mistake, when only lying is possible. The distinction between a mistake and a lie, depends on whether or not the witness is bound to know the real facts.

The variety of techniques for challenging credibility on the ground of inconsistency, will be explained in later chapters, but one or two possibilities are mentioned here.

One approach is to create inconsistency in the evidence of one or more witnesses by indirect tactics which lead them into invention.

If lying is suspected in part of one witness's evidence because of inconsistency, a cross-examiner should try to extend the taint to all his disputed evidence. To charge one such witness with lying is easier than imputing lies, mistakes or accuracy to two or more witnesses who disagree.

But, as will be seen, it is sometimes better to press an attack home, and at other times to let inconsistency pass, so that neither the witness nor the opponent can correct it. It can then be stressed in the final argument.

Where two or more witnesses give inconsistent evidence, one can be confronted with what another said; this may lead to unimpressive retractions, thus discrediting the evidence further.

Instead of clashing, the evidence of two or more witnesses may seem too uniform, so that collusion may be suspected. Here, the identity of wording or content should be brought out and highlighted. Such witnesses may usefully be asked if they have discussed their evidence. Even reasonably honest witnesses often deny this, or that it influenced them. This is often surprising where they see each other frequently. If one witness admits and another denies discussion, further inconsistency may arise.

*(b)   Impossibility.*   Evidence-in-chief of facts which are clearly impossible, is rare. Obvious nonsense should have been eliminated during preparation. Impossibility usually emerges from other facts, e g recognizing a suspect shown to have been round the corner. Here the cross-examiner's task should be simple.

*(c) Improbability.* Improbable evidence is common. Improbability may be apparent in the evidence-in-chief, or it may only emerge under the pressure of cross-examination.

Individual facts, combinations of facts, or the whole story may exhibit improbability. Perhaps the most common issues of this kind are those which concern human nature and behaviour.

The test of improbability is ordinary experience of life. Probability is a matter of degree but it is only quantifiable in special contexts, e g in technical evidence like fingerprints or the frequency of blood groups.

For ordinary evidence, the attempt of some thinkers to create a mathematical model of probability, is only of academic interest. It has no practical value in court.

Yet the degree of improbability does matter. Evidence of a rather unlikely fact may be believed, but evidence of an absurd fact may be rejected. Part of the art of the cross-examiner is to convert what seems unlikely into what seems absurd, by increasing the degree of improbability. This is done by expanding both the story and its context, so that it will be seen that they do not fit together.

By controlled questioning, a cross-examiner may intensify the improbability of evidence by drawing out its assumptions and consequences, and exploring its implications. The incongruity of what is asserted should become more and more obvious as the contacts of the evidence with reality are increased.

A witness, challenged about some initial improbability, may, in trying to justify it, add further unlikely details, to the point of absurdity. The same effect may be achieved by encouraging one who is over-talkative, either because of confidence or anxiety, to ramble on freely until he develops an improbable story to an unacceptable point.

The question arises as to when improbability will lead to rejection of evidence or not. Obviously, such a general question cannot be answered too specifically. No rules can be stated, but the following two approaches set out parameters within which a fair and sound decision may be reached.

A court must maintain an open mind, and apply some degree of imagination. Many strange facts are true. Odd and unlikely happenings are reported every day in criminal courts. Some may only seem strange to jurors because of a cultural gulf, although they are commonplace in some social groups. Evidence should not be rejected automatically just because it refers to unusual facts.

On the other hand, if the evidence is contrary to what happens in reality and suggests facts, ways of thinking and modes of conduct that are so unlikely as to be an affront to common sense, a court would be entitled to reject it.

For a court, there is no substitute for practical judgment based on experience of life, and applied to the particular circumstances. The proper decision cannot be worked out logically. After wrestling with parts of the issue, it will, finally, be seen as a whole, one way or another. What usually helps in difficult questions is to consider other evidence, to use a variety of approaches, and to have more facts. As in all judgments, the improbability of evidence should not be the sole basis of decision. But if it is combined with other factors, increased grounds for confidence in the assessment develop, e g where improbable evidence is also inconsistent, and, after being weakened by cross-examination of obviously motivated witnesses, it is contradicted by other acceptable evidence.

A decision whether improbable evidence which is rejected, arose from mistake or lying, has consequences for trust or distrust of witnesses.

Sometimes, error cannot be excluded as a possible reason for an isolated piece of unlikely but not unreasonable evidence, which only becomes absurd in relation to the whole picture, known to the court but not to the witness.

In such a situation, the nature of the event, conditions of observation, state of the witness, or passage of time may seem to explain an error in the honest evidence of an independent witness.

But where a strongly motivated witness, who must know the reality, gives extensive evidence (the whole story or a major part of it), which is obviously improbable in itself, he may well be held to be lying.

*(d)   Lack of realism.*    The form of statements may seem sincere or false, i e having or lacking the 'ring of truth'. This does not refer to their content, consistency or probability. It is a way of assessing forms of expression, by analysis, intuition, and comparison with what is likely in a true account. There are no rules for this impressionistic approach to evidence, but it can help. Typically unrealistic features of false stories are lack of factual detail and colouring, or of personal involvement, and a tendency to be all one way.

The lack of factual detail and colouring arises because false stories often focus anxiously on the central theme alone so that, unlike true stories, they may be bare and lack surrounding detail. Facts are always related to others, often causally. True accounts often mention related facts spontaneously, whereas lying stories omit them because they did not exist, and have not been invented.

For similar reasons, false stories may lack any element of personal involvement of the witness. People normally react to events; they are not video cameras. Many persons find it hard to sort out what they saw from their impressions and feelings. Normally, in describing an event, they would include their responses to it. The lack of any human vitality in an account may be suspect. It may be missing because the event never happened, and the natural feelings aroused by a real situation, and reflected in a true story, have not been invented.

Of course, some truthful evidence may be given in a dry, impersonal and objective way, without factual detail or personal involvement, for various reasons.

The subject of the evidence may be something neutral like skid marks or documents in a fraud, where elaboration is not to be expected.

The court situation, or the advocate, may be inhibiting, or the witness may be of a class from whom impersonal reports are expected, eg a police witness describing a traffic accident, or a pathologist giving a post-mortem report.

Details may have been forgotten, or repeating statements during enquiries or in preparing for trial, may have blunted the witness's feelings about the event.

Despite these qualifications, when a lay witness gives a bare account of some dramatic event, a court may, intuitively, be put on its guard by the unconvincing form of testimony (although it may be quite consistent and probable). Obviously, on the basis of such a quality of evidence alone, a court should not conclude that the witness is lying. But a cross-examiner who is alert to the possible significance of lack of realism in the form of evidence, may probe it for lies, sometimes with useful results.

Lying may be suspected when a witness gives one way evidence, inappropriately.

Firm evidence, in a consistent direction, is often truthful and convincing, eg a report of a clear-cut event, observed and remembered accurately. But if all the evidence points dogmatically in one direction, where there is room for doubt, probing to see if it is untruthful may be prudent.

True accounts of uncertain facts, do not always follow one consistent line; they may include doubts or elements which seem unnecessary, odd, irrelevant, unexpected, or inexplicable, just because they happened; they may omit important items to which the witness cannot speak, or spontaneously add to or correct previous testimony. Such points are seldom found in false accounts, as they would complicate them needlessly.

Such realistic imperfections and inconsistencies are usually missing in invented stories. They tend to cover the essentials, directionally and dogmatically, without deviating from the main theme, omitting what does not help the general thrust. The purposiveness of the evidence stands out clearly. Its form is explained by its intended effect.

For a court, lack of realism in the form of evidence, as discussed above, may suggest lying, but not in terms of rules, conscious formulation, nor as the sole basis for deciding credibility. Although this may not be an intentional approach, e g in the minds of first-time jurors, an intuitive response to lack of realism, that testimony seems unconvincing, may find its way into the final holistic evaluation of all the evidence.

This approach is part of the psychology of persuasion, and the art of advocacy. Cross-examiners should be alert for the openings suggested by such clues. If they then probe and challenge evidence as untruthful on such grounds, subtle though they may be, they may find the court receptive to it, because of its intuitive response.

Sometimes, if the opponent's witness is allowed to tell his story again in his own words, its lack of realism may be highlighted, and this can then be followed up by leading questions.

## 3   Holistic assessment

To leave the subject of lie detection at this point would be misleading. It is not exhausted by the above separate accounts of the guidance given by a witness's personality, character, motives or demeanour, or the inconsistency, impossibility, improbability or lack of realism of evidence. As was said, no one approach is reliable by itself.

In practice, all this must be put together by advocates and by the court, to expose lying, and so that evidence may be rejected on that ground.

A broad approach is required for lying, even more than for mistakes, where the co-operation of honest witnesses sometimes makes a narrower focus possible.

To confront the problem of lie detection, head-on, the stark and inescapable fact is that when honest communication stops, people cannot read each other's minds. There is no direct way of knowing if someone is lying or not. A liar's inner experience is private and impenetrable. Thus, the credibility of evidence is never self-evident. It is a conclusion derived indirectly from various facts, with variable degrees of confidence.

To do this confidently, requires the total approach of a criminal court to all the witnesses and all their evidence. A holistic, integrated evaluation which surpasses the sum of its parts, is how sound decisions are made about credibility.

Generally, the greater the number of witnesses, the easier it is to challenge or to decide credibility. The tasks for advocates and courts are more exacting in convictions based on the uncorroborated evidence of one Crown witness, or acquittals following from a reasonable doubt raised by one defence witness.

A major factor in testing and deciding credibility is the normal adversarial conflict between prosecution and defence evidence. After each party has put his version to the opponent's witnesses in cross-examination, to accept one version is to reject the other.

This is of crucial importance for the outcome. It may often seem that nothing is wrong with evidence, looked at by itself, yet, it may be confidently rejected as false, if it is contradicted by other accepted evidence. Likewise, a witness may seem to be trustworthy, yet he is contradicted by an opponent's witness who seems even more trustworthy. Then, to trust one, means distrusting the other.

The conclusion may be that the rejected witness was lying. Without the guidance given by this conflict between evidence and witnesses, it might not have been possible to reach that conclusion with confidence.

For a cross-examiner to show, or for a court to decide, that a witness is lying, may be complicated and may involve hard work. There are no magic techniques whereby this can be avoided.

# CHAPTER 5

# Examination-in-chief

I   Introduction
II   Witnesses
III   Questions
IV   Anticipating cross-examination

## I   INTRODUCTION

### A   Relationship to cross-examination

Cross-examination can only be understood properly in relation to examination-in-chief, which is the subject of this chapter.

For conviction, the prosecutor must both prove his version of the facts and destroy the defence. For acquittal, the defence need only destroy the Crown case, by legal criteria, but in practice they generally support this by leading evidence of an alternative version of the facts. Thus, success usually depends on the strength of one's evidence-in-chief, as well as the weaknesses in the opponent's evidence.

Bearing in mind these twin requirements, when a cross-examiner challenges testimony as mistaken or untruthful, a realistic aim would be to weaken it, so that it is overcome by his own contradictory evidence-in-chief. A related technique is to put his case to the witness under cross-examination, and to confront him with the facts spoken to in conflicting testimony.

However, an advocate's evidence-in-chief is not only the basis of the cross-examination which he conducts; it will itself become a target for cross-examination by the other advocate. Accordingly, in carrying out the examination-in-chief of his witness, an advocate ought to anticipate the attack which will be made on it in cross-examination, and should rob it of its effect so far as he can.

### B   Aims of examination-in-chief

As a stage of criminal procedure, examination-in-chief consists simply of questioning one's own witness, however he answers. This

71

gives no guidance as to its aims. The testimony may be disputed, undisputed, favourable or unfavourable.

A party calls a witness to support his case—although an adverse witness may do the opposite. The aim is to elicit all the admissible, relevant and material evidence which the witness can give in relation to the issues.

Admissibility depends on the rules of evidence. Relevancy is a matter of logic—usually inductive logic. Materiality is a question of weight.

Much evidence-in-chief is undisputed. But on disputed issues, effective evidence-in-chief should support the party's theory of the case, and be comprehensible and persuasive.

## C   Theory of case

A party's theory of the case is his consistent and integrated view of all the undisputed facts, his version of the disputed facts, and what he must prove in law for the verdict which is his objective. It represents a party's position, fully thought-out, rather than an assessment of the evidence.

Sometimes, depending on what will be proved, alternative theories of the case must be held; if so, each should be self-consistent.

An advocate's theory of the case creates a frame of reference, for a consistent and purposive presentation. It is best to draft the theory of the case as his proposed final argument, which will shape the aims of his examination and cross-examination of witnesses.

To conduct any case, strong or weak, without such a theory, is less than professional, as would rapidly become obvious. A court, looking at the case as a whole, would see that the advocacy was not serious, thus impairing prospects of success.

An advocate's insight into his opponent's theory of the case will help him to anticipate, and perhaps to frustrate, lines of cross-examination.

The theory of the case will vary according to circumstances. Chapter 2 'The Anatomy of a Criminal Trial', outlined the possible nature of the issues.

The prosecution theory will always be that the crime was committed by the acts of the defendant as set out in the indictment or information (sometimes including the possibility of commission of a lesser offence). For conviction, a prosecutor must prove his whole case, i e that the crime was committed, and that it was the accused who committed it.

Although one or other of these two issues is generally uncontested, this does not relieve the Crown of the obligation to prove everything, unless the defence admit the uncontested facts formally. These facts, whether or not contested, must be established by evidence which is admissible, relevant, sufficient in law, and of enough weight, to prove guilt beyond reasonable doubt. This will determine the content of the prosecution examination-in-chief of each of the Crown witnesses.

Commonly, eyewitness evidence is led about the crime, and eyewitness or circumstantial evidence is led to implicate the accused.

Before the trial, in foreseeing defence cross-examination, a prosecutor may be limited by how well he can predict the defence theory of the case. His pre-trial information about the defence may depend on whether the trial is on indictment or is a summary trial, and on other factors. However, the line of defence will emerge early in the trial, in opening speeches or initial cross-examination.

There may, of course, be no defence evidence-in-chief. The defence may simply resist the Crown proof by objecting to the competency of procedure, or to the admissibility of evidence, or by submitting that there is no case to answer, or by probing, testing or challenging evidence, without trying to prove anything positive.

It is probable, in most cases, however, that positive evidence-in-chief is led by the defence, with a view to establishing an alternative version of the facts, or at least, of creating a reasonable doubt about the Crown version.

If so, as was seen in chapter 2, any positive defence will normally be one of two alternatives, i e either that the crime was not committed, or else that it was not committed by the accused—but not both. This contention, with the undisputed facts, and relevant legal provisions, would be the defence theory of the case.

Where the defence positively assert an alternative version of the facts, their examination-in-chief will usually include the accused, and perhaps other witnesses, who give direct evidence denying either that the crime was committed, or else that the accused was the offender. Circumstantial defence evidence is less common.

## D  Comprehension

Evidence must be clear; it must be understood. It may be worse than useless if a harmful meaning is conveyed. Apart from leaving evidence in a hazy state, for tactical reasons a vague and general image of an incident is less effective than a sharp and detailed picture etched on the memory.

Some facts themselves are inherently complicated or confusing, and difficult to follow, e g technical information or where several defendants are charged with multiple offences in various combinations. Here, the need for clarity is particularly strong. But even simple facts are often obscured by poor presentation. This is the responsibility of the advocate, not his witness, whom he controls. Advocates, through familiarity with the case often make unconscious assumptions about evidence and fail to grasp its effect when it is first heard.

A judge's questions may clarify isolated points, but not what puzzles jurors; nor is he concerned with the clarity of the overall presentation.

Forgotten evidence has no value. Trials may be lengthy. Jurors take few notes. It is easier to recall evidence which is clear.

The following requirements are essential if evidence is to be comprehensible.

## 1   Speech

An advocate's first concern should be with the elementary basis of oral communication—an acceptable quality of speech from his witness. Common problems in courtrooms without microphones, are marginal audibility, poor articulation, and speaking too quickly. Through variable hearing ability, court layout, relative positions, or other factors, one person may grasp what is said though another does not. Unless clarification is sought, evidence may be missed or misunderstood.

## 2   Language

Any unusual terms used by a witness, from slang to an expert's jargon, should be explained at once in ordinary language. Vague, slipshod or roundabout statements should be probed and the exact meaning extracted. So far as facts are within a witness's knowledge, the advocate should insist on precise and definite answers.

## 3   Place

The scene should be carefully set, from the start. A visual image will normally be created in the mind of the court; the evidence should assist in this. Where physical layout is material, it should be explained carefully. The advocate should ensure that he is not assuming knowledge of something because he is familiar with it.

There should be no possibility that, in the middle of a dramatic account of a fight, the advocate has to divert attention by asking 'Where was the door?'.

## 4   People

After the stage has been set, the *dramatis personae,* the persons whose acts are to be described, should be placed in their respective positions, before describing acts of importance. Again, visualization should be assisted, wherever possible; this could be done by referring to small pictorial details to distinguish people, e g 'the man with the striped scarf'. However, names and visual identifications of persons concerned, whether pre-trial, in the dock, or in the public benches, should not be omitted.

## 5 *Sequence*

A logical sequence, invariably the chronological one, should be followed in describing the incidents and actions in issue. Firmness with the witness may be necessary to achieve this.

## 6 *Visual aids*

Where practicable, an advocate should help the court to visualize incidents exactly, by supporting oral evidence with visual aids, e g plans, maps, diagrams, sketches, charts, photographs, video films, models or samples. They can simplify evidence enormously, and can save much confusion, pointless dispute and waste of court time.

Although such evidence would be admissible, it is not produced as often as it might be. Cost is seldom a major difficulty. Perhaps the reason is often lack of imagination.

## 7 *Repetition*

Simple things may only need to be said once in evidence. But it is often advisable to repeat evidence of complex or crucial facts, to ensure that it has been understood, and to emphasize it.

## 8 *Variation*

Unless inconsistency arises, evidence, if repeated, will be enhanced by varying words, angles of approach, or its form, e g direct, circumstantial, oral, real or documentary, or by calling several witnesses to one event.

## 9 *Expansion*

Facts are always more clear if seen in their context. Within reasonable bounds of what is relevant and material, evidence of the main facts may be expanded to include some explanation of causes, collateral circumstances, and consequences.

If any impression or opinion evidence is admitted, its factual basis should be made explicit.

## E   Persuasion

The object of advocacy and of leading evidence is to persuade. The Crown seek to prove their whole case. The defence, if they lead evidence, need prove nothing, but generally, they will try to persuade the court to accept their alternative version of the facts, or at least to feel reasonable doubt about the Crown version.

To ensure that evidence-in-chief fulfils the requirements of being comprehensible and remembered, is the foundation, but beyond this, techniques of good presentation should be employed. These include features which are found in other fields than advocacy, although they take a muted form in criminal trials.

The main qualities of persuasive evidence may be stated briefly. It should consist of a human story, realistic in quality, and strong in visual content. The main theme should recur, for emphasis. Criticisms should be forestalled.

### 1   The story

The most persuasive form of evidence is a human story which integrates all the facts meaningfully. This holds interest, and explains what happened in terms of human conduct which the court can imagine. Facts are best grasped and recalled in relation to each other. A mass of unrelated details would have no impact, especially in a long trial.

If few, or none of the witnesses can tell the whole story, it should be built up by several, including those who give circumstantial evidence.

### 2   Realism

The story should seem vivid and real, and not like something which happened to robots in a vacuum. It should not sound like a police report.

An advocate cannot manufacture dialogue like a playwright. But by guiding a witness without leading or editing testimony, he can contribute to such a convincing 'ring of truth' as it may have.

Having regard to the discussion of realism in the previous chapter, the advocate may encourage his witness, within permissible limits, to enhance his account with natural elements, including factual detail and colouring, and personal involvement.

He may allow suitable witnesses to give some evidence by means of a free narrative with minimal questioning, to maximize its animation and spontaneity.

## 3 Visualization

The visual elements of a story, are aspects of its realism. But this is worthy of separate mention if only to emphasize the advantage of expressing things visually where possible. If a witness claims that he arrived at the locus by public transport, this is less vivid than saying that he took a blue bus.

When evidence becomes heavy, pompous and abstract, it will be sharpened if it is converted to simple, concrete images, as in this example.

## 4 Theme

Although a realistic and convincing story needs some colouring by detail, this should not be overdone, so that the essentials are obscured by minutiae.

The main theme of a party's case should dominate his presentation, and should recur.

Knowing what to select or omit is a key to advocacy. Evidence-in-chief should cover all the material facts known to a witness, thoroughly, and in enough detail. Omitted facts of importance, which emerge later in cross-examination may seem sinister.

Cases usually turn on two or three crucial points, which should be kept in the forefront. They should be expressed consistently in the most forceful way, and should be brought out as quickly as possible. The court should be reminded of them constantly in the evidence.

To avoid diluting a strong case, weaker points should stay in the background, and evidence with only a remote bearing on the issues should be omitted, even though it is admissible.

Most pre-trial witness statements contain too much, including background and inadmissible material, much of which should not be led.

## 5 Weaknesses

Even a persuasive story may have weaknesses, which can do more harm if the cross-examiner brings them out. If that is likely, it will be more impressive to anticipate them in evidence-in-chief. This subject will be considered below.

# II WITNESSES

It is assumed that advocates are familiar with the rules governing the competency and compellability of witnesses.

## A Selection of witnesses

The selection of witnesses is a matter for the tactical judgment of advocates.

A prosecutor should call at least those who are needed to avoid a 'no case to answer' submission, or, exceptionally, for corroboration. He is expected to call, or to have available, all his material witnesses, even if their evidence may be adverse to his case—unless their veracity is suspect. He might call a witness just to be cross-examined.

The defence, of course, need not call any witnesses. However, if they make serious imputations against Crown witnesses, they may be criticized if they lead no supporting evidence.

It may seem best for either party to call all their good witnesses. But the weight of evidence on disputed facts may depend more on the quality of evidence and its resistance to cross-examination, than on mere number. Calling more than a few good witnesses on one issue should only be done after careful assessment.

There are no rules nor any substitute for good judgment in a particular situation, about which witnesses to call. Flexibility is the keynote. Some who attend may be kept in reserve.

Points to consider include these: too many witnesses may suggest lack of confidence in any; adding witnesses increases the risks of cross-examination and inconsistency; if one strong witness resists cross-examination without damage, another weaker witness giving the same evidence may lose the favourable effect; to overprove facts, especially if they are secondary, wastes court time, dilutes other good evidence and may divert attention from what is more important.

These are all reasons for limiting the number of witnesses, but there is no reason for not calling a sufficient number to reinforce a strong case.

## B Sequence of witnesses

Apart from the accused as first defence witness to the facts, the best sequence of witnesses is a matter of tactical judgment. It should take into account the best sequence of evidence. The various considerations which relate to the order of witnesses and the order of evidence, may differ and the best compromise must be reached. There is no one 'right' order, but any logical or natural order is better than none.

Witnesses called, or evidence led, in a chronological order, are easiest to follow. This should be chosen unless other reasons prevail. That is often so, as the following tactical considerations show.

Generally, the first witness called by a party should be a good one, who can, if possible, tell the whole story, and stand up to cross-examination. In any event the main contentions should be put to him as early as possible. The impression made then, when attention is at its peak, may persist and add to the effect of later evidence which would build on this foundation.

What the opponent selects for cross-examination of a witness who speaks to the main facts, will reveal any vulnerable areas, as a guide to the further evidence which will be led.

It is also desirable to call a good witness last. The final impression is likely to be strong; if it is favourable, this is likely to endure. It is best if the last witness, also, knows the whole story, so that he can draw the threads together, and can correct weaknesses which have emerged. To end with a weak witness, whose evidence is damaged in cross-examination, could be extremely harmful to the case.

Witnesses may be weak because of personal inadequacy, or difficulties in their evidence. They should not be called first or last. If possible, a weak witness, should be called after a strong one who made a good impression, and before another strong one who can repair any damage done.

Within the evidence of any particular witness, each topic should be taken in turn, usually in a chronological order, and exhausted before proceeding to the next topic.

## C  Anxious witnesses

Even truthful witnesses may be tense, if they are naturally anxious, or fear to give evidence. Although they are rarely tongue-tied, anxious witnesses may be inaudible or excited, or apt not to answer questions properly, or to have lapses of memory. This may worsen as the evidence proceeds.

An anxious demeanour may be mistaken as a sign of lying in an honest witness, and he may be more vulnerable to cross-examination.

There may be little that an advocate can do about anxiety which has some substantial cause, other than not to make it worse. But it will improve the evidence, if he can relax the witness by means of tact, his tone of voice and manner, and suitable questions.

Instead of leading in introductory questions, as he could do, the advocate might ask non-leading questions about the witness's personal details, and how he came to be connected with the facts which he observed. Making positive statements, instead of just replying 'Yes' or 'No', accustoms the witness to answering questions and to the sound of his own voice.

Sensitive topics should be approached gradually, letting the witness see the objective and giving him plenty of time to answer. If a witness's memory is blocked, the topic should be left until later, when he is more relaxed. If it is then approached gradually, the material may be recalled naturally, by association of ideas.

## D   Unfavourable witnesses

If advocates obtain incomplete, unexpected, unfavourable or even harmful evidence from their witnesses, they should show no reaction which could influence the judgment.

Imcomplete evidence about known facts, may simply be due to lapse of memory, and may be overcome in the way previously described.

Unexpected departures from written statements, may just be due to the normal fallibility of memory. But they may create inconsistencies between witnesses, and expose them to cross-examination.

To forestall this, an advocate may try to have his witnesses admit that they may be mistaken on such points. The lines of questioning might stress their agreement on essentials, rather than their differences on secondary matters.

If the expected evidence is given, but has become so exaggerated as to be liable to cross-examination, the aim would be to moderate it and extract concessions which the cross-examiner would obtain anyway. If the evidence has been unduly weakened, it would be reinforced.

Even when unexpected and unfavourable evidence is given, the general rule is that a party cannot cross-examine his own witness, or put previous inconsistent statements to him, although he may call contradictory evidence.

But if the departure from the expected evidence is shown to be due to animosity to the party who called him, so that the witness is unwilling to tell the truth, or is giving unfair evidence, the court may allow the advocate to treat him as hostile. He could then cross-examine him, ask leading questions, and put previous inconsistent statements to him—apart from calling contradictory evidence. If the witness seems at first to be hostile, it is best to make him reveal this, to justify such an application. Even if it is not granted, the witness may be discredited by disclosure of his motivation.

## III   QUESTIONS

Knowledge of the rules of evidence concerning questions in examination-in-chief is assumed.

Here, attention should be on the witness and his evidence, not on the advocate. In the interest of spontaneity, he should, so far as he can, examine from his memory of essentials, not the witness's statement.

## A Leading questions

In examination-in-chief the general rule excludes leading questions, i e those stated in a form which suggests the answer, as it may influence witnesses.

Subtly suggestive questions may not be leading, but should be objected to if they overstep the boundary. The court situation may itself be suggestive regardless of the form of question, e g dock identification or identification of exhibits.

To direct a witness's attention to a disputed topic, or to ask him to choose one of two alternatives, is not leading, if it is neutral in its context, e g asking if he admits or denies a conversation spoken to by an opponent's witness. Letting a witness see the relevancy of a line of questioning and evidence, by non-leading questions, may be helpful and admissible.

Exceptions to the rule prohibiting leading questions include the following: the witness's personal details; how he got involved; introductory narrative; preliminary matters not directly connected with the issue; undisputed facts; topics where advocates agree to, or do not object to, leading; dealing with facts proved by other evidence; and where an advocate questions his own hostile witness.

In practice, leading is time-saving and efficient in a great deal of evidence-in-chief, and goes on as a matter of course, so that the real point can be reached as rapidly as possible. As the real issues emerge and become more specific, the scope for leading on undisputed matters usually increases.

Objection should be taken to improper leading at once; even if the question is excluded and unanswered, it may be harmful by suggesting the answer to a witness, and facts to a jury. An answer given before objection was taken and sustained, may be admissible, but it would have less weight.

Advocates should not take objection to questions as leading, without justification, merely for tactical reasons, e g to interrrupt a harmful line of evidence, or to harass the witness. This would invite judicial reprimand.

For various reasons, it is common for an advocate to allow his opponent to lead his witness, even where he would be entitled to object. He may be sure that the desired answer is inevitable however the question is framed. He may hope that the evidence may seem weaker if elicited by leading—as if the witness were coached. He may wish to avoid giving the impression to the jury that the evidence is important, or that he has something to hide.

A typical motive is that advocates who wish to have freedom to lead themselves, may tolerate it in their opponents.

Apart from rules of evidence, to refrain from leading even where it is allowed, may be a good tactic; evidence freely given may have more weight. If obtained by leading, doubt might have arisen as to whether it would have been given otherwise.

Leading stresses the partiality of evidence, as the advocate, not the witness, seems to be its source. It may confine answers to a formal 'Yes' or 'No', stripping the witness of spontaneity or character, and his evidence of substance. This eliminates much of the basis for assessing reliability or credibility, as the ground for trusting the witness. He may remain a cipher. But even if evidence is obtained by leading, the court might still think that the witness is honest, and would not give that evidence if he thought it was inaccurate.

Leading questions suggest answers by being too specific, e g 'Did the accused come into the pub around 9 pm?'. This can be avoided by taking a step or two back from the desired evidence and generalizing the questions, e g 'Did anyone come into the pub after you got there?'; 'Was he a stranger or did you know him?'; 'Who was it?'; 'About what time was that?'.

## B   Controlled questioning

A witness may be examined under strict control, or allowed to tell his story freely, or both methods could be combined.

In practice, the controlled method is employed in examination-in-chief, with few exceptions. The witness is taken through his evidence by tightly framed questions, in small steps, and in an orderly and deliberate way to ensure that all material facts are covered, and to avoid inadmissible, irrelevant, harmful or prejudicial evidence.

This lets an advocate edit evidence for persuasive reasons, by selection, omission, and subtle shaping. This is only proper within ethical limits. The Crown must disclose facts material to the defence. The defence must not knowingly mislead the court by giving an impression which is not based on, or contrary to, their information.

Deciding whether to use controlled questioning will depend on the witness, and the nature of his evidence. It is the preferred method where the evidence is important, where caution is advisable, or where the witness might be unable to sustain an account of the facts without detailed prompting. These reasons, among others, explain why it is used almost invariably.

Controlled questioning tends to make the evidence more complete because the witness stretches his memory, in compliance with the pressure on him. Studies suggest that this may reduce accuracy in marginal areas of recollection.

For reasons already given concerning leading questions, too much control in questioning may limit a court's confidence in stark, impoverished, forms of testimony, not enriched by factual detail or personal involvement. This offers less material as a basis for assessing reliability or credibility.

## C Free narrative

Evidence-in-chief may consist of a free narrative in which the witness tells all or part of his story in his own words, with few questions. The scope for this is usually limited by advocates' caution. It may begin with a request, e g 'Please tell the jury in your own words, what you saw from the window'. The aim is for the story to be told naturally, spontaneously and conversationally, so that the event, recreated by living evidence, can be imagined vividly, thus enhancing trust in the witness.

If evidence-in-chief is genuine, this is often the most convincing way to present it. It eliminates the impression of coaching given by stilted 'Yes' or 'No' or other short answers to controlled questions.

Very few non-suggestive preliminary questions are needed to guide the witness's attention to what is to be reported. After he has told his story, it could be most impressive, to ask no further questions, but it is usually necessary to deal with omitted points or explain something; the fewer the questions the better.

The advocate does not abandon control; this is always essential, although it may be kept in the background. He must be ready to intervene with a corrective question at once, if something inadmissible, irrelevant, damaging, prejudicial or otherwise undesirable is said or may be said, or if the witness starts to ramble or become garrulous.

Whether to elicit testimony freely, partly depends on the witness. Those who seem honest, confident, intelligent, likely to be at home with the jury, and unlikely to stray into undesirable areas, would be suitable, but not those who lack such qualities or who present risks.

However, allowing evidence to be given freely is seldom free of the danger of harmful disclosures, e g if a Crown witness revealed an accused's previous conviction or a defence witness gave away some incriminating fact. This is why it is relatively uncommon as a technique of questioning in criminal trials.

Exceptionally, if an area of evidence and a witness are thought to be safe, and suitable for this, free narrative may be combined with controlled questioning. A witness might first be allowed to tell his story freely, and then gaps could be filled, obscure points could be explained, and apparent inconsistencies could be reconciled.

Studies suggest that since the witness is not pressed to or beyond the limits of his recollection, his evidence may be less complete but more accurate.

## D   Purpose of question

If the examination-in-chief has been properly prepared, there can be no reason for aimless enquiries. An advocate should not be in the position of asking his own witness any question without a clear purpose, which is based on his preparation and furthers his theory of the case.

Naturally, an unforeseen but promising point might sometimes be followed up to see where it leads.

## E   Answer known

A generally accepted maxim of advocacy is never to ask a question to which the answer cannot be reasonably foreseen. The concern is that some unexpected harmful evidence may emerge.

This is a sound rule. An advocate may sometimes have to depart from it in cross-examination, but normally, he should not have to do so in examining his own witness. He should be guided by his knowledge of what his witness will say, although he can never be absolutely sure of this unless the witness has memorized his statement.

Of course unpredictable developments may occur. A witness may depart from his previous statement because he has forgotten what it was. He may have turned against the party who called him, so that he gives adverse evidence, or even qualifies as a hostile witness. In such cases, the advocate, though intending to follow the above maxim, might at first receive unexpected answers.

Again, if the opponent raised some quite new topic in cross-examining an earlier witness, the advocate may feel bound to explore it with his later witness, although he is uncertain of the kind of evidence which he may give.

Generally, the maxim is good, but few rules apply in all circumstances.

## F   Rate of questioning

In examination-in-chief, the questioning should be deliberate and unhurried, unlike cross-examination, where rapidity may help. The pace may be varied. It may be slowed down, and the evidence elicited by small steps, to facilitate the court's assimilation of a complex situation. It may be accelerated to reach the important evidence quickly, or to convey an impression of the swiftness of an incident.

## G  One point

Questions should cover only one point at a time. Compound or double questions should not be put, e g 'What did he shout from the window?'. Such questions make assumptions and produce confusion.

## H  Brevity

Questions should be short. Many brief open-ended questions may be asked in examination-in-chief, e g 'What happened then?'. Lines of evidence should also be concise. The whole examination-in-chief should take no longer than is necessary.

Archaic circumlocutions should be avoided, e g 'Now, would you please cast your mind back, if you will, to the night of the first of June?'.

## I  Clarity

Questions should be clear, direct and precise. Major evils are circumlocution, verbosity and pomposity. If the witness answers only 'Yes' or 'No' to a confusing form of question, it becomes part of his evidence.

The meaning of anything in doubt should be clarified at once.

## J  Simplicity

To some extent simplicity and clarity overlap. Questions should be framed as simply as possible in plain language. Complex facts should be broken up into simple ones and approached by small steps. The main outlines should be prominent and unobscured by unnecessary detail.

Frequently, simplicity may be achieved by having the witness express something in visual or concrete terms, avoiding abstractions.

## K  Detail

Judgment is always needed as to how much detail to include.

Everything need not be proved. A party need only prove the essentials of his case to the extent necessary.

The evidence should provide sufficient information for the court to understand the facts and be convinced of their accuracy. Further details are superfluous, and to seek them may even be tactically harmful, unless they can be proved conclusively.

To ask several persons about exact times, distances, the position of vehicles and so on, may elicit as many versions as there are witnesses.

Often such details would not assist the case even if they could be proved objectively; they may simply prime the cross-examiner with material for an attack based on inconsistency.

## L   Repetition or comment

Once an answer has been given, that is that. An advocate can only ask further questions. He should not repeat the answer without a good reason, and he should not comment on it at that stage.

It is objectionable to repeat an answer in different words which insinuate a subtle and more favourable meaning.

It would not be a good reason to repeat an answer for emphasis.

It might be a good reason to repeat the answer as part of a new question, e g 'When he said "Give me the car keys", what did you do?'. Here the quoted answer is a necessary basis for the next question.

# IV   ANTICIPATING CROSS-EXAMINATION

Examination-in-chief as the way of presenting a positive case has been discussed. But this case will be challenged in cross-examination. It must be protected against this challenge, in advance, by anticipating cross-examination, and reinforcing the evidence where necessary. Thus, to 'anticipate' here, means both to foresee, and to forestall, lines of cross-examination.

## A   Disclosure of weaknesses

Most cases have some weaknesses. A common dilemma is whether to face up to, and deal with, them in evidence-in-chief, or to risk their being raised in cross-examination, with the hope of repairing them in re-examination.

This is a separate question from where and how to fortify the evidence against cross-examination. This can be done at vulnerable points, without necessarily revealing weaknesses in doing so.

It is assumed that advocates will comply with their legal and ethical duties. A prosecutor must disclose any material facts which may help the defence, and the defence may not knowingly mislead the court. The subject is therefore discussed solely as a question of the best tactics.

Tactics obviously depend partly on the nature of the case and the evidence, which may be infinitely variable. But in general terms, the following are the arguments for and against confronting difficulties in examination-in-chief.

## 1   Advantages of disclosure

To raise difficulties in the evidence-in-chief has many advantages.

*(a)   Candour.*   To have one's witness admit a point in the opponent's favour, creates a helpful impression of candour in the witness and the advocate. Dogmatism may be counter-productive, especially if contrary facts are or become obvious.

If adverse facts are not admitted, or denied, without good reason, confidence in the witness and in the advocate will suffer, if they emerge later.

*(b)   Emergence of difficulties.*   It is unsafe to lead evidence on the assumption that a competent advocate on the other side will not see its difficulties.

*(c)   Scope for topic.*   A topic can be dealt with more fully and favourably in examination-in-chief, than in re-examination which is limited to what arises directly from cross-examination.

*(d)   Preparing witness.*   In questioning one's own witness on a matter, he can, in effect, be prepared for cross-examination on the subject. He can derive guidance as well as the benefit of rehearsal.

*(e)   Reducing impact.*   To introduce a topic in evidence-in-chief can take the wind out of the cross-examiner's sails. He will be in the unfavourable position of repeating questions already answered, and by evidence which is against him. His cross-examination may lack force and seem pointless.

## 2   Disadvantages of disclosure

There are fewer disadvantages in disclosing problems in the evidence-in-chief.

*(a)   Forcefulness.*   Where possible, evidence-in-chief should be positive and persuasive, leaving it to the adversary to challenge it.

*(b)   Suggesting challenge.*   It is imprudent to put ideas into the head of an opponent who may not see the difficulty.

*(c)   Inadmissibility of challenge.*   The opponent may only attempt to cross-examine in some inadmissible way which can be prevented by objection.

*(d)   Adding weight to challenge.*   To put an opponent's contention to one's witness may seem to take it seriously, and to give credence to something unreasonable. It may be better to leave the cross-examiner with the embarrassment of introducing some challenges, e g an absurd attack on police witnesses.

## 3   Conclusions

The most successful evidence-in-chief presents a case clearly and convincingly, and destroys the cross-examination in advance.

It is submitted that, except where the above or other disadvantages are substantial, it is generally best to reveal difficulties in examination-in-chief and to meet them head-on, before the witness is cross-examined.

It is best not to raise the problems until a firm foundation for one's case has been laid. A suitable stage may be in the middle of one's witnesses, and just before a strong one, who can counteract any harmful impression.

The topic should not be omitted from the evidence of a witness who could have spoken to it, and then raised later in the evidence of another. This may seem like an afterthought rather than candour.

In one situation, not of weakness, but where the evidence is strong, to withhold it may be a good tactic. This sets a trap for the cross-examiner if he is sure to raise the topic. When the opponent brings out the evidence, which is adverse to him, unexpectedly, it will have maximum impact.

## B   Reinforcing evidence

Whether or not weaknesses are disclosed in evidence-in-chief, it should be fortified where possible, both to frustrate constructive cross-examination seeking positive evidence, and where it is vulnerable to destructive cross-examination.

It can usually be foreseen, or known from pre-trial procedure or earlier cross-examination, whether the reliability or the credibility of evidence will be the target. Either way, the aim is to deprive the cross-examination of any force. This can contribute powerfully to a case.

Prosecution evidence-in-chief about one issue—the crime or the accused's implication in it—may need to be strengthened against attacks on reliability or credibility. Defence evidence-in-chief, again, may require reinforcement in regard to the same issue, but usually against an attack on credibility alone. This would be the typical situation.

## 1 Reliability

As was seen, either external facts or mental processes can cause errors in observation or memory.

*(a) Observation.* If the accuracy of observation is going to be attacked, it is easier to support this by showing that the external facts were favourable, than by reference to mental processes. The evidence should be as objective and as tangible as possible.

Both the advocate who leads evidence and the cross-examiner, are likely to have similar difficulties with intangible factors, e g the effects of stress, distraction, or expectations.

Trust in the witness and his assertions will, of course, count as well, but inferences from objective circumstances are also important.

In seeking to support the accuracy and reliability of evidence which will be challenged, an advocate should fortify it objectively wherever possible.

As an illustration, a cross-examiner may suggest to a witness who drove a car in lashing rain, that he has wrongly identified the accused as the driver of an oncoming car, at high closing speed. Such facts are easily visualized and are acceptable. Motorists in the jury will understand the situation.

In anticipation of this, the identification might be supported by contradictory objective evidence. This might be to the effect that the rain had stopped, that the cars were going slowly, that powerful headlights shone on the accused's face, and that he had been known to the witness since they were at school together. These too are easily visualized, acceptable facts.

To support accuracy of observation in such ways, preparation of evidence should assemble any helpful objective data, e g lighting, distances, times, weather, amount drunk and so on.

Where practicable, visual aids or exhibits, and precise oral or documentary evidence could support the accuracy of observation objectively, e g plans, diagrams, measurements of distances, the location or absence of obstructions, photographs of layouts, the number and location of street lamps, weather reports, or medical reports on injured witnesses.

In practice, the value of providing such supporting evidence is insufficiently realized, as seen in so many trials, where assertions and counter-assertions compete.

Notwithstanding the desirability of supporting accuracy of observation by objective data, the warning may be repeated that witnesses should not be asked in examination-in-chief, for exact figures or details, unless they can state them correctly and consistently; otherwise this simply exposes them to cross-examination as inconsistent.

*(b)  Memory.*   A challenge to the accuracy or reliability of evidence may be expected, on the ground of forgetting or influence. That evidence might be supported by any objective material which is available (including, perhaps, objective facts about the observation, e g how long someone was watched, where identity is in issue).

Time plays a part in forgetting, but accuracy of memory cannot be proved or disproved by any given period of delay alone. But if the case was properly prepared, a witness should be able to specify exact and important time intervals, e g, when he was first asked to point out the suspect or direct his attention to the facts, when this was repeated, and when he gave the police a statement.

Notes made at or shortly after the time by police, might support accuracy of recall strongly—unless they are attacked, as invented.

How suggestion, or a witness's mental processes, may have affected his memory, are beyond direct enquiry, but related facts and circumstances may be established from which inferences favourable to the proper recall of the facts may be made.

An advocate might have his witness admit that he discussed his evidence with other witnesses, where this was inevitable, in order to overcome the usual reluctance to admit this, which the opponent might exploit.

*(c)  Trust in witnesses.*   Despite the emphasis, so far, on supporting the accuracy or reliability of evidence liable to challenge, with objective material, it is not always available. Often, it is a question of accepting or rejecting a witness's assurances about the accuracy of his evidence. In effect, he assesses the quality of the evidence himself, and if the court decides to trust him, it relies on that self-assessment. If so, this would supersede any doubts caused by various impediments to observation and recall.

It is therefore essential to create and maintain the court's trust in the witness, as a bulwark against possible attacks in cross-examination. To do this, the advocate should try to show that the witness is fair, reasonable, and unbiased. This should be kept in mind in eliciting evidence which is likely to be challenged. It should be taken firmly, but reasonably. Obvious points which favour the opponent should be freely conceded.

## 2   Credibility

In areas where evidence is susceptible to attack in cross-examination as untruthful, steps should be taken to strengthen it. The factors on which credibility depends were discussed in the previous chapter. A few salient points have been selected here for emphasis.

*(a)   Previous convictions.*   It was seen that the scope of attacks on character is limited by law and by the court situation. Where such attacks are allowed, and made, it is usually on the ground of the witness's previous convictions. If they are known to the opponent, who is likely to bring them out, the tactical problem is how to reduce their impact—especially if they are substantial.

Leaving it to the cross-examiner to bring out the previous convictions involves risks that the examination-in-chief may seem deceptive, and that the convictions will be revealed in a way which worsens their effect.

An advocate normally tenders his witness as creditworthy. Failure to disclose his previous convictions may seem like a lack of candour, which can damage the court's impression of that witness and his evidence, as well as of the advocate and his case.

A witness may be unsure about the cross-examiner's knowledge of his criminal record or be embarrassed about it. He may disclose his convictions reluctantly and evasively. There are ways of cross-examining skilfully which could convert this into a transparent attempt to deceive the court in the current trial. This could be more destructive of the witness's credit than the previous convictions themselves.

But if an advocate brings out the previous convictions of his own witness, he eliminates both of these dangers. The advocate has been frank, and a good impression of the witness may have been formed.

But in addition, the advocate can present these convictions in the most favourable light, which the cross-examiner would not have done, e g as youthful folly which did no great harm, and which happened a long time ago since when the witness has married, started a family, obtained employment, and has become a model citizen. If an advocate discloses the previous convictions of his witness, and handles the matter properly, the cross-examiner may be left with little or no ground for attacking that witness's character.

If he returns to the topic of the previous convictions, it may seem to be unnecessary and unfair to focus on this secondary material with a view to creating prejudice against the witness. He would be asking questions which had already been asked, and answered.

*(b)　Motivation.*　A witness who is not independent may be exposed to challenge in cross-examination on the ground that his motivation has led him to lie.

The advocate who called him may anticipate this by disclosing the witness's interest, by eliciting his evidence in a convincing way, and sometimes, by asking him to confirm that he is telling the truth.

It is better to disclose the witness's interest in examination-in-chief, if it is not obvious, but is likely to be raised by the cross-examiner. However, it should be done incidentally, and as a matter of course, without creating an impression that his interest has any sinister significance.

The witness should be encouraged to give his evidence in such a way that it does not seem to be motivated. It should be seen to be realistic, in the sense discussed in the previous chapter. Excesses and exaggerations should be restored to balance; concessions should be made where proper; a reasonable and moderate tone should be maintained.

Conveying sincerity by the way in which evidence is given on the issues, can sometimes be reinforced by the response to a direct question inviting the witness to confirm that he is telling the truth, despite his interest in the case. If his evidence is genuine, this may evoke a spontaneous reply which is convincing. But the form of answer cannot be dictated. The question may be omitted if there is doubt about its probable effect.

To be persuasive, the question should relate to the present trial and not invite a claim to permanent veracity. To assert the latter might seem exaggerated and unreal, e g a mother's alibi evidence, which is otherwise acceptable, may be impaired by protests that she would never lie to save her son.

If the evidence of his witness is likely to be attacked as untruthful, to the extent that an advocate can anticipate this in the above ways, he may be able to remove the sting with a degree of success which will vary according to the circumstances.

*(c)　Demeanour.*　In the previous chapter, a critical view of demeanour as a method of lie detection was stated—but this might not be accepted universally. Any court is free to attach what weight it thinks fit to a witness's demeanour in a particular trial. Advocates should therefore do what they can so that their witnesses'

demeanour will be convincing if the cross-examiner accuses them of lying.

While an advocate cannot coach his witness or control his demeanour, it is not outwith his function to relax the witness, to take his evidence in the most convincing way, and to meet difficulties in advance. This should contribute to a witness's more favourable bearing under challenge.

An advocate can help a tense witness to relax by a reassuring manner and tone of voice, and by the content of his questions.

He would begin to elicit his evidence by controlled questioning, but if and when the witness is ready for this, his confidence may be developed and his evidence may be made more convincing, if he is allowed to give it freely with minimal questioning.

If the witness is sincere, signs of this may be evident in his demeanour. Spontaneous and natural forms of expression and realistic indications, as discussed in the previous chapter, should carry weight. Of course it sometimes involves risks to take evidence in this way, but if possible, this natural note should be introduced.

Finally, the advocate should anticipate and try to deal with difficulties which may arise in cross-examination, as discussed elsewhere.

Such steps may help, but of course there can be no guarantee that anxiety may not, after all, impair the testimony.

An advocate should, of course, be ready to object to any lack of consideration by a cross-examiner, or if his witness becomes unduly distressed.

*(d)  Inconsistency.*  It is to be expected that a witness will be cross-examined about any inconsistency in his evidence-in-chief; it should not be completed without correcting this. The consequences of not doing so could be serious; if lying is taken to be the explanation, the whole of that witness's evidence may be tainted or rejected.

The best remedy, where this is possible, is to reconcile the two alternatives, by some explanation which shows that they were not really inconsistent at all.

If this cannot be done, the witness would have to elect between one alternative and the other. However, it would still be necessary to explain how the inconsistency arose, e g as the result of misunderstanding, uncertainty or mistake.

Whether the inconsistency has already done any damage or not, may depend on the extent to which explanations are accepted. Some harmful effect may remain, but this is at least better than leaving the raw inconsistency for the cross-examiner to exploit. It is certainly better to face up to the problem in the examination-in-chief.

Where inconsistency arises on comparing the evidence of two or more witnesses for a party, it may range from minor discrepancies to conflicts about material points.

Minor discrepancies arising from the common fallibility of observation and memory mean little or nothing, as signs of lying, although their importance is often exaggerated in cross-examination and in speeches.

Typically, an opponent's argument that the differences between witnesses indicate lying, is met by the argument that they mean the opposite, since lying witnesses would have made up a uniform story. Assessment would depend on the circumstances.

If an advocate notes that his witness differs from one of his earlier witnesses, on a point which he regards as minor, he may either ignore the variation or else seek a concession that the current witness may be mistaken, if that might be so.

It would be more serious if the differences between two or more witnesses on the same side were material; this might create a risk that any of them may be taken to be lying, or that none of them will be trusted. Important variations in Crown evidence may result in an acquittal because of the standard of proof required for conviction.

To forestall the inevitable cross-examination here would be difficult, since the earlier witnesses have already testified and been cross-examined. They are out of reach. If any of them diverged from the evidence expected, that should have been dealt with at the time. The advocate's options are limited with the current witness.

An advocate's difficulties in anticipating cross-examination of a witness whose evidence differs materially from his earlier witness or witnesses, include the following. The advocate cannot lead his witness in the desired direction. He can only ask him about facts, and should not give him information about what his earlier witnesses said. Even if he manages to extract a concession from his current witness that he may be mistaken, or if he can bring him to alter his evidence, to conform to what his earlier witnesses said, this would be adverse to credibility, and would itself invite cross-examination on the ground of self-contradiction.

In such a situation, re-examination is unlikely to help. Once serious inconsistency emerges from the comparison of the evidence of several witnesses for a party, the final argument may offer the only hope of meeting it, but with little prospect of success.

The position would be rather different if the current witness could be treated as hostile, with the court's permission, so that leading questions could be put to him, and he could be challenged about the inconsistency directly, or about previous inconsistent statements. This, of course, would become the cross-examination of that witness, rather than an anticipation of cross-examination.

*(e) Improbability.* If evidence-in-chief contains something which is so improbable as to be virtually impossible, it may be treated like self-contradiction, i e by guiding the witness to the topic and giving him a chance to explain or modify his evidence spontaneously. If he is cross-examined about this later, he will, at least, be prepared for it. If such a difficulty is not tackled beforehand, in the examination-in-chief, a cross-examiner might exploit it in a damaging way.

An advocate can usually foresee which parts of his evidence-in-chief will be challenged as improbable, and which should therefore be reinforced against cross-examination. Since improbability is a matter of degree, he will try to reduce it, whereas the cross-examiner will try to increase it. In either case, the story will be probed, and expanded by adding circumstantial details and surroundings facts, in order to colour it in the direction of being more or less likely. This is what an advocate should do with his own witness, by foreseeing the directions of attack. This often reduces the impact of later challenge; it may seem pointless and futile to go over what was already covered. The advocate should build up the story, providing explanation of any odd points, until it seems reasonable, and likely to be true.

*(f) Realism.* As was seen, the realism and 'ring of truth' of evidence, are related to its richness of factual detail, and inclusion of the witness's personal reactions to events. Lack of these realistic qualities is not so much a specific danger which may expose the evidence to cross-examination and which must be dealt with in advance. It is rather a matter of poor presentation, viz the evidence will be less persuasive than it might be.

However, as a measure to be taken to strengthen his case generally, an advocate should be aware of these factors in the evaluation of evidence, and should allow them to permeate his examination-in-chief.

By allowing honest witnesses to testify freely with minimal control, where practicable, factual detail and the witnesses' personal involvement are likely to be included spontaneously, thus adding to the persuasive effect of the evidence.

Lying may be suggested by evidence which is dogmatic, over-purposive, and over-directional in a situation where some deviations or elements of uncertainty might have been expected.

This situation should be distinguished from another, where untruthfulness would not be suggested by the form of evidence, i e a firm report of a definite incident, seen under good conditions of observation.

Where it is clear that evidence-in-chief falls into the former unrealistic, over-purposive category, it should be toned down and the one-sidedness and exaggeration should be corrected. It is better to do this than to leave a skilful cross-examiner the opportunity of exposing evidence as being unrealistic and unreasonable.

*(g)   Contradiction.*   One party's main witnesses normally contradict the other party's main witnesses on the essential issues. This takes the form of different versions of a connected story, although some may only be able to speak to parts of it.

In examining his principal witnesses, an advocate should anticipate that his opponent, in cross-examination, will put his case to them on facts which they know. The advocate should therefore put his opponent's case to his own witnesses. He should not do this in a challenging way, but rather in some way which tends to weaken it. He also has the opportunity of developing whatever answers they may give, which he would lose, if he did not anticipate the cross-examination. This is a valuable way of forestalling the opponent.

# CHAPTER 6

# Cross-examination: foundations

I General
II Questions
III Strategy

## I GENERAL

### A Planning cross-examination

Before the trial, an advocate should plan his overall strategy on the basis of his evidence and what he knows of the opponent's case, from formal or informal disclosure, statements and inference.

The plan should include a provisional outline of proposed cross-examination, but only in the form of bold headings, and, perhaps, crucial details, based on the theory of the case. It should cover all the important points, but must be flexible to allow for improvisation of suitable questions.

Verbatim lists of intended questions or detailed notes could be a real handicap by interfering with the necessary alertness to the witness, and to the evidence, and its nuances, as it comes out. This could impede the ability to make swift tactical decisions. Pre-occupation with notes may suggest inexperience and lack of confidence. In advocacy, thinking on one's feet is essential. The plan for cross-examination is only an overall guide.

### B Decision to cross-examine

Decisions about which witnesses to cross-examine, on what topics and by which tactics, are made in the trial, according to what witnesses actually say, how they say it, and the context of the trial at the time. The fundamental principle is never to cross-examine without a clear and definite purpose.

Inexperienced advocates regularly ignore this principle. Skilful advocates only cross-examine when they must. When they do rise to their feet, the effect of their cross-examinations is enhanced by the expectancy that they will be significant. Like surgery, cross-examination is often crucial, but neither technique should be used indiscriminately. Much of the advocate's skill is negative: it consists of knowing when not to do something, where inaction is more effective. This negative form of skill is really an expression of purpose and control. It should pervade everything in cross-examination, e g keeping it as brief as possible, and stopping whenever the aim is attained, which will be considered below.

Aimless cross-examination may waste time, gain nothing, invite criticism, suggest that an advocate really has no case, emphasize the evidence challenged, or elicit harmful testimony, dilute any gain achieved, or create a new right to re-examine.

Such results, individually or combined, can be seriously damaging or fatal.

The commonest form of futile cross-examination consists of aimlessly going over the evidence-in-chief. There may be a vague hope that some flaw will emerge or that it will be changed somehow in going over it again. An aggravation is to delve into pointless detail.

This is not cross-examination in any meaningful sense; it only qualifies as such in the procedural sense of questioning another party's witness.

Its likely effect is to emphasize the evidence-in-chief, by repetition; the witness has a second chance to assert it more firmly, and to add supporting detail.

This can convert even relatively harmless evidence into a real difficulty. It would be hard to imagine any greater fault in cross-examination, than to achieve precisely the opposite effect to that which is intended.

Such aimless questioning is not converted into anything significant by suggesting finally that the witness is either lying or mistaken, where no foundation was laid for this. The witness will simply deny such suggestions of inaccuracy. Faced with such a feeble challenge, it would be a shaky perjurer whose facade disintegrated, or a very timid witness who conceded that he was mistaken.

However, it is quite different, and can be worthwhile, for a cross-examiner to have a witness repeat his evidence-in-chief in nearly identical terms, to show that it is memorized.

An advocate should not cross-examine if he cannot foresee any significant helpful result, or more than a minor gain, e g if the evidence to be challenged is merely neutral, unhelpful, or only slightly or remotely unfavourable. It is often best to disregard trivial points, even if they are contested, to avoid diluting what counts.

To ignore evidence minimizes its importance; to cross-examine on it emphasizes it.

Cross-examination is not designed to discredit truth. If unfavourable evidence will obviously be accepted as true and accurate, it may be more effective to concede it with good grace, than to challenge it or pretend that it does not exist.

Despite these reasons for not cross-examining, a party is expected to put his case to his opponent's witnesses who know the facts, partly as a legal duty and partly for tactical reasons. Texts on the law of evidence should be consulted for the obligation in law, and consequences of failure to comply. Sometimes an advocate who fails to challenge evidence at the time, may be deemed to have accepted it, which may become an impediment to later forms of challenge.

The position may differ in trials on indictment and in summary trials.

Within the ambit of these requirements, a case may be put in ways which range from asking about one point after another, in full detail, to one global and comprehensive question, so framed as to elicit a 'Yes' or 'No' answer.

Where the rules of evidence leave the matter open, a tactical decision should be made. If the case is only put for formal purposes, the more briefly this can be done the better, viz by one comprehensive question, or as near to it as possible. This minimizes the harm which an adverse witness can do. The danger of emphasizing adverse evidence by cross-examining a resistant witness in detail should be avoided. It may be better for the cross-examiner to contradict him by relying on the evidence which he will lead himself.

## C  Aims of cross-examination

The aims of cross-examination are not specified by law. They are tactical, and are either constructive or destructive.

The aim of constructive cross-examination is to build or strengthen one's case with positive and favourable evidence obtained from another party's witness, which supports one's evidence-in-chief.

Witnesses called by another party are not necessarily hostile, biased or unco-operative. If they are honest, they may be expected to concede favourable facts where this is justified. Even if they are partisan or untruthful, the context may oblige them to admit some indisputable facts.

The techniques of constructive cross-examination are the subject of the next chapter, viz: emphasis; new meanings; new facts; and alternative case.

The aim of destructive cross-examination is to weaken, and if possible to destroy, harmful evidence given by any witness (including one's own, if this is allowed) in order to defeat the opponent's case. To achieve this, often requires acceptance of the cross-examiner's evidence-in-chief to contradict the evidence which he attacks.

While cross-examination per se may not destroy the opponent's case, its contribution is indispensable. To confront one point of view with another in cross-examination is the heart of the adversarial process. It is an essential factor in persuasion. It is the most natural reaction to ask 'Well, what do you have to say to this?' and to evaluate the reply. Failure to challenge adverse and material evidence, can be fatal. A court should not be left simply to adjudicate on competing versions of facts without putting the conflicts to witnesses.

The techniques of destructive cross-examination will be dealt with in chapter 8. The overall approaches are either to challenge the witness as a mistaken or untruthful source of evidence, or else to attack the evidence itself as inconsistent, improbable or unrealistic. While these two main approaches are separable on analysis, one implies the other and in practice they are normally combined to some extent.

## D   Witnesses liable

Any witness called by an opponent is liable to cross-examination once he has been sworn, even if he is not examined in chief. Sometimes a Crown witness is called only to give the defence this opportunity.

Co-defendants may cross-examine each other and their respective witnesses, within certain limits.

As a general rule, an advocate may not cross-examine or discredit his own witness even though his evidence is unfavourable. He would do well to bring such testimony to an end as quickly as possible, and he could lead other evidence to contradict it. But exceptionally, a judge may hold the witness to be hostile, and grant leave to the advocate to cross-examine him, if the witness is seen to be testifying unfairly and without an intention to tell the truth.

This right of cross-examination includes putting previous inconsistent statements to the witness.

Familiarity with the rules of evidence governing the cross-examination of co-defendants, their witnesses, and one's own witness, is essential, and reference should be made to appropriate texts for that purpose.

## E   Subjects of cross-examination

Within the bounds of the rules of evidence, a witness may be cross-examined on any subject which is relevant to the issues of fact or his credit, although it was not raised in examination-in-chief.

The issues of fact in criminal trials were analysed in chapter 2: almost always, the two main issues of whether the crime was committed or whether the defendant was the offender, are limited to the one which the defence choose to dispute, the other being proved formally.

Crimes were classified into result-crimes, conduct-crimes and object-crimes, and issues of identity into those in which the accused claimed that he was, or was not, at the locus, or pleaded alibi. Cross-examination on the issues will either refer to the facts involved in these forms of crime, or alternatively, in these questions of identification.

Cross-examination as to credit is designed to show that the witness should be disbelieved. Thus he may be questioned about his character, previous convictions, bias, or previous inconsistent statements, on reasonable grounds, and if the imputations may affect credibility materially.

This differs from similar fact evidence tending to show a defendant's disposition to commit an offence of the type charged, and which is only admissible in exceptional circumstances.

The general rule excludes evidence in rebuttal of facts affecting a witness's credit which he denies in cross-examination, since this raises collateral issues. But exceptions exist. If bias, previous convictions or previous inconsistent statements are denied in cross-examination, evidence may be led to prove them.

Complex rules, which should be known, restrict rights of cross-examination as to character. A prosecutor can only attack the accused's character in the specific circumstances set out in the Criminal Evidence Act 1898. This also deters the defence from making imputations against Crown witnesses, or attacking co-defendants, lest the accused lose the shield afforded by the Act.

A cross-examiner may suggest that testimony is mistaken or untruthful without attacking character generally, but the shield may easily be lost.

## F  Sequence of cross-examination

Cross-examination should follow the best tactical sequence, whether or not it is understood by the witness or the court. No one type of sequence is best in all situations; it depends on the aims in the given context.

A chronological or logical order helps the comprehension and retention of evidence. This may be best where the advocate's approach is open and direct, e g if he is eliciting helpful and positive evidence from a co-operative witness, or is trying to have him concede that he may be mistaken. Here, the aim will be clear to the witness and to the court.

But a cross-examiner must often conceal his disbelief of a witness suspected of lying, and his intention to expose the deception. If so, he may follow an indirect and tactical sequence which the court does not understand, and he may ask some questions whose point is not obvious. A cross-examiner should be prepared to justify his line, if objection is taken, or the court intervenes—either in the absence of the witness, or by assurances or circumlocutions which do not give away his purpose.

Where an indirect sequence is followed, to conceal the aim from the witness, it will be followed by a direct challenge, at the proper stage.

In such an indirect approach, the cross-examiner may follow an unpredictable order, perhaps with rapid questioning. He may switch unexpectedly from one topic to another, swing back and forward from crucial to secondary facts, or change the angle of approach. This can disrupt a memorized story, or interfere with attempts to improvise, leading a lying witness with no foundation of reality on which to rely, into confusion and inconsistency.

Yet another order is best where the cross-examination begins with an attack on the evidence as untruthful, viz to go from the strongest to the weakest point.

Success with earlier points may eliminate the need to go on to later ones. Also, a good first impression on the court is important; it may shake the witness and cast doubt on his further evidence.

Apart from its general sequence, the opening and ending of cross-examination are significant.

The opening often has maximum impact since interest is at its peak, and attention and expectancy are focused on the confrontation. The sooner a cross-examiner puts forward an alternative version of the facts to those stated in the evidence-in-chief, the better, especially if the witness is the first important one. Ideally, the first questions should state the whole issue and lay a foundation for the rest of the cross-examination.

A good way of beginning cross-examination is to do so as forcefully as possible. A striking approach, assuming that the evidence merits this, is where it is challenged at once, as untruthful, on the strongest grounds available, e g manifest inconsistency or improbability, or confrontation with some strong material which contradicts it. If the witness can be taken by surprise, the impact may be even greater.

Of course, as has been said, cross-examination must sometimes begin indirectly, in order to lead a lying witness into a trap. At other times, preliminary probing may be necessary to find the best approach—but this should not be allowed to deteriorate into the kind of aimless enquiry described above.

Where the aim is constructive, i e to elicit helpful evidence, the opening of cross-examination should reassure the witness, showing him that he is trusted: it should seem as if he is merely being asked for additional information. To open tactfully, is also desirable where it will be suggested that the witness is mistaken.

A neat way to open, which shows alertness, and exploits continuity, is to ask a first question which follows on directly from the last answer in evidence-in-chief.

The choice of opening depends on the situation.

How cross-examination ends is also important. It should stop as soon as the objective has been attained and should not go on beyond the point at which everything material has been covered thoroughly.

It is desirable to end with a good final impression which may persist into later argument and the verdict. It is particularly helpful if the last answers sum up as much as possible of the cross-examiner's case, in a favourable way.

A good ending would be a victory over the witness in the form of a trap which exposes lying, inconsistency, statements contradicted by other credible evidence, or obvious improbability.

If the trap is inescapable, the cross-examination might exploit it from as many angles as possible, but this may involve risks.

Generally, on receiving a desired answer, it is safest to stop the cross-examination or to turn to an unrelated topic immediately. The temptation to gild the lily by asking further questions for confirmation, emphasis or development of a favourable answer should be avoided. It could ruin the whole result. Generally, the risks of going on exceed the possible gains. It gives the witness a chance to qualify or retract what he said. It reminds or stresses to the opponent the need for re-examination or to lead further evidence to meet his difficulty.

For obvious reasons, no sign of satisfaction with the evidence should be shown.

Unless the effect of a valuable admission is reduced by re-examination or further evidence led by the opponent, it is often unwise to endanger it by asking other witnesses the same question—apart from the situation, of course, where the cross-examiner must do this as an aspect of putting his case to them. Other witnesses may confirm the favourable evidence, but on the other hand they may weaken or contradict it.

Again, this reminds the opponent of the significance of the

evidence, while he can still re-examine, or call other witnesses to the topic. It is better to conceal its importance until the final argument, when it is beyond rebuttal.

A refinement of stopping with a triumph is to stop just before it occurs. Proof does not always require an explicit statement from a witness provided that the evidence is sufficient for the desired conclusion. An example of restraint is not asking a witness questions which would allow him to clear up an inconsistency. It might be better to highlight the inconsistency in the speech.

Instead of asking a final question designed to obtain a desired answer explicitly, cross-examination may be ended just before that stage. The purpose is to let a jury reach the desired conclusion themselves, by inference, with more force, as it is the result of their own process of reasoning. Even if they did not themselves draw that inference, it could be put forward in the speech.

Advantages are that: (i) the witness cannot defeat the aim by giving an adverse answer or by modifying or withdrawing his evidence; (ii) the adversary may not realize the danger, and re-examine; (iii) similarly, he may not lead further evidence in rebuttal; (iv) if his final argument precedes that of the cross-examiner, he may omit the point.

Possible disadvantages of not asking the final question are that the point may not be seen, or that it may be regarded as weaker because it was not conceded expressly. The opponent may argue that the witness was not given the opportunity to contradict or explain the evidence, since the matter was not put to him. This might reduce the weight of the evidence, but it would not invalidate an inference drawn by the court.

Again, it is assumed that the question is not one which the cross-examiner is obliged to put to the particular witness.

Whether or not to ask a final question is always a question for good judgment in the particular circumstances. Perhaps most advocates prefer express evidence, to leaving a point to inference.

## G   Brevity

Witnesses often persist in their adverse evidence, perhaps because it is true, honestly mistaken, or perjury to which they must adhere. If so, instead of turning away from an insuperable obstacle, an unskilled cross-examiner may go on for too long.

This increases the damage to his case. The longer cross-examination goes on, the more it emphasizes the advocate's view of the importance of the evidence attacked and the more it emphasizes adverse evidence by repetition, often supported by added detail. Moreover, even more harmful evidence may emerge unexpectedly.

Also, attention may ebb whereas brevity maintains expectancy that the cross-examination will be significant.

A brief cross-examination, even if unsuccessful, tends to minimize the importance of the evidence. The cross-examination of any witness, and on any topic should be as swift as possible. It should last no longer than is absolutely necessary to cover the material thoroughly. The advocate should select and concentrate on the few essential points on which a case usually depends, presenting them as early as possible to colour what follows favourably, and keeping them to the forefront, trying to achieve his objective as rapidly and as efficiently as he can. Success on major points, if properly selected, should have the effect that the minor points will not matter. Enquiry into every disputed fact or detail is unnecessary.

Brevity is not only a matter of the topics covered. It is assisted by short questions, avoiding those which are unnecessary, needless repetition or elaboration. If the only purpose is to show that evidence is not accepted, a question such as 'Is your story not completely untrue?' might suffice where it is unnecessary to be more specific.

As soon as the desired answer is given, cross-examination of that witness, or if there are other topics to explore, that line of enquiry, should be brought to an end, lest the evidence be qualified or withdrawn.

## H  The story

Almost every criminal trial is really a conflict between two stories about a human event, not a legal debate. All the advocate's arts, including the techniques and devices of cross-examination, should converge to tell a party's story, in such a way as to persuade the court that it is true. Belief or disbelief in a story is the ultimate test.

The main way for an advocate to tell his story is through his own witnesses, but he should also seek confirmation and support by constructive forms of cross-examination or by destructive challenges to the competing story. Cross-examiners should try to do more than just score isolated points; they should be promoting their whole version of the facts whenever they can.

With any witness, the relationship of the topic of cross-examination to this story should be introduced at the earliest stage, and kept to the forefront wherever possible. The main theme should recur, again and again. It is in cross-examination that one story confronts another, albeit that only parts of each version come into contact.

## II   QUESTIONS

### A   Purpose of questions

It should hardly be necessary at this stage to emphasize that no question should be asked in cross-examination without a clear aim.

A special aspect of this is the generally accepted maxim that no crucial question should ever be put in cross-examination to which the answer is unknown and cannot be reasonably foreseen, lest this elicits damaging evidence.

Sometimes, if a cross-examiner thinks that he must disregard this maxim, he should approach important matters and essential questions cautiously by small steps, testing the ground. Any risk taken must be as calculated and under as much control as possible. Questions about unknown aspects of minor facts are common enough, and are often safe.

### B   Form of questions

The law excludes some types of question at any stage, including cross-examination, e g those which would elicit inadmissible or irrelevant testimony. The main permissive rule in cross-examination is that leading questions are allowed. Otherwise, common sense and tactics settle the form of question.

There are no magic formulae or trick questions which guarantee success in cross-examination. Questions are framed spontaneously and intuitively as the advocate's personal response to the total situation, including his aims, the previous answer, the meaning of the question, and the context. Individuals may put equally effective questions in different ways. But some common phrases should be avoided, e g 'I suggest that . . .', or 'I put it to you that . . .' which are really statements, or 'My information is that . . .' or 'My client will say that . . .', which really give evidence.

### C   Control

By its nature, destructive cross-examination tends to be highly controlled, allowing as little freedom as possible. To let an adverse witness tell his story freely might be damaging or disastrous. But in cross-examining a co-operative witness constructively, the credibility of testimony may be enhanced if control is relaxed so that it is given spontaneously and naturally.

Free narrative by a witness may also be helpful where an over-confident lying witness is allowed to elaborate on his story as he wishes.

He may develop it to such a point of exaggeration and improbability that it can be easily discredited—even without contradictory evidence. If several lying witnesses are encouraged to do this, literal similarities in their stories may suggest that they have been memorized in collusion, or inconsistencies may show that they are false.

## D Leading questions

Leading questions, i e those which suggest the answer, are the normal form in cross-examination; in effect, the advocate asserts the facts, and the witness agrees or disagrees.

One form of cross-examination is to lead the witness forcefully on one point after another, keeping maximum control over him and his testimony with a view to excluding harmful statements. Any deviation from the point of the question, or evasiveness, may be countered by warnings, reminders, repetition of questions, and insistence on proper answers. Non-compliance exposes the witness's partiality or reluctance. Restricting the witness by narrow questions and small steps, prevents him from dealing with the whole issue.

The cross-examiner would avoid open-ended questions, e g, 'How?'; 'Why?'; 'What did you see then?'; 'How did that happen?'. He would avoid general questions seeking explanations or reasons which would open the door to wide and harmful statements.

Alternatively, a comprehensive leading statement covering a whole incident may be put for acceptance or denial, which prevents the witness from disputing the details, one by one.

But any kind of forceful leading will be less effective if it gives the impression that the evidence is coming from the cross-examiner, not the witness. Thus, it is desirable to conceal the extent of control and leading, so far as possible, while maintaining it to the necessary extent. It is a matter of striking a balance.

## E Clarity of questions

Since evidence obtained by destructive cross-examination consists mainly of accepting or denying leading questions, its comprehensibility as a whole will depend on the clarity of the questions. Evidence which is not clear will be neither remembered nor convincing. Moreover, a witness should not be allowed to escape from a trap by claiming that a question was confusing, and that he did not really say what is attributed to him.

Questions should be put in simple and ordinary language. Points should not be befogged by circumlocutions, pomposity, ambiguity, technical terms, or police jargon. They should be as brief as possible. If unusual or obscure terms must be used, they should be explained as part of the question. Questions should be precise, and should cover only one point at a time (apart from comprehensive leading questions of the type described).

Other impediments to clarity are questions which assume or imply facts which are themselves not clear or are unproved. This, of course, includes double questions.

## F    Repetition of answers

In principle, cross-examiners should only ask questions, and should not, for emphasis or other reasons, repeat answers. The mischief which can flow from non-compliance includes restatement in a slightly different form to insinuate a more favourable meaning, and comments or argument—which should be left for speeches.

At times, repetition of answers is unobjectionable. The almost inaudible reply of a timid witness or a child may be repeated so that it can be properly heard, and put to the witness for confirmation.

The exact words or gist of a helpful answer may be incorporated in the next or a later question.

A question may really be a comment on a repeated answer, conveying an advocate's personal reaction, explicitly or subtly, in an ostensibly interrogative statement, made in a sarcastic, scornful or incredulous tone of voice, eg 'Do you actually say that you jumped out of an upstairs window?'.

No attempt is made here to define the boundaries. Cross-examination requires reasonable latitude. Reciprocally, advocates often tolerate minor or borderline impropriety in their opponents without objecting. If objection is taken, it is a question for the bench in the particular circumstances.

## G    Misleading questions

Professional ethics take account of the interests of justice. They do not prevent a cross-examiner from misleading a dishonest witness, within acceptable limits, eg the advocate must not lie or misstate evidence which has been given, or make use of prejudicial or unfair material. But a degree of simulation is not only permissible but is often the only way in which the truth can be attained and justice done. The following are useful tactics; others may be devised as required.

A cross-examiner, having mastered every detail, may, without saying so, by his tone, manner, or form of question, give the impression that he has only a vague acquaintance with the facts. As a result of a false sense of security, an overconfident and dishonest witness may then invent or exaggerate evidence until his story can be easily exposed.

An advocate's tone, manner, or form of question may intentionally suggest that he seeks a certain answer, which in fact is the opposite of what he wants. A liar, to frustrate what he thinks is the advocate's purpose, may give the answer which is really desired.

The witness's attention may be distracted from the importance of a question, by asking it in a casual way, or by surrounding it with trivial ones asked in such a way as to appear crucial.

## H  Series of questions

Questions in a series may have a powerful cumulative effect which they would lack separately; they could make a mountain out of a molehill, which is part of the technique of cross-examination.

A good point may be maximized if, instead of exhausting it rapidly with one or two questions, it is built up to a climax by a series of narrow questions, advancing by small steps, or with a slightly new element each time.

Alternatively, a topic could be put in parts to different witnesses, so that none is asked the essential final question, or can answer it adversely, although the conclusion is clear to the court. This could be done where the cross-examiner is not bound to put the question as a whole to any individual witness, as part of his case.

An answer may be harmful or evasive in general terms. Generalization is a common way of avoiding reality in any argument. If so, a series of questions may be put about the particular facts which lead up to the conclusion. It will be more difficult to deny the truth, or to avoid the point of such specific and concrete questions.

A witness caught in a trap from which he cannot escape, may be asked a series of questions from various angles, to exploit and intensify his defeat.

## I  Rate of questioning

Varying the rate of questioning is useful in cross-examination. The hindrance of note-taking should be minimized. Noting evidence in detail interrupts the flow of questions, reduces impact, and gives liars time to think. In jury trials, it should be left to an assistant, and in summary trials, without an assistant, only essential notes need be taken. Personal abbreviations could include initials, e g 'P' for police, 'c/c' for caution and charge, or symbols for verbs of motion, vision and hearing, etc which can speed up note-taking enormously.

The best rate of questioning for a co-operative witness, giving helpful and positive evidence, is that of normal conversation which creates no strain.

Rapid questioning, especially in an unpredictable order, may give a liar too little time to invent answers related to earlier evidence and the hidden truth. If he repeats a question to gain time, this may be obvious. Off balance, he may be led into inconsistencies, improbabilities, or into testimony which can be contradicted by other evidence.

Alternatively, slow, deliberate questioning of a liar at crucial points, allowing ample time to answer, may highlight hesitations and difficulties, and demonstrate the falsity of his answers. To emphasize pauses, questions may be repeated or, even better, read back from the court record.

# III   STRATEGY

Guidelines to the strategy of cross-examination emerge from choices or a balance between various major alternatives.

## A   Witness and court

Janus-faced, a cross-examiner has to look in two directions—at the witness and at the court.

He seeks to induce the witness to give certain testimony, and to persuade the court that a certain version of the facts is true. The best steps towards either objective may not always be identical.

To extract desired evidence from a witness may require challenge, and open distrust, e g in a direct attack on the perjury of a police officer. But this may not impress the court. Knowing of no ground for this, the court may be critical, feeling that respect and courtesy would be the proper approach.

On the other hand, a cross-examiner may conceal his suspicion and mislead the witness, so that he can lead him into a trap by indirect methods. But the court may be mystified about the purpose of the line of enquiry; yet if open tactics were used for the court's benefit, the witness would also understand them, and they would be frustrated.

Generally, getting the desired evidence, is the primary and main consideration. Here the focus must be on the witness, and this determines the tactics.

But there is no point in eliciting testimony on which the court is unwilling to rely, because of the way in which it was obtained. To persuade the court to accept or reject what the witness was led to say, is the essential and ultimate aim. For this, the focus must be on the court, and this must qualify the tactics used with the witness.

The conclusion is that a cross-examiner's strategy should always be based on the best balance between manipulating the witness, and presenting the case to the court.

## B  Constructive or destructive tactics

In constructive cross-examination, the aim is to elicit positive and favourable evidence to support one's case, and in destructive cross-examination, the aim is to weaken or destroy evidence which is harmful to one's case. The tactics, themselves, will be described in later chapters. Here, the question is whether they may be combined in cross-examining one witness or, if not, which should be selected.

A constructive approach to a witness may sometimes be combined with a destructive approach which does not go too far.

If the challenge goes no further than to suggest some reason to regard the evidence as unreliable or honestly mistaken, this would leave the witness's credit intact. The door would then be open to the use of constructive tactics with a view to obtaining positive and favourable testimony.

However, since some people dislike even a suggestion that they are mistaken, considerable tact should be used in this situation. If possible, it may also be better to obtain the positive evidence before criticizing other evidence.

However, if the witness is accused of lying this will both alienate him, so that he will not co-operate, and may undermine the court's trust in favourable concessions which might be obtained. Here, the prognosis for combining constructive and destructive tactics would be poor.

A choice between seeking helpful evidence or attacking the witness as untruthful, depends of course on the relative value of the evidence in the particular circumstances. Favourable and material evidence is often preferable to attacking evidence. Helpful concessions from an opponent's witness usually make a strong impact. Cases are generally won by proving, not by disproving facts. Moreover, to weaken evidence is not necessarily to destroy it, and to destroy it is not necessarily to prove the contrary. But, despite this general comment, the actual situation must settle the matter.

## C  Challenging witness or evidence

In destructive cross-examination, either the witness may be

challenged as an unsound source of the evidence, e g as lying because of his motivation, or the evidence may be attacked as intrinsically unsound, e g inconsistent and improbable.

These approaches complement and imply each other. If a witness is mistaken or is lying about something, that part of his evidence must be inaccurate; on the other hand, any inaccuracy in his evidence must be due to a mistake or lying on that matter. So challenging either the witness, or the evidence, are different modes of contending that evidence should be rejected. Generally, both forms of challenge are combined, although greater emphasis may be placed on one or the other.

## D   Mistake or lie

The dichotomy between mistaken and untruthful evidence is not always respected and brought out clearly by cross-examiners. There should be no doubt about the kind of defect which is suggested. Since his tactics and presentation are shaped by the appropriate alternative, a cross-examiner should decide whether to contend that inaccuracy is unintentional or intentional, and should adhere to that consistently.

If the witness knows the facts which he reports wrongly, the inaccuracy must be intentional, i e he is lying. But even where this is obvious, cross-examiners are often reluctant to charge witnesses expressly with lying. Some reasons for this may be pointed out.

In indirect tactics (discussed below), a cross-examiner conceals his intention to treat the witness as untruthful until the proper stage.

Some advocates may think that to allege that a witness is lying may make their performance seem less polished or that it may antagonize a jury. But neither need be the case. A cross-examiner can suggest lying, without abuse, and by diplomatic language or circumlocutions. He might even, in a suitable situation, where it is obvious that the witness is lying, leave the topic without pressing it home by an explicit allegation. Then, the witness cannot retract or qualify his lie. It is not emphasized to the opponent, who may yet correct it in re-examination or further evidence. An unintelligent witness may also be misled into thinking that his deception has succeeded, which can help in cross-examination on other topics. The inference that the witness is lying may be left to the jury at that stage, and can be argued in the final speech.

However, to leave any doubt about whether the witness is said to be mistaken or lying, is weak advocacy. This should be made clear either during the cross-examination or in argument. Otherwise, it gives the court no help on the vital questions of how the witness is related to his evidence, and whether or not he is to be trusted.

To say that a lie is a mistake is even worse. Where a witness must know the truth, to suggest to him that he may be 'mistaken' as a euphemism for lying, is tainted with insincerity.

Disbelief in one's own challenge seems to explain much reluctance to accuse witnesses of lying. Advocates should present cases without judging them, but they may be half-hearted about some unreasonable and highly improbable suggestions. Formal ethics do not eliminate human nature. Common examples are some extreme defence attacks on police officers alleging seriously criminal conduct, in which the advocate appears to have no faith. Such accusations are sometimes true, but less often than they are made.

To challenge evidence as mistaken or untruthful is only meaningful after prior enquiry into the factors which were discussed earlier. A few casual questions, followed by 'I suggest that you are mistaken about this' or 'I put it to you that this is untrue' are inept and only indicate a cross-examiner's formal stance.

There is usually no aversion to claiming that evidence is mistaken, so that it is reluctantly converted to an accusation of lying.

## E  Friendly or hostile tactics

Apart from the standards of conduct expected from all advocates, deliberate role-playing, viz 'friendly' or 'hostile' tactics, are typical forms of approach to witnesses in cross-examination. Friendly tactics give an impression of trust and belief. Hostile tactics suggest distrust and disbelief.

Apart from these tactics, cross-examination today is generally quiet and moderate without the histrionics of earlier times. Witnesses, as 'captives', must be treated considerately even if some may be perjurers or rogues. The bench prevents abuse, harassment, or needless offence. Advocates should seek their goals objectively, by intellectual power, keeping control at all times. They should be professionally detached, on the court's level of thinking, and without excessive partiality or identification with their cases. They may be forceful and firm, but should combine this with fairness, reasonableness and courtesy. These ideal qualities are not universal.

Friendly tactics are suitable in seeking the co-operation of honest witnesses from whom helpful evidence, or concessions that they may be mistaken, are sought. Such tactics may disarm a defiant, but not necessarily dishonest, witness, making him less determined to do as much harm as possible.

Friendly tactics, in their most calculating form, may be employed to prevent a dishonest witness from realising that he is being led by an indirect approach into a trap; the tactics would become hostile at the proper stage.

Friendly tactics are often the best way to start cross-examining any witness—even those who are seriously biased, partisan or untruthful.

If hostile tactics become necessary later, it should by then have become increasingly clear that the witness, not the advocate, has caused this. The need for open challenge and firmness should have emerged from the witness's evasiveness, partiality, inconsistencies or improbabilities. If this has been well done, in rapport with the court, hostile tactics will then be seen to be fully justified.

Starting cross-examination in a hostile way is usually advisable only if there is strong contradictory material with which to confront the witness. This would show the court at once that such hostile tactics are necessary.

## F   Direct or indirect tactics

In direct tactics, an advocate allows the aim of his line of cross-examination to be seen by the witness, and in indirect tactics, he conceals it.

Various combinations of direct or indirect with friendly or hostile tactics, may be employed.

A combination of direct and friendly tactics would be appropriate in cross-examining honest witnesses, where, quite openly, helpful evidence or an admission of mistake, is sought.

Direct and hostile tactics would be chosen for cross-examining defendants; indirect approaches are unlikely to succeed with them.

Direct and hostile tactics would also be employed with any lying witnesses where the cross-examiner was at once able to put strong material to them, e g any self-contradiction or improbability in their evidence, previous inconsistent statements, the contradictory evidence of other witnesses on either side, exhibits, documents, or facts not in dispute. Forceful leading questions would be put in a challenging tone and manner, about one point after another, of which the aim is to make the witness commit himself firmly and precisely by admission or denial. The objective of this frontal attack is to drive the witness, inevitably, to concede helpful facts or inaccuracy in his evidence. It is more a matter of compulsion than of subtlety.

A dishonest witness may respond to such a direct initial attack in various ways. An unfavourable outcome would be that, having been put on his guard, he may become more cautious, and may insist on his story more firmly. Yet, under pressure of this kind, he may be unable, to invent persuasive facts quickly enough—especially circumstantial details.

Some witnesses might be less inclined to lie further after a successful initial attack, but few can be expected to withdraw or modify any previous false evidence.

An immediate attack still has advantages. The court would realize the need for this approach at once, from the nature of the material put to the witness. Any success in this confrontation may make a strong impression on a court when attention is at its peak. The challenge contradicts the evidence-in-chief at once, with an alternative version of the facts. It may shake the witness, and make him more vulnerable in further cross-examination. Such flaws as may emerge in this evidence initially are likely to colour the rest of the cross-examination.

If the attack does not succeed fully or at all, in its immediate objectives, it may be that, in resisting it, the witness becomes entangled in such inconsistencies, improbabilities or evasions, as to discredit his evidence, when it is compared with acceptable and contradictory testimony led by the cross-examiner.

In indirect tactics, a cross-examiner conceals his intention from the witness. The result may also be to conceal the intention from the court, although it has a better chance than the witness to see the whole picture. However, a cross-examiner should always be ready to justify the relevancy of his line of enquiry, if the opponent objects, or the bench intervenes—preferably in the absence of the witness and a jury.

Typically, indirect tactics are used in cross-examining seriously biased, partisan or lying witnesses, where the cross-examiner does not have strong material with which he can confront them. Without such material, simply to ask leading questions suggesting that a witness is mistaken or untruthful, would achieve nothing. The aim of indirect tactics is to acquire material for the purpose of challenging the witness directly. Thus, it is common to begin cross-examination indirectly, and to switch to direct tactics later.

Naturally, this approach will be as friendly as possible to reduce the witness's alertness to the risks which he incurs. Even though a dishonest witness knows that he will be challenged, he cannot foresee exactly how this will be done. He may not see the point of a question or a series of questions, until it is too late.

Indirect tactics are seldom needed or desirable with honest witnesses. There would seem to be no point in concealing the intention of a line of questions from them. But even honest witnesses may dislike, and may unconsciously resist, having to change their evidence. If so, a little indirectness may sometimes help in the approach to securing an admission of some mistake, or in insinuating a new meaning for observed facts.

Leading the witness into a trap often requires skill, subtlety and imagination. Where possible, the questions should concern facts for which he is unprepared, drawn from the collateral circumstances which precede, accompany or follow the main incident, or matters arising from the conduct of those involved. Details should not be probed needlessly where nothing is to be gained.

The cross-examination should proceed by steps in which the witness, who should be kept in ignorance as long as possible, is made to commit himself firmly to facts which the advocate knows he can contradict later by turning to direct tactics, and confrontation with material of the kind described above. The flaws which would be revealed then are those which follow from various forms of contradiction. As has been reiterated, even if this does not destroy the evidence under challenge, it may so weaken it that it is overcome by positive evidence led by the cross-examiner.

CHAPTER 7

# Cross-examination: constructive techniques

## I  INTRODUCTION

Cases are won by proving, as well as by disproving facts, i e as a result of the strength of one's case, as well as the weakness of the opponent's case. The importance of cross-examination is not limited to weakening or destroying the opponent's evidence, although this aspect is usually emphasized. A significant objective of cross-examination is to obtain favourable evidence by means of various constructive techniques. Such opportunities should be grasped. Concessions by an opponent's witness may have a strong impact.

Two questions arise initially for the cross-examiner, viz 'Does the witness know of any helpful facts?' and 'Will the witness co-operate?'.

The state of a witness's knowledge of favourable facts would usually be obvious to a cross-examiner from the evidence-in-chief. Eyewitness testimony about a disputed incident puts the witness at the locus as an observer who saw a good deal, if not everything material. Circumstantial evidence is more limited in scope but may offer opportunities.

In a strongly disputed issue, where some facts may reasonably be in doubt, it might be odd if a witness's whole evidence pointed unequivocally in one direction, i e if it was either totally incriminating, or totally exculpatory, with nothing pointing the other way. If a cross-examiner does not know of any such facts, he might probe the evidence for that purpose. If none can be found, this may mean that none are known to the witness, or that the witness's credit is suspect. Dogmatism in an area where some uncertainty would be reasonable is always open to question.

The opponent's witnesses are expected to co-operate in the cross-examination as an obligation of law. Although the opponent called them to give evidence favourable to himself and unfavourable to the other party, this neither defines their duty nor represents the everyday reality of criminal trials. Witnesses must comply with their oaths wherever their evidence leads, not act as partisans for whoever called them. No difficulty should arise with witnesses who are honest and impartial. Even biased, partisan or lying witnesses are under some constraint. To avoid the law's penalties, their evidence must fit into a context of other evidence, and a network of uncontested or obvious facts. Usually, even reluctant witnesses must give answers which are relevant whether or not they are accurate.

While, by definition, the aim of constructive techniques of cross-examination, is to obtain positive and favourable evidence, as with so many distinctions, the boundary between constructive and destructive techniques is not absolute. The classification is practical, not philosophical. Sometimes, an affirmative answer about one fact is also a negative statement about another, i e it is destructive.

Also, in practice, constructive and destructive techniques may overlap or be combined, or there may be swift transitions from one approach to the other.

Reference is made to the discussion of the relationship between constructive and destructive techniques in the previous chapter.

Generally, if favourable evidence is sought from a witness, co-operation is more likely if this precedes any challenge; depending on the results, it may then be better not to challenge the witness, or to do it only formally if there is a duty to put one's case.

The main constructive techniques progress from accepting evidence-in-chief to contradicting it, viz: (i) emphasis; (ii) new meanings; (iii) new facts; and (iv) alternative case.


## II  EMPHASIS

In the technique of emphasis, the cross-examiner finds something in the evidence-in-chief which favours his case. He accepts it, and does not try to change it in any way, although he may draw out some additional details. He makes the witness repeat it for emphasis. Naturally he would do it in such a way as to highlight the favourable aspect. The evidence-in-chief on that topic is what the cross-examiner builds on. He simply focuses attention on it to make it more prominent.

This may be illustrated in a charge of robbery where masked men enter a shop, terrorize the staff with hammers, empty the till, and escape in a car. A sales assistant, claiming to have recognized one robber as a customer, by his build, hair colour, and typical way of walking, says, in evidence-in-chief, 'It was over so quickly'. A cross-examiner may seize on the brevity of the event for emphasis, adding detail to build up a picture of how many things the witness seems to have attended to in a short time, leaving little time to study that robber. Here, the advocate accepts and focuses on one element of evidence of this, and perhaps other witnesses. To emphasize the brevity of the event supports his attack on the identification as unreliable or wrong. It is usually easy to find at least some favourable aspect for emphasis, even in evidence which is generally adverse.

One tactic for doing this, is to use the principle of relativity, by comparing evidence actually given with more harmful evidence which might have been, but was not, given. The difference may then be emphasized to the effect of suggesting that the facts are less adverse than they seem to be.

A police witness may speak to finding the stolen goods in the living room of the accused's house. A cross-examiner may elicit, and emphasize that the officer was invited into the house, without a search warrant, and that the goods were lying openly on a table. The absence of evidence that the accused objected to the witness's entry, or that the goods were hidden in the attic, when compared with the actual evidence, is favourable to the accused, and may be emphasized.

Often enough, even incriminating circumstances are not as bad as they might conceivably have been, and a skilful cross-examiner may extract some advantage from emphasizing this. The same approach may be taken to any kind of evidence, eg the conditions of observation which are rarely perfect, but where the absence of even worse conditions may be stressed.

None of these approaches requires any challenge to the witness and he will often be co-operative.

Some objections to the method may be considered.

In theory, it is enough for something said in evidence-in-chief to be heard once and understood. Repetition should add nothing. Also, as has been said, repeating the evidence-in-chief is one of the most common faults in cross-examination. But in this technique only one or two helpful points in that evidence are repeated—not all of it. Repetition ensures that they receive attention and are recalled; it figures in all forms of persuasive communication from advertising to teaching.

Again, the advantages of dropping a topic as soon as helpful evidence is given, have been pointed out. On that view, favourable points in evidence-in-chief are best left alone until the final speech. If there is any risk that the helpful evidence may be qualified or retracted, if it is repeated, it would indeed be better not to cross-examine on the point. But if the evidence is likely to remain intact on repetition, and a worthwhile gain is foreseen, to emphasize it may help, especially if it is developed by eliciting additional details, so that its favourable effect is intensified.

To emphasize part of an opponent's evidence, is useful, especially on starting to cross-examine. It may disarm a witness and make him easier to manage. Focusing on what is common to parties should lead to acceptance of the undisputed evidence by the court.

In this method, part of the evidence-in-chief is accepted. For emphasis, the witness is sometimes made to repeat that testimony, or sometimes to amplify it by adding details, but there is no attempt to change it. This should be distinguished from the next technique to be considered, where the cross-examiner tries to change the meaning of evidence-in-chief which he accepts. In practice, these two techniques may be combined, or they may overlap to some extent.

## III NEW MEANINGS

In cross-examination new and favourable meanings may be given to facts stated in evidence-in-chief, which are accepted as accurate. Such meanings are also facts but they are derived from other facts and not perceived directly. They range from a witness's impression or interpretation of what he observed, to the inference drawn from circumstantial evidence.

Issues of admissibility can arise in this type of evidence. However, they should have been settled in the course of the examination-in-chief. Whatever was admissible then, whether or not objected to, should be subject to cross-examination.

Texts on the law of evidence should be consulted for exceptions to the general rule which excludes evidence of opinion from lay witnesses.

Evidence of identification, or a witness's view of his own mental or physical condition, motives or feelings, may involve opinion, but are admissible, and open to change of meaning in cross-examination.

So too is evidence of impressions which are ways of conveying material and relevant facts perceived by the witness, or which interpret meaningfully, observations which were too vague, obscure, subtle or ambiguous, to be otherwise described and communicated effectively.

In practice, it is difficult to apply rigid tests to this kind of material. The strict technical rules are not pressed to the point of absurdity, and are qualified by practical considerations, common sense, and necessity. Witnesses often give impression evidence in marginal circumstances, which is admitted because no objection is taken, e g an opinion which is so obvious from the evidence given that it would be artificial to exclude it.

Impression evidence is often given about persons, their ages, condition, motives and conduct, e g that someone had been drinking, or was distressed, that a man was threatening others with a glass, that youths were acting suspiciously in a car park, or that physical contact had a sexual intention.

Impression evidence may also be given about physical things, or situations, e g that there was a good deal of traffic about, or that a crowd of football fans were in a wrong area seeking trouble.

These are examples of general statements of facts derived from observing other specific facts, which the witness may not be able or required to report.

Expert opinion evidence is open to this technique and is considered in a later chapter.

The effect of circumstantial evidence depends on the inference drawn from it. It is for the court, and not for witnesses, to make such inferences. But if any statement which a witness was allowed to make in evidence-in-chief contains some element of inference, it should be open to cross-examination, and to modification. Even if the inference is not referred to expressly by either the witness or the cross-examiner, the pattern and relationship of the facts may still be altered so that the court's final interpretation of them will be favourable.

The aim of cross-examination, then, may be to give a new meaning to any adverse and material impression evidence or to any circumstantial evidence which may otherwise yield an adverse inference.

It should start with friendly and indirect tactics which proceed gradually, step by step. By careful leading questions, the witness is made to accept minor adjustments to the evidence here and there, stressing this and toning down that, so that the balance and pattern are altered subtly in the direction of the desired new meaning.

Little pressure is needed with reasonable and co-operative witnesses, but greater firmness, and perhaps reference to some contradictory material, may be required with those who are resistant. With both types, the objective should be concealed for as long as possible.

A general conclusion, which the witness would not accept at first, may be reached indirectly, e g by building it up from specific points, or by combining separate facts which converge to give that result. The important area of evidence should be approached with caution, while a view is formed of the witness's likely response to the objective. At the proper stage, the cross-examiner must use his judgment as to whether or not to put the proposed new meaning to the witness expressly.

The advantages and disadvantages of asking a final specific question, discussed earlier, arise here. To stop just before that, leaves the point to the court's inference; the result of its own judgment may be more impressive than a witness's view. The point can also be made in the final speech. Also, the witness has no chance to weaken or destroy the desired interpretation, by qualifying or withdrawing his earlier evidence. Moreover, emphasis of the risk to the opponent is avoided; he is then less likely to meet it by re-examination, calling other evidence, or final argument.

On the other hand, asking the final specific question, also has advantages.

The witness may accept the new interpretation as the correct one, conceding that what he said on the topic in evidence-in-chief was wrong. If so the technique has been successful.

If the witness concedes only that the meaning put to him is equally consistent with the facts, or at least a possibility, this is also a worthwhile achievement. An alternative and favourable version of the evidence-in-chief will have been presented to the court out of the mouth of the opponent's witness.

If the witness rejects an interpretation put to him, dogmatically, and it is a reasonable one, his credit, and not the proposition, may suffer. He may be seen to be biased or untruthful.

This technique may contribute much to a case, although the witness does not accept the cross-examiner's interpretation. A story may be given a new orientation, without altering the basic facts. The evidence-in-chief may be so weakened by it that it is rejected in favour of evidence led by the cross-examiner; a reasonable doubt may be created about a fact which is essential for conviction. Although the witness denies the points, merely putting them is suggestive.

The technique is essentially constructive, since the aim is to build up one's case, but it combines this with weakening or destroying harmful evidence. Advantages are that it can be done without challenging the witness as mistaken or untruthful, thus gaining his co-operation, yet impressing the court, since the concession comes from a witness called by the opponent.

# IV   NEW FACTS

A common and important approach in cross-examination, is to bring out new and material facts, which were omitted from the examination-in-chief. Opportunities for this will depend on how thorough the examination-in-chief was, and on how far it anticipated cross-examination.

This differs from probing collateral facts, looking for flaws in the evidence, or from simple requests for additional information, e g the width of a road.

Any material facts which may be relevant to the defence, and which are known to the prosecutor, should be disclosed in the evidence of Crown witnesses. But something may be omitted in good faith, because he does not think that it is significant or does not know about it. The prosecutor is not required to look for or to construct a defence.

Material facts may be deliberately omitted from the defence evidence-in-chief. The advocate is not obliged to disclose incriminating facts, provided that his presentation of the case does not assert what he knows to be false, deny what he knows to be true, or mislead the court intentionally. To omit adverse facts from defence evidence for tactical reasons incurs the risk that if the opponent knows them, and brings them out for the first time in cross-examination, the harm will be increased by the defence lack of frankness.

A cross-examiner should not ignore the possibility that sometimes an omission may be a trap designed to increase the harm to his case if he raises the point. If he does not, the opponent will lose the benefit of that evidence, because of his misjudgment.

Apart from deliberate omissions, any advocate may miss out something important as a result of simple oversight. This would not be surprising in the pressing circumstances of a criminal trial. Advocates often ask their assistants if they have omitted anything.

Thus both the evidence-in-chief of either Crown or defence witnesses may offer scope for bringing out new facts in cross-examination. The merits of doing this should be weighed up before embarking on it.

Sometimes it is better to leave something alone or in doubt. Advocates should avoid the lawyer's tendency to want everything to be express and stated in words. New facts should only be brought out if they are likely to be helpful and material, and not simply because some area of evidence is incomplete, as a result of failure to state something. The omitted facts may only be important to the opponent, or they might open up an area of evidence where the cross-examiner's case is vulnerable. To raise an omitted point in cross-examination allows the opponent to deal with it in re-examination. A cross-examiner may regret it if he enters into such questions. Whether to cross-examine for new facts, when to go on, and when to stop, calls for judgment.

If the cross-examiner ignores the maxim of never asking

questions to which he cannot foresee the answer, and explores unknown territory, he will incur risks. If so, he should proceed very cautiously, trying to form a view of what the likely answer will be to the significant question.

With a co-operative witness, evidence obtained without leading, although it is permissible, will be more persuasive; however, if there is resistance, leading is sometimes necessary. The evidence will also be more comprehensible if it follows some logical order—usually chronological.

New and material facts which emerge for the first time in cross-examination are likely to have a strong impact, as they come from an opponent's witness, and this may reflect adversely on the opponent's lack of candour in the examination-in-chief.

If the new evidence is really helpful and important, the benefit may be negated by trying to discredit that witness in other respects.

# V  ALTERNATIVE CASE

Whether or not he uses other constructive methods, a cross-examiner should put his alternative version of the case to any witness who knows the facts, giving him a chance to accept or deny it, and to explain any contradictions. Failure to do this may be taken as acceptance of what was not challenged. Sometimes results may follow by law, e g a bar to cross-examining other witnesses on the same facts, or to leading contrary evidence, or to challenging that evidence in argument—with possible differences between jury trials and summary trials. This aspect of the law of evidence is not entirely clear or fully developed, but only tactical questions will be considered here. Even where legal restrictions do not follow, not to put one's case is to lose a vital tactical opportunity.

It is a general rule of tactics that if a cross-examiner has led, or intends to lead, evidence to contradict a witness, he should give him a chance to explain that contradiction. Although this has been done with one witness, it is advisable to do it also with later witnesses whose evidence is similarly contradicted.

The situation will determine how and to what extent the alternative case should be put to the witness. Sometimes, one comprehensive question, asking for a 'Yes' or 'No' may be enough and at other times, the case should be put, point by point, in detail; within these extremes there is a range of possibilities.

If the case is only being put for formal purposes, to show that evidence-in-chief is not accepted, the more briefly this is done the better, viz by one comprehensive question, or as near to it as possible. This minimizes the harm which an adverse witness can do.

To put every point in one's case in detail, to an unyielding witness, allows him to repeat his evidence, more firmly, perhaps with elaboration and more support from circumstances, scoring in one respect after another. This will only emphasize the damaging evidence. Putting one's alternative case in detail should be avoided unless success on material points is being achieved. If it is seen to be futile, such cross-examination should stop. To undo the harm caused by such a witness, and to contradict his evidence, it is better for the advocate to present his alternative case in cross-examination, as briefly as possible, and then to rely on his own witnesses.

Clearly, the extent to which an advocate may put his case in cross-examination, is limited by the witness's knowledge of the facts. If the witness knows enough to enable the whole case to be put to him as a connected story, rather than as unrelated facts, this would be best. A trial is essentially a matter of resolving a conflict between two stories about a human event, not a legal issue. Everything should converge on the story, in the most convincing way, including cross-examination, where one story confronts another, in whole or in part.

Unless the defence story is disclosed in an opening speech, the court may only learn what it is in cross-examination of Crown witnesses, when it is put forward as a meaningful story which anticipates the defence evidence to be led.

If an eyewitness, or participant in the incident is called by either the prosecution or the defence, the whole alternative version can usually be put to them in cross-examination, in contradiction of their direct evidence.

Sometimes a prosecutor will cross-examine by putting the Crown version of the facts to the witness in detail. He might do this with a co-operative witness from whom concessions are being obtained. On the other hand, he might do it with a stubborn and unreasonable witness, who exposes his partiality with every answer. At other times, a prosecutor will dismiss an obviously lying witness after only a few questions, by suggesting that his evidence is quite untrue, and that the facts were as charged.

When defence advocates put their case to eyewitnesses called by the Crown, they often do this in detail, accepting rebuff after rebuff. It is not recommended that this should be done beyond the point where it is productive.

Since Crown witnesses who only give circumstantial evidence did not observe the whole event, the defence cannot put their whole alternative case to them.

Presentation of the alternative case usually comes at the end of the cross-examination of any witness. It usually follows destructive challenges in which the cross-examiner tries to show that the witness is mistaken or untruthful, or that the evidence in question is defective and implausible. When the ground has been prepared, the cross-examiner puts his own alternative case.

Putting the alternative case is essential, even where, as is usual, the witness denies it. It shows exactly where a party stands, focuses the issue, integrates isolated or secondary points, shows that there is an alternative version of the facts, confronts the witness with that and demonstrates his response.

Its effects have something in common with cross-examining for new meanings. If, exceptionally, a witness accepts the cross-examiner's case, when it is put to him, success has been achieved. If he only concedes that it is a possibility, that too accomplishes something worthwhile, e g if a Crown eyewitness admitted this about a crucial fact, it may be enough to raise a reasonable doubt and lead to acquittal. If a witness rejects the case put to him, unreasonably, his bias or untruthfulness may become obvious.

In any event, merely putting that alternative story has a suggestive effect per se, which can add to the persuasiveness of the case.

# CHAPTER 8

# Cross-examination: destructive techniques

## I   INTRODUCTION

The main aim of cross-examination is to weaken or destroy harmful evidence. Skill in the art depends on insight into the process, not mastery of a set of tricks. In various contexts, a cross-examiner must know what he can do, how he can do it, and the probable effects of doing it: he will then apply this insight in the particular situation.

The development of a cross-examiner's natural ability by practice and experience should be based on an understanding of the processes of destructive cross-examination, which are described in this chapter.

There are no rules or verbal formulae whereby anyone can acquire instant expertise or demolish any evidence automatically. There are, however, principles which can be applied flexibly as required. In planning and in conducting any cross-examination, nothing can replace the need for the advocate's good judgment in the particular circumstances.

## II   DESTRUCTION OF EVIDENCE

'Destruction' of evidence, here, simply means that the court rejects it, i e does not base the verdict on it. This is what counts, whether it is due to total disbelief including acceptance of the opposite state of facts, or a reasonable doubt.

127

Although the destructive effect of each step may vary, the complete three-stage model of destroying evidence is to weaken it in cross-examination, contradict it by other evidence, and attack it in argument. But if no defence evidence is led, that, and cross-examination by the prosecutor, are missing from the process.

If cross-examination is so effective that the opposed evidence would be rejected even if it were not contradicted by other evidence, this cannot be known, or predicted with certainty, at that stage. It is a safer working rule that the whole trial process is necessary to destroy evidence, and not to leave anything undone which could contribute to this.

Whether or not to lead evidence is a classic problem for the defence. Without it, they are unlikely to establish any version of the facts in competition with the prosecution. But it may be felt that the evidence available could be harmful or risky, or the accused, for his own reasons, may decide that evidence should not be led.

If the defence rely on cross-examination and argument, they need only raise a reasonable doubt about the Crown case to succeed. Depending on the state and significance of the evidence to be challenged in the context of the Crown evidence generally, and the cross-examiner's skill, such a defence may succeed at times, but to omit helpful evidence which could be led involves some risk.

Although the defence complete their cross-examinations before deciding whether or not to lead evidence, they may be uncertain about whether the court will eventually reject the evidence which they attacked. The defence advocate must calculate the risks in deciding whether or not to imperil his case on cross-examination without leading evidence.

Realistically, a cross-examiner should not expect a lying witness to retract his story or to substitute the truth. His original strong motive for lying is reinforced by fear of penalties that may follow if he admits it. Moreover, lying witnesses seldom become incoherent or silent, to the extent of demolishing their testimony.

Mistaken evidence is sometimes retracted, or doubts about it are conceded, by impartial witnesses, although even honest witnesses, from bias, partisanship, vanity or other reasons, may show resistance. But a cross-examiner should certainly try to get favourable concessions of this kind.

Destroying evidence only establishes the contrary, if that follows logically, e g, to destroy the accused's evidence that he was not driving the car makes him the driver. But in other cases, destruction of evidence about one assertion leaves other possibilities open, e g, to destroy an accused's claim that he was in Leeds does not place him in Watford or prove that he committed the crime.

# III BELIEF AND DISBELIEF

Since the aim of destructive cross-examination is to produce disbelief, it is relevant to consider how belief in evidence develops. It depends on three elements—if any one is missing or deficient, evidence may be disbelieved: the witness must be trusted, his evidence must be reasonable, and his evidence must have weight.

## A Trust in witnesses

To trust or distrust witnesses is a daily reality in courts. It depends partly on direct and natural responses to them, and partly on intellectual assessment. There can be degrees of trust, and it can be selective. The court may trust a witness as being truthful and sound, so that his self-assessment and confidence in his report may overcome any allegation of unreliability or mistake. Some witnesses may be trusted as truthful, but doubted in some other way, e g, memory for details.

Acceptance of the witness's personal assurance in the context of the trial, as to what he saw, is one of the foundations of belief that the facts were indeed so. This belief depends on both feeling and thinking in a certain way about the witness in relation to the trial, e g, 'That nice old lady has not come to court to commit perjury so that an innocent youth should be convicted'.

In court, as in daily life, a report about facts by a trusted person, is well on the way to being believed. There is no absolute reason or compelling process of logic which dictates that any piece of testimony must be believed; it simply happens—but only if the essential feeling of trust exists.

## B Reasonableness of evidence

Trust alone, is not enough for belief. Even a trusted person might talk nonsense. To lead to belief, what a person says must be reasonable.

In daily life, if a trusted person reports something unlikely, faith in his sincerity and reliability may prevail so that it is accepted. If what he says is highly unlikely, his good faith may be accepted, but he might be thought to be mistaken. But an incredible statement about which he could not be mistaken would be rejected as a lie.

In daily life, statements, even from an unknown source, may be acceptable because they are reasonable, i e they conform to existing knowledge. Their truth and accuracy may be self-evident, e g, geometrical axioms, or highly probable statements, such as that there was no major earthquake in London this year.

But testimony in court refers to fortuitous facts which could be true or not, and about which the court knows nothing. Whether or not evidence is reasonable must be approached in a different way.

For evidence of a single witness to be reasonable, i e acceptable in itself irrespective of who gives it, it must not be self-contradictory or improbable. Either defect would obstruct belief in it. But the absence of inconsistency or improbability just removes barriers to belief. It does not necessarily make evidence true or accurate. It simply means that it could be true. For belief, something more is necessary.

## C   Weight of evidence

The phrase 'weight of the evidence' is used in various senses in courts and in legal literature, mostly with reference to the effect of a whole body of evidence, or perhaps all the evidence in the case. Here it is used narrowly, to denote the value or significance conferred on individual items of evidence by comparison with all the other evidence.

Belief in evidence, then, depends on trust in the witness, the reasonableness of his evidence, and the weight of his evidence in this sense. This means that his evidence seen in the light of all the other evidence becomes more persuasive than it would have been alone, as a result of comparing the testimony of one witness with another and discovering that in essentials they are identical, or of noting how the evidence under consideration fits into a complex network of other testimony and facts. The weight attaching to a particular piece of evidence is enhanced by the context. The factors of trust, reasonableness and weight, then, combine to produce belief in the particular testimony.

## IV   CONTRADICTION

The destructive function of the cross-examiner is to interfere with this process of forming belief by undermining trust in his opponent's witnesses, showing that their evidence is unreasonable, or attacking its weight in relation to other evidence.

Destructive cross-examination is based on the concept of contradiction, the dialectical principle at the heart of the adversarial process. Starting from the self-evident truth that a thing cannot both be and not be at the same time, the aim of one advocate is to deny what the other asserts, or to assert what the other denies—

where this is based on his information and relevant to the issues.

Applying this to the question of trust in a witness, a cross-examiner may attack character, expose motives for lying, question sincerity, highlight bias or partisanship, or try to create doubt about the witness's competence as an observer, or his memory.

The attack on the reasonableness of the evidence will focus on self-contradiction, improbability or lack of realism in the evidence of the witness under challenge.

The weight of that witness's evidence will also be brought into the contest by confronting him with facts which are inconsistent with his assertions, spoken to by witnesses on the same side, or contradictory facts derived from the cross-examiner's witnesses.

These lines of challenge usually proceed simultaneously, and one enhances another, e g, by exploring lies objectively on some point of improbability, the liar is revealed by his manner of answering.

The cross-examination of one witness after another should be orchestrated into a closing argument which is the ultimate contradiction of the opponent's case.

# V   WHEN TO CHALLENGE

The aims of destructive cross-examination should be clear and attainable. An advocate should have a realistic understanding of what he can hope to achieve. Otherwise, he may cross-examine where he should not do so, or he may go on too long with increasing damage to his case, when he should stop. The questions are whether to challenge a witness at all, and if so, on what parts of his evidence.

## A   Negative indications

The main reasons for not challenging evidence are either that it has caused only minor harm, or that cross-examination is not the best way to counter whatever harm it caused. Moreover, it may be better to sacrifice the possible gain from challenging harmful evidence for the benefit of obtaining favourable evidence.

### 1   Minor harm

Slightly unfavourable evidence may not merit challenge—trifling points, or those which are only remotely harmful, should be ignored. Minor discrepancies due to normal eyewitness fallibility rarely justify attack to show that evidence of the main facts is unreliable, mistaken or untruthful. But sometimes small points of evidence can be important. If the question is whether an incident occurred at all, e g, in the case of an alibi, slight differences in evidence could be sinister and might be probed by a prosecutor.

Facts which seem unimportant in themselves, may be highly significant when linked together as circumstantial evidence, and if so, adverse evidence about details may have to be attacked.

With regard to other matters of no great moment, to ignore something is to treat it as having no importance. Then, the court may well disregard or forget it. But to cross-examine on the topic, especially at length, may emphasize its significance. This could turn a minor point into a real obstacle.

## 2 Alternatives

There are ways in which an advocate can deal with unfavourable evidence sometimes, other than by challenging it.

Evidence which is unacceptable may be so weak in itself that it is not worth challenging. Even strong evidence may be contradicted successfully by still stronger evidence. But in deciding not to challenge evidence, since it is expected to be ineffective anyway, it is for the advocate to judge if he is taking any material risks.

A cross-examiner may let some evidence pass if he has successfully challenged similar evidence when it was given by an earlier witness. On the other hand, he might defer a challenge for a weaker witness who is expected to give similar evidence.

Some evidence may be so strong that there is no hope of weakening or overcoming it by cross-examination. Also, apart from the strength of the evidence per se, its reiteration by a resistant witness might intensify the damage. The only prospect of meeting that evidence may lie in leading contradictory evidence, or in argument.

Nothing said in this section about alternatives to challenge by cross-examination is intended to mean that a party should not put his case to an opponent's witness so far as he knows the facts.

## 3 Favourable evidence

Even reluctant concessions, or favourable evidence obtained from an opponent's witness, are usually convincing. They should be sought before he is challenged in any way, when the witness is likely to be more co-operative and more likely to seem trustworthy.

If no helpful admissions are obtained, the advocate would then proceed to challenge the witness on other matters.

But if the cross-examiner elicits any helpful evidence, he should weigh the possible reduction of that benefit against the possible gain from going on to challenge other evidence. Sometimes, to abandon the challenge is worthwhile.

The benefit of favourable testimony may be impaired if it is followed by any challenge other than a suggestion of honest error.

## B Positive indications

### 1 Putting the case

For reasons which are partly legal and partly tactical, a cross-examiner should put any material part of his case to witnesses who know about those facts and should challenge any adverse evidence to show that he does not accept it, to avoid possible difficulties in trying to do so later.

Often, a challenge need only be formal. At one extreme (as an exception to the rule of keeping questions to one point at a time) the advocate may ask a single comprehensive question, which can only be answered by 'Yes' or 'No', or their equivalents, e g. 'It is the case that your story about what happened in the lane is an invention?'. This may satisfy the obligation to put one's case and, at times, may be the best tactic.

### 2 Harmful evidence

Any evidence which is both harmful and material should be challenged. Whatever the strength of his case, an advocate should not refrain from cross-examination because of complacency. Even a good case may be vulnerable in some way.

Sometimes harmful evidence may be made worse by persistent cross-examination which only causes it to be repeated, and reinforced with emphasis and elaboration. If so, a single global question of the kind indicated in the previous section may be better.

But at other times, to put detailed and specific questions, point-by-point, may be the best tactic where progress is being made. Here, the repetition and its suggestive effect, may work for the cross-examiner and not against him.

The category of adverse evidence which should not be allowed to pass unchallenged would include eyewitness evidence of the crime if it is disputed, evidence of visual identification of the defendant as the offender, if that is in issue, alibi evidence, evidence of confessions and admissions which implicate the accused, and any other material evidence.

### 3 Vulnerable witness

Harmless evidence may be given by a witness who is in a position to know about matters on which other witnesses gave or may give damaging evidence but who is himself weak.

A cross-examiner might exploit this opportunity for attacking the other adverse evidence retrospectively or in anticipation, by questioning this witness about the same facts.

# VI   WHEN TO STOP

In regard to particular topics or witnesses, it is as important to know when to stop destructive cross-examination as when to undertake it. To some extent, this can be planned, but unforeseen reasons for stopping may emerge.

A planned point for stopping would, of course, be when a specific aim is attained. The value of ending with an explicit victory on some topic has been pointed out above. When some desired concession is obtained, the cross-examination on that topic should stop at once. The gain can be emphasized in the closing speech.

But encouraged by his success, a cross-examiner may be tempted to drive home what he has achieved, by further questions to make it even clearer or stronger. He may regret doing so. A witness, given a second chance, may withdraw or modify his answer, thus nullifying the gain.

For each witness, a cross-examiner should constantly bear in mind the question of whether he has sufficient material for his closing speech, where he can make the most of evidence which he has elicited. When he has sufficient, he should not try to score additional points lest he lose what he has. He should stop to prevent retraction or qualification of the testimony by the witnesss, or alerting his opponent to the need for meeting the point by re-examination, leading further evidence or argument. This is a crucial test of the judgment and skill of the advocate.

Exceptionally, a cross-examiner might go on after getting a favourable admission, where the witness is trapped and cannot escape, so that his situation can be exploited from various angles, but not if he could conceivably invent some way out.

A variation is where the aim is attained insofar as answers have reached the stage where a final question would make the gain explicit. Instead of asking it, the cross-examiner leaves the point for the jury to infer, perhaps with more impact. Then it becomes less likely that either the witness or the opponent will try to meet the point.

Some objectives are unrealistic. Where this becomes clear, the cross-examination should not be prolonged unduly in the vain hope of achieving them. It is not the witness, but rather the evidence which should be treated as the target for destruction.

Generally a cross-examiner should stop when he is satisfied that he has contributed significantly to the rejection of the evidence—and not go on unproductively. Cross-examination which seemed necessary at first may turn out to be pointless, or even harmful. To go on may intensify the damage by repetition, emphasis and adding supporting detail. If so, the cross-examination should be ended at once—perhaps by a global question which can only be accepted or denied. Prosecutors often do this.

Occasionally, in suitable circumstances, it may be worth going on although the answers themselves are not those which are desired, e g, for the cumulative and suggestive value of repeatedly getting unreasonable denials of reasonable points, or to commit the witness firmly to statements which can be disproved later, so that he will be discredited.

But generally, where, for any reason, a witness is completely resistant to any modification of his evidence, the cross-examination should not go on beyond the point where it stops being productive, and becomes harmful.

A cross-examination which is cut short, may be replaced, e g, by cross-examining a weaker witness, calling a contradictory witness or by argument.

Where a cross-examiner makes no progress at all, it should not be totally beyond his contemplation that the testimony may be truthful and accurate, and that he should not expect to overcome it.

# VII CHALLENGING THE WITNESS

## A  The context

A complete attack on testimony not only shows why the account of facts cannot be accepted, i e challenging the evidence, but also exposes the mistaken or lying mental processes which explain the inaccuracy, i e challenging the witness.

These go together. Inaccuracy must be due to a mistake or a lie and a mistake or a lie must create inaccuracy.

Obviously, a cross-examiner who can do so, should employ both forms of challenge. He must certainly challenge evidence which he does not accept. To show whether inaccuracy arose from mistake or lying may not be essential, but it can reinforce the attack on the evidence.

As was seen, trust in the witness is the foundation of belief in evidence. To undermine that trust materially, may lead to rejection of evidence which seems quite reasonable. But criticism of a witness per se, unrelated to anything in his evidence, would be an irrelevant personal attack and would be disallowed.

One or other approach tends to dominate at times, but most cross-examination is objective, i e it consists of challenging the evidence. This is the context in which the witness is also challenged. Challenging the witness is usually integrated with challenging his evidence so that personal criticisms are related to specific parts of his testimony. In the course of his main enquiry into the issues, a cross-examiner is likely to suggest that the witness's account of important disputed facts is mistaken or untruthful, and to enquire into circumstances which support such allegations, e g, by showing that it was too dark to recognize the accused, or that the witness previously made an inconsistent statement.

Flaws in a witness may also emerge incidentally in his way of answering objective questions on the issues, e g, the liar is revealed by enquiring into the lie rather than into the person.

## B   Assessment of witness

During the evidence-in-chief, an advocate should assess a witness's mental state in relation to the parts of his testimony which are to be challenged as inaccurate. For this, no better guidance is available than his common sense, experience of life, and intuition. It is usually too difficult to discover much about the witness as a person; the more limited aim is to see where he stands in relation to his evidence, e g, if he is lying or mistaken. He will be cross-examined on the basis of this assessment, unless it has to be modified.

In relation to a given item of disputed evidence, a witness may be truthful and accurate, truthful but mistaken, or untruthful. If he is biased and inaccurate, his testimony may fall anywhere between a mistake and a lie. It is difficult to be more specific without introducing unnecessary psychological complications. It is emphasized that this is not a classification of witnesses into types for which there is neither a theoretical basis nor any need in practice. It merely groups forms of accuracy or inaccuracy in regard to a particular piece of evidence. Even in the same trial, the relationship of a witness to his evidence may vary, e g, from being truthful to being untruthful.

Evidence should not be assessed on the basis of general views about the accuracy of types of witnesses. There are no rules about the credibility or reliability of classes of witnesses either in psychology or in law. A court's view of the accuracy of the evidence of any witness should be formed by what occurs in the courtroom. With that safeguard, it is harmless to say that independent witnesses are often truthful since they have no motives for lying, but could be mistaken. Witnesses involved in the situation in some way may have motives for lying, and may be suspected of this. On the other hand, they may be mistaken or truthful despite their involvement. Both independent and involved witnesses may also testify inaccurately as a result of bias. Initially, the general treatment of a witness will correspond to his assessment. It may change later if the assessment has to be corrected, or as a result of the progress of the cross-examination.

## C   Mistaken witness

The aim in cross-examining a witness who is treated as truthful but mistaken, is, ideally, that he should concede his mistake and accept the facts put to him by the cross-examiner. This is not common. The next best objective is that the witness should concede some doubt which the cross-examiner can exploit, e g, in visual identification of the defendant by a Crown witness. If no such concession can be obtained, the final alternative is for the cross-examination to sow doubt anyway, so that the evidence under challenge will be defeated by contradictory evidence.

If all truthful witnesses were as honest and impartial as their oaths oblige them to be, cross-examining them would become less of a contest and more of an exercise in persuading witnesses, as well as the court, about the real state of facts. But this is hardly the general picture. The basic intention of many witnesses to tell the truth need not necessarily exclude various forms of resistance. To achieve his aims, the cross-examiner must try to overcome these.

If a cross-examiner has decided to treat a witness as honest but mistaken, he should establish a friendly rapport with him from the start and maintain it throughout. He does this to secure the witness's co-operation and to uphold his credit as the basis for any concessions which he may obtain. The tactics should be friendly. The advocate should make it obvious that he regards the witness as sincere and trusts him. He can do this at once by his tone of voice, manner and initial questions.

It reassures a witness, to show that part of his testimony is accepted even if another part is not: 'Mr Wilson, when you noted the registration number, was it not getting dark?'

Many people fear courts, and especially cross-examination. They are afraid that they will be made to look foolish, or accused of being unable to observe competently or of having a poor memory—or worse, of lying. Short of telling the witness that he will not do this, the cross-examiner should convey that impression. By suitable leading questions he should show sympathy with the difficulties that may have led to incomplete or mistaken evidence, and allow the witness to save face. Probing the accuracy of observation might be introduced by a question showing understanding: 'Mrs Davis, you were busy in the kitchen, and you had no special reason to watch these men through the window, had you?'

If the fading of the witness's memory is involved, the line could be commenced like this: 'Mrs Davis, it was well over a year ago, wasn't it?' Everyone in the courtroom knows this, but Mrs Davis, like most witnesses, may be glad of any chance of saying that the incident happened a long time ago, to explain her forgetfulness, or as an excuse for her uncertainty.

Appreciation of the witness's human responses, strengthens the bond: 'Was it quite an ordeal for you to see that?'

Words of encouragement to help a witness over a hurdle should precede key questions of this kind: 'Could the man not just have resembled the defendant?' Here the witness may be anxious about departing from the firm evidence of recognition, and needs to be reassured.

In cross-examining an impartial witness to show that evidence is mistaken, the tactics are mostly direct and open. Usually, there is no need to conceal the aim of a line of enquiry, to mislead or surprise the witness, or to lead him into a trap, as there might be with an untruthful witness. The aim is often quite obvious, even from the first question: 'How far away were you from the fight?' This is clearly the basis of a challenge to the accuracy of observation.

But open tactics do not include pointless repetition of the evidence-in-chief, culminating, without any preparation or foundation, in this: 'I suggest that you are mistaken. Is that not so?'

This inept process simply wastes time and leads to denial, without any persuasive effect. It only shows that the advocate does not accuse the witness of lying. Such weak advocacy is not uncommon. A challenge to a witness, that he is mistaken, must have some substance beyond the cross-examiner's mere assertion.

Having considered the cross-examiner's approach and tactics in relation to honest but mistaken witnesses, attention may now be given to how such a challenge may be built up by showing how the mistakes could have arisen. This is usually done quite openly. Since one of the cross-examiner's aims is to persuade the witness to concede that he is mistaken, and to accept the contrary version of the facts, he should seek the witness's co-operation all the way.

Indirect tactics are unusual with an impartial and sincere, but mistaken, witness. The court may be puzzled if a challenge is approached by a devious route, and may think that it is unnecessary to treat an honest witness in this way. Moreover, the witness may resent such treatment, and become less co-operative.

Probably most challenges to evidence as mistaken, concern visual identification of the accused by prosecution witnesses, intangible elements in result-crimes, or conduct-crimes.

The various sources of interference with the accuracy of observation and memory were fully set out in chapter 3. In preparing for the trial, advocates should be alert for the presence of such factors which may provide a basis for cross-examination. In applying that material, it is helpful to keep certain general principles in mind.

As has been seen, if a court trusts a witness, his self-assessment can overcome objections to the accuracy of his evidence. He was there, and the court was not. If the witness is confident about what he saw and remembered, and both his sincerity and judgment are trusted, then all the barriers to the accuracy of observation and memory suggested in cross-examination, may be defeated. The importance of this is that in the course of cross-examining, an advocate should not focus exclusively on the obstacles which the witness faced; he should also note carefully how he is responding to the challenge, and may adjust his questions in order to undermine his apparent sincerity and judgment if there is ground for this, e g, by showing bias, or inappropriate dogmatism. But if he does this, he may lose the witness's co-operation. Which line to take is a matter for judgment in the circumstances.

If the challenge to the witness is thus extended, it may not be possible to obtain desirable concessions from him, and the attack on the accuracy of his evidence will have to succeed without his co-operation.

Another difficulty which a cross-examiner faces is that he can rarely show that any particular source of error leads inevitably to the conclusion that evidence must be inaccurate. Indeed, many of them are just difficulties not insuperable obstacles, e g, the amount drunk by the witness, poor lighting or lapse of time which may have caused some fading of memory. Certainly, they matter in their time and place, but it is difficult to show this in court long afterwards, from the mouth of someone who asserts that they gave him no trouble.

A cross-examiner should therefore assemble a number of these difficulties, if he can, arising from the nature of the event, the conditions of observation, the state of the witness, delay, discussion of evidence and so on.

It is also very difficult to probe into the private psychological processes of a reluctant witness, whatever their role. This refers to such matters as what he was giving his attention to, whether his expectations influenced his perceptions, the effects of discussion, his self-induced errors, and the degree of confidence which he feels in his evidence, e g, of visual identification.

To meet these difficulties, the cross-examiner should, where possible, elicit from the witness under cross-examination, and from others, evidence of any objective facts from which these private psychological processes may be inferred.

To illustrate this, if the witness was being menaced with a knife in a bank, his attention would not be on the registration plate of the robbers' motor car outside. If a store detective stopped a customer almost immediately when she took a scarf from the counter, his expectations might seem to have jumped ahead of his observations. If discussion of evidence is suggested as a source of distortion of evidence, it would help to know the details of time, place, persons present and subject.

In the context of the difficulties faced in this type of cross-examination, an advocate should concentrate on the really material points on which he wishes to show that the witness is mistaken. He may not succeed with the minor points, and if he did it might not matter.

While this section is concerned with challenging the witness rather than the evidence, it is relevant to note that a cross-examiner may be able to establish that a witness is mistaken because of probative defects in his evidence, i e self-contradiction, inconsistency with other witnesses on the same side, or manifest improbability.

An advocate cross-examines on the basis of his information about the accuracy of evidence. This is a working assumption, not a judgment which only the court can reach. On that basis, he may think that an honest witness is resisting correction unreasonably because of bias. This may not be so. An impartial witness may feel that he is telling the truth as he sees it, is confident that his testimony is accurate, and is simply being firm. It is difficult to distinguish firmness from mild bias and unnecessary to do so.

Where bias is strong, however, a witness may or may not have some awareness of his partiality as a reason for resisting modification of his testimony. Although he still believes that he is telling the truth, he may be prepared to bend his evidence somewhat to support his view of the facts, e g, by exaggeration or by becoming argumentative.

Bias may be shown by the witness's language e g, words or phrases like 'out of the question', 'absolutely', 'impossible', 'positive', 'never at any time' in contexts where milder or more qualified terms would correspond to the situation more appropriately. This suggests subjective involvement and a lack of objectivity in the evidence.

Witnesses may become biased for a variety of reasons, only some of which may be detectable. Over many months, what a witness recalls and what he imagines, may have fused into a rigid but wrong view of the event, which he believes to be genuine. If mistakes arose between the incident and the trial, from any cause, e g, the suggestive effect of a discussion with other witnesses, they would tend to become frozen in the witness's memory, and to persist into the trial.

A witness may feel committed to a view by what he said before the trial, e g, to the police, or in statements which were taken from him. Witnesses generally do not wish to seem irresponsible or inconsistent by changing their minds at the last minute.

Sources of bias may be tendencies to see things in black and white, or to take sides uncritically, or for witnesses to side with the party who called them, with some degree of partisanship.

Fixed attitudes or prejudices, or seeing people as stereotypes, and the indirect effects of the media generally, may also influence witnesses. Lay witnesses for the Crown may be hostile to types of criminals, e g, drunken motorists or sexual offenders. Defence witnesses may have preconceptions about police brutality. Any witnesses may be prejudiced against teenagers or wealthy people, and so on. Such causes of bias and their effect on testimony are difficult to expose.

A cross-examiner must know of such possible causes for unreasonable resistance to his contention that evidence is mistaken. Bias itself, can sometimes cause inaccuracy, e g, by creating expectancy about something seen in darkness. But mostly, inaccuracy is caused by something else, e g, poor conditions of observation, and the effect of bias is to make the witness unwilling to admit that the evidence is or may be mistaken.

The general tenor of the earlier discussion of suitable tactics for honest but mistaken witnesses, viz that they should be friendly, direct and open, must now be qualified for witnesses whose evidence is biased to a material extent.

Mild bias is fairly common but may be ignored where it is not expected to affect the essentials of the evidence materially. Here, a cross-examiner may employ friendly, direct and open tactics, as he would with completely impartial witnesses.

But strong bias may affect evidence. At its most extreme, the state of mind of witnesses may be as close to lying as to mistake. While they think that, on the whole, they are being truthful, they may be partly aware of their resistance.

Where bias and resistance are material, the cross-examiner may treat the witness in a firm or even hostile way, keeping strict control by narrow leading questions, and using indirect tactics to manipulate the witness into making concessions.

It is best to start the cross-examination of such witnesses in a friendly and open manner and to continue in this vein until the need for more forceful tactics becomes clear to the advocate and to the court, from the unsatisfactory answers.

Some sources of mild bias might be detected, and possibly removed, in the context of a friendly form of cross-examination, e g, a witness's fear of departing from what he told the police or solicitors who took statements from him, by reassuring him that if honest doubts have emerged, they should, and can, be stated without repercussions. But sources of strong bias cannot be eliminated like this.

Where facts can be drawn out to support an inference that the witness is biased, e g, some link with the defendant, whether or not previously revealed, these facts may be explored objectively, but at the right time. If such enquiry is made at the outset, it might put the witness on his guard, and make him defensive and unco-operative. It would seem to be undesirable to do this until it becomes clear that there is no hope of obtaining any concessions from a strongly biased and mistaken witness, and that it would be best to discredit him. It should then be done as soon as possible, since this may colour the rest of his testimony unfavourably. The attack may be weaker if it is left until the end of his evidence.

One way to discredit a biased witness is to lead him into showing his bias fully by relaxing control of his evidence and encouraging him to elaborate freely. The aim is that he will reveal his bias more and more until his evidence is suspect and he discredits himself. But if, instead, this leads to harmful statements which are persuasive because they are spontaneous, it may be curtailed.

Again, a seriously biased witness may be drawn into displaying this by provocative or sarcastic leading questions.

Where a really partisan witness will say almost anything to support his side, a tactic already described may work. If the advocate wants an answer, A, but the form of question suggests that he seeks an alternative answer, B, the witness may fall into the trap by giving the wanted answer, A.

Challenging a witness as mistaken can have a variety of results. The overall intention, if the circumstances justify it, is to weaken or destroy trust in the witness's judgment (rather than his sincerity) and not only to attack part of his evidence. Otherwise the witness's self-assessment and confidence in his evidence, may gain the day. Despite all the criticisms of the accuracy of an item of evidence, if a trusted witness assures the court that the facts were so, this might still be accepted.

So far as the evidence itself is concerned, the best result would be if the witness conceded that he was completely mistaken and accepted the cross-examiner's version of the facts. This would be exceptional. The opponent is unlikely to call such witnesses. If it did occur, it should have a highly persuasive effect on the court, although other evidence would have to be considered also.

The next best result would be that the witness concedes some doubt about his evidence, which the cross-examination created or intensified. This is a realistic objective in cross-examining an impartial witness. As was seen, challenging a witness as mistaken is aimed at persuading him, if he is impartial, as well as the court, of the mistake. This is unlikely to succeed with a biased witness.

Such a concession of doubt, if attained, will be valuable. But if the witness will not go so far, the cross-examiner should strive, at least, to have him admit that another view is possible. Even to agree that an alternative is within the realms of possibility is a weakness in the opponent's evidence. But if the witness's rejection of even such a possibility is unreasonable and dogmatic, he may, thereby, contribute to the cross-examiner's desired conclusion after all.

Concessions by the witness are helpful, but a challenge may succeed without them, if it satisfies the court that the evidence is mistaken or, at least, unreliable. If essential Crown evidence is held to be unreliable, that is all that the defence need to show. Even if cross-examination alone does not establish that the evidence is mistaken or unreliable, it may be so weakened, that it will be overcome by other contradictory evidence on comparison.

Generally, the more reasonable and moderate a cross-examiner's contentions are, the more impressive they will be. In particular, when attacking bias in evidence, it does not help to show it oneself by overstating the argument.

To show that evidence is mistaken does not per se establish the truth unless this follows as an inevitable logical conclusion, e g, if a barman wrongly states that the accused was in the bar at a particular time. However, where it is shown that evidence is biased, a court might infer what the evidence could have been if it were fair.

## D   Lying witness

This section deals with cross-examination in relation to the personal aspects of false testimony, i e lying witnesses, their characters and motives. A wider view is taken than in cross-examination as to credit, which aims to show that the witness should not be believed on his oath and focuses on his character on the assumption that the witness is a bad person, with a disposition to lie.

This is derived from former views that people are either truthful or untruthful persons. It has some merit of course, but it is too unrealistic and too simple for court purposes. Innumerable witnesses, of apparently good character, lie in criminal courts, because they are motivated to do so in the particular situation. It is thought that a person's motives in a particular situation lead to false testimony much more often than a general disposition to lie.

Cross-examination of a lying witness will therefore be based both on such discrediting evidence as to his character, as may be elicited, and on exploring his motives in the situation. It must be accepted that this approach to lying evidence has both legal and tactical limitations.

Only some attacks on character are allowed by law. If he testifies, the witness whose character probably matters most, the defendant, can only be cross-examined about bad character in circumstances defined by statute. The defence may refrain from making imputations against Crown witnesses in case the defendant loses that protection.

Where character is attacked, it cannot be blackened without restriction. Some criticisms, even if true, would not be allowed. The cross-examination must be relevant to the witness's standing with the court, and not be merely vexatious.

The general rule is that answers concerning credit and other collateral matters are final. This prevents a cross-examiner from calling contradictory evidence, except where a witness denies previous convictions or previous inconsistent statements, or to show that he is biased. Questions might arise of the admissibility of some contradictory evidence concerned with the witness's motives as being collateral matters or as being too remote.

Other limitations on challenging the character or motives of witnesses are tactical. Trust or distrust in witnesses as the sources of evidence is crucial for belief or disbelief. Cross-examination confined to character or motives rarely establishes per se that a witness is lying, although, without being decisive, it might create doubt or distrust.

The effects of distrusting a witness may vary. Distrust of a Crown witness who testifies to some essential element in the case, e g, a police officer's visual identification of the accused, could be fatal to the prosecution.

But mostly, doubt or distrust of the truthfulness of a witness is only conclusive when the evidence given is also shown to be defective, in the context of all the evidence in the trial.

Leaving aside the dubious polygraph, if psychology had discovered any reliable method of diagnosing lying, by purely mental means, the legal profession would have seized on it long ago. Psychology has not done so. In the courtroom, lying cannot be confidently diagnosed either, by considering the character and motives of a single witness. The superiority of the criminal trial, over a psychological interview, is its massive approach to questions of credibility which requires study of all the evidence from all the witnesses, and from all points of view after thorough testing, which makes a sound and integrated holistic judgment possible.

A witness's personal qualities and relationship to the situation, are usually clearer from his answers about the issues, than about himself. But personal questions are usually asked first, to colour the rest of the evidence. The aim is to insinuate these personal doubts into the context of an objective attack on the accuracy of evidence, so that the flaws are attributable to dubious motives.

A cross-examiner who intends to show that a witness is, or may be, lying, should not attempt too much by way of a personal attack beyond drawing out the main facts about his character and circumstances, from which the court may infer his lack of scruples, and motives for lying, despite the witness's denials.

The cross-examiner should create a background of scepticism or distrust of the witness's evidence on the issues which he will attack. In practice, after the main personal facts are elicited, suggestions to the witness that he is lying may be interwoven with questions on the issues.

The evidence-in-chief should have given a cross-examiner a view of the witness's personality, character, motives and demeanour and should have enabled him to decide whether to challenge harmful evidence as mistaken or untruthful.

This decision should be unambiguous. Witnesses who know the facts and testify wrongly, do so intentionally and can only be lying. But for reasons discussed elsewhere, cross-examiners sometimes suggest that lying witnesses are only mistaken, not untruthful. A cross-examiner should not accuse a witness of lying, irresponsibly, or without reasonable grounds. But if he can only be lying, a cross-examiner should make the nature of his challenge explicit, even if he chooses to do so diplomatically. It misleads the court to suggest that a lying witness is mistaken, where that is not how he is related to his evidence.

A cross-examiner who does this invites the court to see the witness as honest and his inaccuracies as unintentional and attributable to a range of possible sources of error in observation or memory—excluding motivation. But a lying witness makes inaccurate statements intentionally, because he is motivated, so that the court would have different factors to consider. Cross-examination in which an advocate does not show his position clearly by distinguishing mistake from lying, is invariably weak or ineffective.

On the other hand, a cross-examiner achieves nothing by merely indicating his approach to evidence per se: there is little point in saying to a witness, 'I suggest that you are lying about this', or something similar, without laying some foundation and leading up to it. Few perjurers confess when confronted with such a charge.

A cross-examiner's tactics in challenging a witness as lying, partly depend on whether he is called by the prosecution or defence, and is independent or has personal motives; the subject of lying, viz the commission of the crime or the accused's implication; and the form of deception, viz affirmative or negative statements, reluctance and evasiveness, omissions, or false qualifications. These topics are discussed fully in chapter 4 and elsewhere, but some important points are particularly relevant to character and motives.

Prosecution witnesses who are most often challenged as untruthful are accomplices, occasionally victims of some crimes, and police.

There are usually grounds for attacking both the character and motives of accomplices.

Where an attack on the veracity of a victim is relevant and material, grounds for attacking his character depend on the individual's history, and for attacking motives, on his circumstances and those of the crime. Most victims of most crimes have no reason to lie.

Where police witnesses are challenged as untruthful, there are normally no grounds in their past history for attacks on character. Moreover, the defence usually have difficulty in showing motives for lying where there are no obvious reasons for doing so, and especially in view of the disastrous consequences of discovery for the witness. But a motive which is often suggested is that the police witnesses are lying to justify the malicious and wrongful arrest of the accused for the crime charged.

Cross-examination as to the character or motives of the police witnesses is unlikely to help the defence here. Their challenge may only make progress if serious inconsistencies emerge in the evidence of two or more police witnesses about the issues, or as a result of other significant evidence.

The accused, if he gives evidence, is the defence witness who is invariably attacked as lying. Attacks on his character are prohibited by law, except in special circumstances, which are infrequent. Whether he is innocent or guilty, he is probably the most motivated witness in any trial, and this needs no elaboration.

Other defence witnesses, deemed to know the facts because of their association with the accused, e g, if they speak to his alibi, are also commonly charged with lying. If they have criminal records, as is not uncommon, these will usually be brought out in cross-examination. Association with such witnesses is not favourable to the accused. Their motives stem from their connection with him.

It is most unlikely that obviously independent witnesses for either the prosecution or the defence, will be challenged as untruthful, or that their characters or motives will be criticized.

An exception, where an independent witness might be challenged as untruthful could be where he is not directly concerned about the situation or the outcome of the trial, but has some personal motive for falsifying his evidence, e g, to avoid the embarrassment of admitting that at a certain time he was at a certain place, when he was supposed to be elsewhere.

With regard to the subjects of alleged lying, viz the commission of the crime or the visual identification of the accused, eyewitnesses who were involved in the incident in some way and their associates who were present are the main category of those likely to be challenged as untruthful. This would exclude independent witnesses.

Typically, mutual accusations of lying are made by a prosecutor against an accused who testifies, and his friends who were at the locus, and by the defence against police witnesses who were also there, and perhaps took some part in the incident.

Circumstantial evidence, typically, consists of isolated items which only become significant when they are put together as a basis for an inference.

Police witnesses are sometimes accused by the defence, not only of lying about such matters, but of having gone further, e g, by 'planting' incriminating real evidence where it can be attributed to the possession of the accused. A defence challenge of the more extreme kind would go beyond an allegation of perjury into one of a criminal conspiracy to convict an innocent person.

A similar situation is the common attack on police evidence of confessions and admissions, as untruthful.

In such challenges, the question of establishing motives for such criminal conduct by police officers would be a major one for the defence.

Witnesses other than the accused (except in special circumstances) may be cross-examined as to bad character and previous convictions. A conviction which is denied may be proved against the witness. The attack should be relevant and fair. Restrictions imposed by law should be known. Some convictions should be ignored.

Merely to show that a witness has previously been convicted does not prove that he is now lying, but might reduce the trust in him, which is essential to belief in his evidence.

The weakest method is to put the convictions to the witness directly for him to admit or deny, with no opening to lie, if he is so minded. The best way illustrates how indirect tactics can lead a witness into a trap formed by lying, viz about his previous convictions, in which he can then be exposed immediately by direct tactics.

A casual and seemingly unimportant question as to whether the witness had ever been in trouble, suggesting ignorance of the position, might encourage an untruthful witness to deny any previous convictions, whereby he becomes vulnerable to exposure and to being discredited. He should be made to commit himself firmly to his denial, after which only one previous conviction should be put to him. His lie can then be exploited, e g, by questions about why he denied the conviction, how he had forgotten one for which he was imprisoned and so on.

The process could be repeated for one conviction after another until the witness becomes ready to admit them all. By giving him the impression that they were all known, he might disclose some which were not.

By such tactics, a witness can be shown not only to be of poor character, but also to be ready to lie in his evidence, the effect of which may be to discredit him totally.

The motives of many witnesses are often quite clear, independently of cross-examination, because of their connections with the issues or parties. The prosecutor should have brought out any such significant facts about his witnesses, of which he knew. If he suspects that there are undisclosed interests in defence witnesses, he would probe these areas to bring them to light. If any material facts emerge from which a motive on the part of the witness may be inferred, failure to disclose it in the evidence-in-chief, will not impress the court.

In any event, in cross-examining any witness, facts suggesting motives which could affect their evidence, may be highlighted and emphasized. So far as relevancy allows, relationships could be put in story or visual form, to make them more striking.

A cross-examiner, knowing of a witness's undisclosed connection with the case, might, by indirect tactics, lead one who lies into denying such facts, with which he then confronts him by direct tactics.

As was seen, it does not follow from the existence of a motive in a certain direction, that evidence to that effect must be untrue. However, it may raise a question. The demonstration of motives may not discredit a witness, but it may weaken his evidence.

Without focusing specifically on the relationship to the case which may motivate a witness to lie, this could be left to the inference of the court, supported by argument in the closing speech.

Having discussed the character and motives of lying witnesses, it is not intended here to refer to questions of the witness's personality otherwise, or to his demeanour in giving evidence, which were discussed in chapter 4. They are hardly suitable as subjects for cross-examination.

It is, however, useful to consider the matter of the tactics to be employed for various forms of deception.

Lying in its most stark form, i e making affirmative statements of what is not true, or denials of what is true, is perjury. Here, the original motive to commit perjury, which must have been strong in itself, is reinforced by fear of the penalties which may follow from exposure. Such a witness will be most resistant to cross-examination. Nevertheless, the cross-examiner should try to bring his motives to light, if they are not already apparent. Retractions, concessions or confessions, should not be expected from this type of witness.

In suitable instances, it may help to allow such a witness to give his evidence freely so that he might display tension, dogmatism and one-sidedness. But exposure of his falsehoods will generally depend on forceful cross-examination on the issues, especially if he has thought out and planned a consistent story.

Reluctant or evasive witnesses demonstrate these dubious qualities by their way of answering questions. They may answer with hesitation, or repeat questions to give themselves time to think. They may avoid the obvious point, or answer points not asked.

Their evasiveness would be a poor prelude to convincing perjury; it is too obvious to the court. Such witnesses are not prepared to commit perjury although they are unwilling to tell the truth, or all of it.

Suitable tactics could include emphasizing their evasiveness. This could be done by asking the witness to listen very carefully, asking questions very slowly and deliberately, repeating them for effect, or having the court reporter read questions back. Such measures should prevent a witness from claiming that he did not hear or understand a question, and should make his evasiveness even more obvious. More forcefully, a cross-examiner could insist on direct answers to important questions, or refer to previous inconsistent statements. Warnings from advocates and from the bench may also help.

If desired evidence cannot be obtained from reluctant and evasive witnesses, they could simply be discredited. The obvious effect of their unsatisfactory performance may be intensified in the closing speech.

Omission of material evidence is another compromise in a witness who is motivated not to reveal all the truth, yet unwilling to incur the risks of lying. This, of course, refers to intentional omissions, not merely to incomplete evidence as a result of limited observation or forgetting—or incomplete questioning.

The remedy is to frame questions which force the witness to

disclose the whole truth as an alternative to committing perjury, which he is unwilling to do. A narrow leading question may allow a witness to escape, e g, 'Did you see her put the watch in her bag?' to which a truthful answer, 'No', might be given. But a wider and more general leading question, e g, 'Did she touch the watch in any way?' would oblige the witness to say what she did see, or risk prosecution for perjury.

Such witnesses may, of course, take refuge in pretended amnesia. This is very difficult to overcome in cross-examination because there is no material to challenge, and no way of knowing or demonstrating that the claim is false.

Again, if the evidence sought is withheld, the witness should be discredited, so that the court may draw an inference favourable to the cross-examiner about the evidence which is concealed.

To do this, note should be taken of the points which the witness claims to have forgotten, which considered together may form a pattern. Also his unhesitant performance in evidence-in-chief, with little amnesia, may be compared with his halting testimony under cross-examination, where the condition came on.

The witness could be cross-examined on these matters, and they, and his responses to them could be helpful material for a forceful closing speech, in which he might be discredited.

False qualifications in evidence, by intentionally colouring it one way or another, or by overstating or understating the degree of confidence in it, are subtle forms of deception which are difficult to detect and to overcome. The same facts may be stated in many different ways even in honest evidence, and witnesses must be allowed to testify in their own natural language.

Where such evidence is considered to be false, it may itself be coloured by eliciting background facts. The character and motives of the witness may be brought out. The witness may have made a previous inconsistent statement which puts his current testimony in an adverse light, e g, if he previously had no doubt whatever about the identity of the offender, which he claims to be very uncertain about in the trial.

Close attention should also be paid to the exact language of the witness, and its nuances, which he might be asked to explain, e g, 'as far as I recall'.

With lying witnesses certain miscellaneous tactics are sometimes helpful. Liars cannot foresee all the possible questions which may be asked. When something quite unexpected is put to them, they may become anxious, hesitant or confused, and uncertain about which direction to take. Therefore a cross-examiner may often achieve some helpful result, without incurring any risk, if he asks a few questions which must be totally unexpected by the witness.

They may indeed have little point, except the cross-examiner's intention of disturbing a lying witness, and of producing some useful reaction of a general kind which might increase distrust in him. Sometimes to ask two or more witnesses such questions, may lead to glaring inconsistencies which could damage their credit. It is really a question of manufacturing tests of veracity.

Examples would be questions about where the witness went for lunch, with whom, what they talked about, what he did on the previous evening, whom he met, when he first told his story, when he was interviewed by the police, whether he has discussed his evidence, and if so where, when and with whom, or whether he knows a particular place or a particular person. Such questions would be designed to suit the particular circumstances of the trial. Some might be calculated to worry a witness, although there is little or nothing behind them in reality. However, the witness does not know that. To avoid objection, such questions should not be too numerous or asked too often, and they should seem to be reasonable.

Challenges to the credit of lying witnesses are usually insufficient in themselves to do more than weaken their evidence. Even an untrustworthy witness could be speaking the truth on a given occasion. It would not seem reasonable to contend in a speech that this could not be so. But where the distrust sown in the witness is combined with showing that the evidence itself is defective, the basis for disbelief in that evidence is much stronger.

In the course of cross-examining the witness about the issues, his personal qualities which may have been explored earlier would recur spontaneously. That a witness is lying might be revealed most clearly when he is trying to substantiate his version of the facts.

Just as exposing flaws of character, lack of scruples and motives for lying are usually not enough in themselves to destroy evidence, without objective enquiry into the evidence itself, so too even that does not complete the process of destroying evidence. It is completed in most cases by leading contradictory evidence which, together with the closing speech, overcomes the evidence under challenge. A cross-examiner should therefore be content if he can make a significant contribution to that process and not expect instant victory.

# VIII  CHALLENGING THE EVIDENCE

Whether destructive cross-examination is conducted by the prosecution or the defence, the essential purpose is to challenge evidence about the central issue of fact in a trial, viz whether the crime was committed, or whether the accused was the offender: criticisms of witnesses as mistaken or untruthful, and other issues, are incidental.

## A   Nature of process

As was seen, for belief in evidence, the witness must be trusted: how trust may be undermined was considered. This section is concerned with attacking the basis for the other two requirements of belief, viz that the evidence must be reasonable, and that the evidence must have weight.

To show that evidence is unreasonable, the challenge should expose inconsistency, improbability or lack of realism. Specific areas of evidence where any of these defects are shown sufficiently, would be rejected. Sometimes other areas of evidence or even the whole case would be rejected as a result.

The aim of the other attack on evidence is to reduce its 'weight' which was defined as 'the value or significance conferred on individual items of evidence by comparison with all the other evidence'. The technique is to oppose the acceptance of disputed evidence by reference to other evidence. Its essence is contradiction. This must be distinguished from a usage where 'weight' refers to evidence which has already been accepted, and its effect in deciding a verdict.

In this approach, a cross-examiner puts his case to the extent that the witness knows the facts, and confronts him with material which contradicts his evidence.

## B   Unreasonable evidence

Evidence which is inconsistent, improbable or unrealistic, may be described as unreasonable.

These are mainly inherent qualities of evidence, which can be seen or exposed without depending on comparison with other evidence.

### 1   Inconsistency

Inconsistency means that two statements cannot both be true at the same time. The starkest form is self-contradiction in the evidence of one witness.

It may also arise on comparing the evidence of two or more witnesses who purport to give similar accounts. Normally they are on the same side, but some may testify in favour of the other side.

Inconsistency is a logical flaw, i e, in the relationship between statements, irrespective of the underlying facts. If a witness claims that he saw a motor car in his neighbour's garage at 9 p m but later says that the garage was empty at that time, logic requires that one statement or the other must be rejected, but cannot specify which. Indeed, both statements might be false, e g, if the witness was far from home at 9 p m.

Inconsistency throws no light on the facts, but it shows that something is wrong with the evidence, viz that part of it, at least, must be mistaken or untruthful; it weakens the impression of evidence, but without destroying any particular element, or establishing the truth.

The cross-examiner's tasks are to expose inconsistency, or to create it if possible, and then to expand its effect beyond its immediate area, in order to inflict the greatest damage.

Unless it is obvious, to expose inconsistency which exists already, requires careful listening, notetaking, which should be verbatim for important points, and comparisons of evidence. Advocates should be, and usually are, alert for this.

Glaring inconsistencies in the evidence of a single witness would generally be eliminated in taking statements for the trial.

If any inconsistency survives this, or arises in the evidence-in-chief, an advocate will generally try to correct it as it is given, by having his witness explain it and elect for one alternative where two statements clash. But if, in this critical area, he leads his witness in any way in the examination-in-chief, objection should be taken at once. Even if he succeeds in patching up the inconsistency, it may still be a vulnerable point for attack by the cross-examiner.

Objection should also be taken to any attempt to undo cross-examination on inconsistency, by leading in re-examination.

To compare the evidence of two or more of the opponent's witnesses is a fertile source of inconsistencies. But it is pointless to exaggerate minor discrepancies which arise from the fallability of observation or memory in everyone.

People do not register events like video-cameras. Trifling differences which abound in the accounts of any two witnesses to the same scene do not usually mean that their evidence as to the central facts is unreliable or untruthful. An advocate who has to rely on that, has a weak case.

Minor inconsistencies of no importance should be distinguished from others which are significant because of their context, e g, where there is an issue as to whether the witness saw anything at all of the incident which he describes.

If a Crown witness testifies that he saw the accused attack someone, but differs from others on details, this may not matter unless the defence claim that the witness arrived after the incident, in which case the differences may be crucial.

In alibi evidence, minor differences about circumstantial details or collateral facts may be sinister where a prosecutor contends that the event never occurred.

Facts whose significance is derived from the context include those which are part of a chain of circumstantial evidence, and about which, inconsistency may be important.

Inconsistency about material facts, e g, the main facts of the commission of a crime, or visual identification of the accused, should not be allowed to pass without being exploited.

Generally, any inconsistency which suggests lying rather than error, would invite challenge. Self-contradiction does not offer the excuse that one witness may be truthful although another is not.

Mistaken or untruthful evidence under close scrutiny has no sound basis of fact, and must be in conflict with reality somewhere. In cross-examination latent inconsistency can often be made explicit, or, with untruthful witnesses who add to their lies, inconsistency can even be created by direct or indirect tactics.

An untruthful witness can be induced to contradict himself by leading him to invent new evidence beyond the relative safety of his prepared story about the main facts, so that he commits himself firmly.

Obviously, the witness will not do this intentionally. Therefore his control must be overcome, as in direct tactics, or he must be misled, as in indirect tactics. The point is to make the testimony move and expand, and to keep the witness off balance, or unaware of the aim, until unintentionally he modifies his evidence so that it becomes inconsistent with what he said previously.

In direct tactics, the cross-examiner, who does not conceal his challenge, in as firm or even severe a manner as is necessary, may fire unexpected questions at the witness, rapidly, and in an unforeseeable order, so that he becomes confused and cannot relate the direction of his invention to what has gone before. The cross-examiner may also challenge the evidence on grounds other than inconsistency, e g, as improbable, or confront the witness with contradictory material.

In indirect tactics the cross-examiner has a similar objective, which he conceals. Instead, he encourages the witness to be overconfident, careless and talkative, and leads him into elaborating and developing his evidence with more and more circumstantial details of the false story.

Several lying witnesses can be cross-examined, whether by means of direct or indirect tactics, and led into committing themselves to statements which are inconsistent on comparison.

Whether similar or different questions are put to each, none of them is in a position to understand the overall aim. The greater the number of witnesses, the more vulnerable they are.

In any group of untruthful witnesses, some are often found to be less motivated, and less well prepared, than others; this may be exploited.

If several defendants are separately represented, their advocates could, by arrangement, cross-examine in different directions, but with a common purpose.

In any situation involving the cross-examination of several untruthful witnesses, the cumulative impact in terms of inconsistencies, can be striking. This can be intensified by putting a story told by one to another, which may lead to unimpressive attempts to reconcile the differences.

Once inconsistency in evidence has been shown, it should be exploited in order to inflict maximum damage. There are two broadly alternative ways of doing this, irrespective of whether a single witness or several are under consideration, and the choice of method is one for practical judgment in the particular circumstances.

One method is to go on with the cross-examination in order to press the advantage home explicitly, by giving witnesses a chance to explain the inconsistencies and to correct the evidence. If this is done, they may intensify the damage to the evidence by their efforts to reconcile the inconsistencies, e g, by creating further inconsistencies or improbabilities.

The alternative is to terminate the cross-examination as soon as inconsistencies have been exposed, without giving witnesses a chance to explain them or to correct the evidence, and to leave the matter for the court to decide after hearing arguments in closing speeches.

This prevents witnesses from giving plausible but false explanations for inconsistencies, or from correcting them. The opponent may not be sufficiently aware of the need for re-examination or for leading further evidence on the topic. Inferences which the court itself makes at the time, may be strongest, although the cross-examiner will argue the point in his closing speech. If the opponent comments adversely on the lack of an opportunity for his witnesses to explain the alleged inconsistencies, it can be pointed out that he could have re-examined them to that effect.

The position is similar with one or several witnesses, but a number of them would be more vulnerable to even further exploitation.

An additional point in favour of ending the cross-examination as soon as inconsistency has been exposed, is that evidence led by the cross-examiner will generally be available to contradict the witness. Two tactics related to inconsistency may be mentioned.

The opposite of inconsistency, viz unnatural consistency, may suggest that the evidence has been memorized by witnesses in collusion.

Among the signs are unusual similarities in language, topics and their sequence, points remembered and forgotten, and stilted ways of giving the evidence.

One way of exposing memorization is to ask witnesses to repeat their evidence-in-chief in their own words. If it has been memorized, the said similarities or others, should be apparent on comparing witnesses.

Such witnesses may be questioned rapidly about that evidence in a random order. If it is not based on reality, this may lead them into inconsistencies and improbabilities.

Repeating these procedures with several such witnesses, may have the effect that the suspect evidence is rejected.

To refer a witness to a previous inconsistent statement is often highly effective to the extent of discrediting him and of defeating his testimony in the trial.

As with putting previous convictions to a witness, the benefit is minimized by just putting a previous inconsistent statement directly to a witness, so that he realizes that the cross-examiner knows about it: he is then likely to admit it—although if he denies it, it can be proved.

The best approach is the indirect one, in which an untruthful witness is given an opportunity to lie as a result of which he can be discredited.

The cross-examiner, in a friendly manner, may lead the witness to commit himself firmly to his untruthful testimony in the trial. Then, a casual enquiry as to whether he has always said that may lead him into the trap of confirming it. He could then be confronted directly with his previous inconsistent statement and cross-examined forcefully about his departure from it. This is likely to defeat trust in the witness and to lead to the rejection of his disputed evidence in the trial, irrespective of the truth or otherwise of the previous statement, which is inadmissible as evidence of what it states.

It may be observed, generally, that cross-examination in which the evidence is challenged is often prolonged because advocates expect too much from it; very often, cross-examination is completed in its effect, not while it is going on, but only later.

A substantial amount of cross-examination would be more effective, if the advocate merely tried to obtain limited concessions on material points, and then dropped the matter; the temptation to press an attack as far as possible may have unproductive results, and should often be resisted.

In many, although not all, cases the effect of cross-examination is to weaken the evidence, which is then overcome by the contradictory evidence of the cross-examiner, supported by argument.

The destructive effects of exposing inconsistency in evidence vary. In the Crown case any material inconsistency would probably be fatal to conviction because of the burden of proof. In the defence case material inconsistency would be serious, but the consequences might be less critical.

In the case of either the prosecution or the defence, minor inconsistencies may not count for a great deal except where they have some special significance in the context, as was seen.

In his questions and in his later argument, a cross-examiner should be explicit as to whether his contention is that the inconsistency is due to mistake or untruthfulness. Their effects are different.

If an honest mistake is shown in part of the evidence given by a witness, generally that part will not be accepted, but the witness will not be discredited.

But if the nature and gravity of the mistake, or a number of mistakes made by the same witness, raise doubts about his general reliability as an observer, his memory, or the soundness of his way of reporting facts, the effects of inconsistency may be wider. Some doubt may be cast on other evidence given by the witness on facts in dispute, even though that has not been shown to be inconsistent.

If inconsistency is shown to be caused by lying, the effects may be wide. The witness may be discredited. To lie in one part of his evidence does not, of course, mean necessarily that he is lying in other parts. A discriminating approach is always necessary. However, the element of trust in the witness which is essential for belief, would have been damaged. The taint of lying or of distrust might then extend to other disputed evidence given by him, in which inconsistency has not been shown.

## 2 Improbability

Probability, generally, means the extent to which the existence of certain facts is likely; in criminal trials it refers to the likelihood that past facts were as stated in evidence. Although conviction requires proof beyond reasonable doubt, acquittal does not. Probability enters into the decision of many facts in criminal trials. Improbability is one of the inherent qualities of evidence described here as unreasonable; where evidence is sufficiently improbable, this would be a bar to belief in it.

The ultimate nature of probability has baffled philosophers and will not be discussed. For practical purposes, as a criterion for judgment in court, probability applies to disputed questions, the tests of experience of life, intuition and common sense. The commonsense usage is that something is probable when it is more likely to happen than not; otherwise it is improbable.

In the everyday sense, the degree of probability does make a difference to judgment, although it is unquantifiable. Evidence may seem highly likely, odd, or totally absurd. The extreme of impossibility in evidence is hardly a problem for cross-examination in practice. Such evidence would be unacceptable per se and unlikely to survive preparation for trial or the evidence-in-chief. If something is only impossible when evidence is compared, it is better to see this as inconsistency or contradiction.

Mathematical and non-mathematical probability are distinct. Mathematical probability is the degree to which an event is likely to happen as measured by a ratio ranging from 0, meaning impossibility, to 1, meaning certainty. The probability of a six in tossing dice is $1/6 = 0.167$. In theory, any event, however unlikely, has a degree of mathematical probability.

In criminal trials, questions of mathematical probability are usually confined to technical evidence, eg, evidence of the distribution of blood groups in the population. Otherwise the non-mathematical view of probability prevails in courts, viz the likelihood that past facts were as stated in evidence.

To challenge evidence as improbable, is more difficult than to show that it is inconsistent. Inconsistency needs only the self-evident test of logical contradiction. Improbability depends on an evaluation for which there are neither rules nor logical procedures; it is a matter of a judgment based on experience of life.

A judgment that something is probable or improbable is really an inference from facts, not certain knowledge of them.

To be admissible, questions which are directly concerned with probability, can only be put in cross-examining certain witnesses and in regard to certain kinds of evidence. In other cases, witnesses can only be cross-examined as to facts which the court will take into account in evaluating the probability or improbability of an event.

Expert witnesses who give opinion evidence may be cross-examined as to the probability of their conclusions. Lay witnesses who, in special circumstances are permitted to give impression evidence, eg, as the only way of communicating their observations, might be challenged about their interpretations of ambiguous or obscure happenings such as the actions of someone charged with taking part in a theft, as a look-out.

Inferences may be made from items of circumstantial evidence, which involve issues of probability, but although such inferences may be challenged by other means, questions about them should not be put to witnesses who merely speak to such items of evidence.

Typically, criticisms of evidence as improbable involve issues of human nature and conduct, perhaps in regard to the witness, but more commonly, in regard to the accused. Their evidence can be attacked directly as untrue, because of facts and circumstances put to them, from which a different inference is more probable. Such evidence may consist of separate facts in relationship to each other, or a connected story as an account of the event in question.

A cross-examiner who intends to challenge such evidence as improbable, has options. He can dispute any fact on which the story is based, he can attack the claimed relationship between facts, and he can assert a different relationship, as was done in cross-examining the accused in the following case.

A man was charged with abducting a female child who had been left with him temporarily, with taking her to his home, and with assaulting her indecently. He claimed that her mother had abandoned her, that he had no choice but to take her home, and he denied the indecent assault.

The prosecutor disputed facts in the evidence, attacked the alleged relationship between other facts and suggested a different relationship between the facts, to the accused.

He contended that the accused had a choice, since as he knew, there was a police station near the place where the girl was left with him, that he was not just looking after her, since he did not give her any food, and that he acted with a criminal intention from the start. The improbability in the accused's story was exposed, and the jury convicted him.

Cross-examination of a defendant by a prosecutor is a typical situation where evidence is challenged as improbable. Here, the defendant has given direct evidence as to his conduct, which exculpates him, perhaps in the form of a denial that he acted as charged, or that he acted with criminal intent, or that he was the person involved in the incident.

The prosecutor can put to the accused, in this situation, facts in his or other evidence, or extracted from him in cross-examination, which point in a different direction, and from which inferences of incriminating conduct may be drawn, i e, showing that the accused's account is improbable, and that an incriminating inference is more likely.

The prosecutor can also put to the accused various items of circumstantial evidence and incriminating inferences which may be drawn from them. Here, the witness is not being asked for an opinion; he is giving direct evidence, but in response to a view of probability.

Similarly, the prosecutor can put to the accused, any directly incriminating evidence given by other witnesses, and obtain his response.

In these situations, the question is one of probability, which, in cross-examining the accused, can be put to him directly.

A similar approach could be made to any witness whose conduct was relevant to the issue, e g, a complainant in a charge of rape where the defence was that she consented, or police witnesses whose evidence of a confession by the accused is attacked as untrue. Here again, questions of probability of the conduct of the witnesses may arise directly.

However, a good deal of cross-examination which is directed towards the improbability of evidence, does not raise that question directly with the witness who is giving evidence. It consists of assembling facts from many witnesses from which the court may make inferences, in deciding the probability of other facts.

In this respect, since probability is a matter of degree, if it is only slight, this may only cast some doubt on facts. The more improbable the evidence is shown to be, the more it is likely to be inaccurate. The larger the volume of facts connected with the disputed evidence which is brought out, the more it can be seen whether that evidence fits into other facts and reality. This ought to expose any discontinuity which indicates that the disputed evidence is inaccurate, for some reason. So in challenging evidence as improbable, generally, and not only with the witness under cross-examination, the advocate's task is to expand the evidence of significant surrounding facts.

Facts never exist in isolation; they exist in a context in which there are all sorts of connections. What occurred before, during and after a main incident could be probed, together with other collateral circumstances including motives and conduct, or causes and effects. Thoroughness of preparation would help a cross-examiner here, in knowing which way to go.

The surrounding facts may be probed by leading questions, or if a witness is suitable, he may be encouraged to ramble on freely. If he is lying, he may invent further details.

Several witnesses could also be cross-examined by leading or allowed to give evidence freely. What one says can be put to another, with the usual discrediting effect.

One way or another, the aim is to expand the contact of an unlikely story with reality, so that it becomes increasingly improbable to the point of absurdity, as it is seen how the story does not fit together, and its discontinuity with reality becomes obvious.

As wide and as varied a combination of facts as possible should be assembled, to which the test of everyday experience may be applied.

Where admissible evidence contains any element of interpretation, counter-probabilities may be suggested as more acceptable than what the witness states, and built up into a story. It may help to leave part of the new meaning to inference by the court.

As always, judgment is needed on where to end such forms of cross-examination. To do so as soon as the aim is achieved, has the usual advantages of preventing the witness from undoing the gains, and of reducing the risk of adverse re-examination, or further evidence from the opponent's witnesses.

If a cross-examiner has amassed sufficient material to attack the improbability of the opponent's case, he will be in a position to present a forceful argument. For best effect, this should be reasonable. Improbability is not impossibility. Often facts speak for themselves and some points may be made most strongly by simply suggesting them. If the attack on the opponent's evidence as improbable, combined with other objections, does not destroy it, per se, it may so weaken it that it is defeated by contradictory evidence led by the cross-examiner.

## 3 Lack of realism

Lack of realism in evidence as an impressionistic method of assessment was fully discussed in chapter 4. Typical unrealistic features of false stories are lack of factual detail and colouring, lack of personal involvement and a tendency for evidence all to be in one direction. It is mentioned here to complete the list of unreasonable qualities of evidence, but it is background material for cross-examiners, not a technique.

## C  Weight of evidence

Evidence may satisfy two of the requirements for belief, and yet not be accepted. The witness may be trusted, and the evidence may be reasonable in the sense that it is neither inconsistent, improbable nor unrealistic. One view of such evidence may be that it is simply plausible, i e that it could be true, but this alone may not be convincing. On the other hand, this alone might be enough for belief, if confidence in the witness is strong enough. But in principle this question should not arise normally, since there will be other evidence, and a court is bound to have regard to the whole of the evidence, whatever it decides to accept or reject.

A court, in reaching its verdict, will consider all the evidence together, holistically, including how some evidence supports, and some evidence contradicts, other evidence. In closing speeches, parties should also take this comprehensive approach, which determines the 'weight' of a particular piece of evidence, as defined here. But in cross-examination, an advocate is concerned with putting to witnesses whatever contradicts their own evidence, not evidence which supports it. His aim is to reduce the weight of the witness's evidence at that stage.

The principle of contradiction at the heart of the adversarial process, is put into effect in cross-examination where an advocate must put so much of his case to a witness as is within the witness's knowledge, and confronts him with contradictory material derived from other evidence.

How an advocate may put his case to witnesses with the advantages and disadvantages of different methods, was discussed, e g, it may be put in detail or in one global question for assent or denial. In any method, the cross-examiner's overall version of the facts should be prominent.

The key to deciding on these tactics, is which kind of response from the witness is going to be most damaging to the evidence which he is giving, and most favourable to the cross-examiner. An unreasonable response to a reasonable proposition, could damage the impression gained of the witness and his evidence, and may therefore be worth intensifying by a detailed approach. Otherwise, in many cases, the more quickly a case is put to the witness and denied, the better.

In confronting the witness with contradictory evidence, a cross-examiner should observe the rules of evidence, and proper practice. He should ask him about facts, perhaps spoken to by his own witnesses, but should not ask for his opinion on other evidence, or to say whether another witness is mistaken or lying. He should not argue with the witness. Also, the cross-examiner should not, in effect, give evidence himself by such statements as 'My information is . . .' or 'My client will say . . .'.

In any admissible reference to other specific oral evidence, e g, in cross-examining an expert witness, a cross-examiner should be careful to quote it accurately, or if he summarizes it, to do so fairly.

A witness may, of course, be confronted with real or documentary evidence which contradicts him.

The effect of putting his case and of confronting the witness with contradictory evidence or even facts which are not in dispute, varies. The minimum of advantage which can be derived from this, is at least to show the court that another view than what the witness said in evidence-in-chief, is possible. The greatest advantage would be where the witness's response to contradiction, gives the cross-examiner an opening to discredit the witness, and demonstrate that his evidence is inconsistent and improbable, as well as contradicted.

The final effect of this attack on the weight of a witness's evidence, may not be achieved at the stage of cross-examination. It is usually completed when the court makes its comparison of all the evidence, and prefers the contradictory evidence which the cross-examiner put to the witness, and as to which the response was unacceptable.

# CHAPTER 9

# Cross-examination: common problems

I Problems arising from issues
II Problems with witnesses

Despite the variety and uniqueness of situations which a cross-examiner may encounter, many patterns recur, and general observations may be made about them. Some common problems are considered in this chapter, on the basis of earlier discussion.

## I PROBLEMS ARISING FROM ISSUES

As was seen, any defence which consists of a positive version of the facts, almost invariably restricts the real dispute in the trial to the question of whether the crime was committed, or the question of whether the defendant was the offender. It would be exceptional for both to be live issues.

### A Crime as the issue

Crimes were analysed for practical purposes into result-crimes, conduct-crimes and object-crimes. Each class involves typical problems for cross-examiners. Issues of identification are dealt with separately.

#### 1 Result-crimes

Where acts followed by results constitute the crime, the results themselves are often beyond dispute, and if not admitted, are proved by overwhelming evidence, e g, the vandalized motor car, the victim with stab wounds, or the signs of breaking into a house, and recovery of the stolen goods elsewhere. Such physical facts seldom create serious problems for cross-examiners.

But these crimes may raise intangible issues about states of mind or the quality of acts, e g, about the accused's guilty intention, whether he struck the blow in self-defence, whether an alleged rape victim consented to sexual intercourse, or whether the driving which caused death was reckless.

A working guide is to expect that there will be disputes about any intangible elements on which the constitution of the crime depends. Usually, they involve conflicts of direct evidence and offer opportunities for skill in cross-examination.

In a vast number of result-crimes, the results speak for themselves, so that essential facts which are intangible can be inferred from them without need for enquiry, e g, the guilty mind of the person who vandalized the car.

At the other extreme, the results may be neutral or ambiguous as to mental states or the quality of acts and other evidence is needed to establish them.

In intermediate situations, intangible elements may either be inferred or not, according to the view taken of the external results, but other evidence could tilt the decision one way or another.

Intangible issues which are not settled conclusively by the results of an act, can be difficult subjects for cross-examination. Advocates should seek support from anything objective which is available, e g, collateral facts.

An example might be the issue of the mental state of an accused charged with the theft of jewellery found in a box hidden in a friend's motor car which the accused was driving. In evidence he denies that he knew it was there. A prosecutor in cross-examining the accused and other defence witnesses will probe for objective material from which such knowledge may be inferred, e g, the fact that the accused owned the box and had borrowed the car around the time of the theft. By merely arguing with the accused about the point, a prosecutor may not make much progress.

Where the issue is the state of mind of an accused who gives evidence, he will be cross-examined on the basis that he is lying. Since this will not be conceded, the prosecutor's realistic aim must be to weaken the accused's testimony as much as possible. If he is of bad character, this cannot usually be disclosed. The accused's motive hardly needs emphasis. The prosecutor's main attack is likely to focus on any inconsistency and improbability in the accused's evidence which he can expose and exploit.

A complainant will also be accused of lying, where his acts or state of mind are in issue, e g, in a charge of assault where self-defence is the plea. If the accused admits striking the complainant with a pool cue, but pleads self-defence, his advocate might cross-examine the complainant about his state of drink, animosity towards the defendant, and tax him with an attack which he made or threatened to make on the accused. The question will be one of credibility.

Where intangible issues arise in result-crimes, as a rule it is only when independent eyewitnesses are cross-examined that it may be contended that their evidence is mistaken or unreliable, or attempts may be made to employ constructive tactics.

## 2 Conduct-crimes

In relation to conduct-crimes, elaboration is unnecessary in view of what has been said about result-crimes. A situation which is similar to the intangible elements of result-crimes arises here in crimes where the acts need have no physical results, e g, abortive attempts at result-crimes, assaults which cause no injury, or sexual offences without contact. The point is that nothing remains after the incident to suggest what happened, one way or another. The verdict depends on eyewitness evidence.

Independent witnesses, having no reason to lie about the incident, would usually be cross-examined on the ground that they are mistaken, or that their evidence is unreliable. Constructive techniques may elicit helpful evidence from such witnesses.

Some complainants may merit similar treatment, depending on the nature and circumstances of the crime charged, because the transient act left no physical traces to confirm their impression, e g, an act of indecent exposure in a park, and since they have no reason to fabricate a complaint.

Complainants who are hostile to the accused, e g, one who reported him for making a threat, may be charged with lying in defence cross-examination.

When cross-examining the defendant and perhaps his close associates, the allegation will normally be one of lying.

## 3 Object-crimes

Where a crime is constituted by a forbidden relationship to some object, the variety of such charges and surrounding circumstances limits any generalizations about forms of cross-examination.

The nature of the object is crucial, and as it should be in court as an exhibit, this is often obvious on inspection, e g, a bayonet, or may be technically indisputable, e g, material identified as cannabis resin by a forensic scientist. There is little scope for cross-examination here.

But other objects may require interpretation by witnesses, which can be disputed, e g, whether a knife is simply a utensil or an offensive weapon. Cross-examination can make a contribution here.

Wider disputes may arise about intangible matters, such as the defendant's possession of the object, rather than about the object itself, e g, where prohibited drugs are found in a house with many tenants, a dispute may arise about whether the defendant was the possessor.

Vigorous cross-examination on either side is likely on such questions as possession. Lying, not mistake, will be the basis of the prosecutor's cross-examination of the accused and his associates.

It is also not unknown for the defence to attack police evidence about the circumstances in which the articles were found as untruthful.

## B   Identification as the issue

In discussing the issue of identification, it is assumed that the commission of the crime is admitted or proved.

Various forms of identification, viz visual, circumstantial evidence and confessions are considered here separately, although in practice, one such form of evidence often reinforces another.

### 1   Visual identification

In the visual identification of a person whom the witness knows, identity with its personal associations rather than perception and comparison of the patterns of faces is the subject of the evidence. Nevertheless, where the circumstances of observation were adverse, a cross-examiner might still succeed in weakening such evidence.

As was seen, visual identification of a stranger as the offender may consist of evidence of recognition, resemblance, or recall of some special characteristic. Only recognition, i e, 'That is the man' proves the accused's guilt if it is accepted. Resemblance, i e, 'He looks like the man' is only an item of evidence among others. Even if it is accepted, this alone does not prove that the accused was the offender. Many people other than the offender may look like him.

The most common defence contention about the accused's implication in the crime is that identifying witnesses for the prosecution are mistaken. The cross-examiner may probe sources of error in observation and suggest that a witness's memory was weakened by delay, or that his identification has been influenced by factors such as discussion between witnesses or irregularities in an identification parade. Even a large number of witnesses has been known to make the same mistake.

At best, cross-examination of this kind may weaken confidence in an identification, so that it is held to be unreliable, and may become unacceptable because of the burden of proof on the Crown. But by itself, it is unlikely to show that the identification is wrong.

The cross-examiner may also focus on the witness's exact words in pre-trial identifications or in court, to see if there is any room for doubt about whether they mean recognition or resemblance. The two although different in meaning, can blend into each other. If a witness can be brought to concede any uncertainty about his identification at all, the door is opened to increasing this progressively to the point where he is only speaking to a resemblance. If so, the cross-examination has succeeded to the extent that the witness is not now saying that the accused is the offender, but only that he looks like him.

In leading the witness to concede some uncertainty, cross-examination about difficulties of observation and memory may have some persuasive effect on him as well as the court, if he is impartial and fair.

Defence cross-examination may also be helped by the common fear of responsibility for convicting the wrong person. Moreover, some people doubt their own perceptions and memory to such an extent that they are hesitant about many things. On the other hand, some witnesses may be reluctant to retract or qualify earlier positive identifications.

A useful line of enquiry is to ask the witness about the basis of his identification, e g, facial features and if so which, build, hair colour and so on. Faces are really perceived as a whole pattern, and a witness who is drawn into such an analysis and into listing the features on which he relies, becomes vulnerable to further questions asking what is unique about them. He is also exposed to the possibility of converting evidence of recognition, not only into evidence of resemblance, but even more destructively, into evidence of individual features.

But a witness who resists any questions seeking to analyse his identification, may seem to be dogmatic and unco-operative, which can per se introduce some doubt about his testimony. This would also be the case where the circumstances of observation were such that dogmatism is inappropriate.

Evidence of visual identification which is challenged as mistaken, may be supported by other evidence, e g, similar evidence given by a number of unconnected witnesses, circumstantial evidence, or confessions, but on the other hand, it may be weakened or overcome by the defendant's testimony supported by alibi evidence.

Less commonly, defence cross-examination may challenge the evidence of identifying witnesses for the prosecution as being untruthful, viz where the serious allegation is made that police witnesses are lying, or even conspiring to secure a conviction. Where this is so, the question is one of challenging the credibility of evidence, rather than a question of visual identification, and the approach is different.

## 2   Circumstantial evidence

Challenges by a cross-examiner to circumstantial evidence impli-cating the defendant may take different forms and may involve various difficulties.

Frequently, an offender leaves personal traces at the locus or on a victim, or carries signs away with him on his person or on his clothes or both.

His conduct before and after the incident may give rise to inferences.

A number of unconnected and independent witnesses may each speak to details, apparently of little significance until, considered together, they are seen to be incriminating. It would seem unreasonable to suggest a lying conspiracy, and may be difficult even to show that such witnesses are all mistaken.

However, since such witnesses may be expected to be impartial, there may be scope for constructive techniques of cross-examin-ation which can change the factual basis of items of circumstantial evidence, without constituting a challenge, e g, emphasizing some facts, suggesting new meanings, or eliciting new helpful facts. The objective would be to change the balance, even slightly so as to replace a sinister picture with a more favourable one. The defence cross-examination is usually confined to subtle adjustments of circumstantial evidence in this way, although the defence can, of course, lead evidence themselves to contradict any incriminating inference by giving a direct account of the facts.

What the defence advocate really wants to attack is the incriminating inference which may be drawn from the circumstan-tial facts rather than the facts themselves. But that is not a matter for any witness; it is a question for the court which can be argued in closing speeches. This is subject to the qualification that impression evidence is sometimes given, without objection, where the underly-ing facts are coloured by interpretation which can be probed.

## 3   Confessions and admissions

In the present context, although not in law, 'confession' means a full confession of guilt, and 'admission' means an incriminating statement, which falls short of that. Both are normally recorded in writing. Confessions are generally taken in the controlled circum-stances of a police station. Admissions may be made spontaneously or in answer to caution and charge, in a police station, but are frequently made in uncontrolled circumstances, e g, at the locus of the crime or at the accused's home.

Admissions by conduct or silence are possible but only excep-tionally.

Defendants are often implicated by such evidence if it is accepted. There can be few more convincing reasons for finding that a person committed a crime, than that he said that he did it— although people have been known to confess to crimes which they did not commit.

Where other evidence is weak, an admission can make the proof of guilt conclusive.

Because of the crucial effect of confessions and admissions, if proved to have been made, they are often contested strongly by the defence in various ways, e g, that the evidence is inadmissible, that the evidence is mistaken or untruthful in whole or in part, or that, if it is accurate, it is being interpreted wrongly or does not prove guilt.

The admissibility of evidence of confessions and admissions belongs to the law of evidence, for which suitable texts should be consulted. It is referred to briefly here, since the procedure for determining admissibility may itself involve cross-examination.

By statute, such evidence is inadmissible where it was obtained by oppression or in circumstances likely to have made the confession unreliable. On defence objection being taken, or on the court's initiative, the evidence will only be admitted on prosecution proof beyond reasonable doubt that the statements were not so obtained. The question is decided in a 'trial within a trial'.

In cross-examining police witnesses, the defence may construe 'oppression' widely to cover anything which tends to deprive a confession of its voluntary character, e g, not only torture, violence, threat of violence, or intimidation, but also more subtle forms of pressure such as prolonged questioning, or lack of refreshment or of an opportunity to sleep, taking into account the suspect's character and circumstances. 'Unreliability' may include various types of threat, e g, to charge a suspect's wife with a crime, or inducement, e g, a promise to facilitate bail.

Whether or not the more serious allegations of misconduct are true, police officers concerned may be expected to deny them, so that credibility will be in issue.

Less serious suggestions, whatever their truth, may meet less or no resistance, e g, times of arrival or questioning, or provision of meals, whether a doctor attended to examine the suspect and so on.

If the information given by the defendant to his advocate is genuine, the defence cross-examination will be difficult. The defendant may call other witnesses in the trial within a trial, and should do so if they would be helpful, e g, a doctor to testify to his condition on release from the police station, or to his wife's advanced pregnancy and dependence on the accused for help. But usually, the decision depends on the defendant's own evidence in opposition to that of several police witnesses.

The defence advocate should therefore be alert for any weaknesses in the prosecution evidence. In a situation like this, inconsistency between police witnesses may be very significant and should be exploited where possible. The defence argument should emphasize the burden of proof beyond reasonable doubt which is borne by the prosecution.

If it came to a prosecutor's knowledge that there was real substance in the defence objection, it would be proper to concede it. Otherwise, he is likely to cross-examine the defendant on the basis that any serious allegations of misconduct are inventions. Whether complaints of a more minor character, even if established, would justify exclusion of a confession, may be arguable.

Evidence of a confession or an admission which is allowed may be challenged on the basis that it is mistaken or untruthful.

A brief admission made in informal circumstances, and not noted at once, or at all, is more likely to be mistaken than a full confession made in controlled circumstances, and recorded at the time.

Police witnesses may say that an accused made an informal statement against his interest at the scene of the crime, his home, or somewhere other than a police station. A defence cross-examiner might challenge this evidence as mistaken because what the defendant said was misheard, as a result of the kind of impediments considered earlier.

Evidence could be mistaken in the following ways which are not exhaustive: nothing was said; something was said, but not the statement attributed to the accused; the statement was made, but parts of it were wrongly reported; the statement was made by someone other than the accused; the statement was made but meant something different in the situation, which opens up enquiry as to the context; the statement was made but should be interpreted differently.

But it is inept to suggest that the inaccuracy of police evidence is due to mistake, where the witnesses must know the real situation, so that the only possible explanation for any inaccuracy which exists is that they are lying.

A great amount of cross-examination of police witnesses about admissions by an accused is of this unimpressive kind. There may be several reasons for the reluctance of cross-examiners to call a spade a spade here, and charge the witness with lying, e g, lack of confidence in the grounds of challenge, fear that the defendant may lose his protection against an attack on his character, false notions about an advocate's style or courtesy towards witnesses, or allowing the witness to save face in the hope of getting his co-operation. But often a suggestion that such evidence is mistaken merely gives an impression of polished insincerity.

Looking at this question squarely, it is a central issue in evidence. If a person accused of a crime tells police that he committed it, it seems unlikely that they would often be *mistaken* about such a fact. Whether the police or the accused might *lie* about it is another matter.

Even evidence about an informal admission is less likely to be mistaken, where the challenge alleges identical mistakes by more than one police witness. Moreover, where the evidence refers to a full confession, in controlled circumstances, e g, in a police station, recorded in writing, read over to or by the defendant, and signed by him, which is spoken to by several police witnesses, it is difficult to see how any mistake can be made, apart from the odd word or two—although either side may be lying.

It is a sound working rule, that disputes about the accuracy of admissions or confessions nearly always raise questions of credibility. Where this is clear, it is more impressive for the defence to cross-examine realistically, than to make suave suggestions about mistake, which are an affront to common sense and deceive nobody.

Cross-examination of police witnesses on the basis that they are lying about an admission or confession, may have little or no effect unless supported by persuasive testimony by the defendant, who surmounts his own cross-examination.

Confining the discussion to full confessions, this issue of credibility raises major questions of motivation for the court, viz:

(1) Why would the defendant confess?
(2) If he has confessed, why would he deny it?
(3) Why would the police lie about it?

Both the prosecutor and the defence advocate must keep these questions in mind in conducting their respective cross-examinations, although they could not necessarily put them to witnesses directly, e g, the defence advocate could not ask a police witness to explain the defendant's reasons for confessing, although he might elicit evidence of facts and circumstances known to the officer from which inferences about this point might be made by the court after hearing arguments.

Why do suspects confess? The reasons, of course, vary according to the individual and the circumstances, but some general considerations may guide cross-examination in particular situations. The defence should keep this question to the forefront in cross-examination and argument. Often, it is not given the prominence which it might have.

If the defence cross-examination can elicit facts to suggest that there was no reason for the defendant to confess, this will support the defendant's evidence and may put the police evidence in a critical light.

The point to be emphasized is that this must be a genuine question in every case, even where the defendant is guilty. People do not normally commit crimes with a view to conviction and punishment. Why then do they change their intention in a police station? The cross-examiner must probe for facts from police witnesses, to show that there was no reason for confessing. In a way, the cross-examiner is helped by the inadmissibility of any police opinions on the matter, although the prosecutor could cross-examine the defendant directly about his motives, and argue the point in his closing speech.

In unpremeditated crimes committed in hot blood, e g, some assaults or even murder, it is conceivable that remorse per se may lead to confession when the blood cools. But this is unlikely in the vast majority of crimes.

States of mind such as exhaustion, stress, a wish to get the whole thing over, and so on, by themselves, or in association with remorse, might play a part, but may not seem generally to be compelling reasons for confessing to a crime, especially where the consequences for the accused may be serious.

Even in criminal situations, confessions do occur from motives of loyalty, where A takes the blame to protect B, perhaps where A has little or no criminal record, and B has a bad one.

But in most cases where a suspect confesses to the crime, voluntarily, without any improper pressures or inducements, the key to his motivation is his belief that denial is useless because the evidence against him is overwhelming. This has two aspects, viz:

(1) what evidence the police have in fact; and
(2) what evidence the suspect thought that they had, which may depend on what they told him.

A suspect could be interviewed by the police or arrested in various situations, from being caught red-handed to being traced by forensic evidence. If there was incriminating evidence, other than the confession, which would prove his guilt inevitably, and the defendant knew this, the probability of confession is maximized. He might seem to have nothing to lose, or may hope that his co-operation may encourage leniency.

If there was strong incriminating evidence at the time of the alleged confession, to refer to this in defence cross-examination would only emphasize the probability that the accused confessed, and the strength of the Crown case on the other grounds.

But if there was little or no incriminating evidence when the confession is said to have been made, the defence would contend that the other evidence was inadequate, and that the accused had no reason to confess. The defence cross-examination should bring this out from the police witnesses who speak to the confession, and any others who were engaged in the enquiry. If a number of them speak to single elements of evidence, the significance of which they cannot explain, the cross-examiner may exploit this.

A prosecutor who foresees that police evidence of a confession will be attacked as untruthful, should reinforce it in anticipation of that. It is in his interest to emphasize the strength of the incriminating evidence as a reason for confessing, as well as pointing to guilt per se. He might take a similar line in cross-examining the defendant if he gives evidence, tending to show that he knew the strength of the evidence against him, and that denial was hopeless.

The second question, why a defendant who confessed initially should deny it later, is not difficult to answer.

The defendant, after rest, time to reflect, discussion with others, and before taking legal advice, may invent a story to explain the incriminating evidence, and denial of his confession follows.

The credibility of police evidence of a confession is regularly attacked. The court must decide whether police witnesses are reporting this truthfully or committing perjury. This involves the final question of motivation, viz why the police would lie about this. Since there are many obvious reasons why a police witness would be truthful about this, a defence challenge which fails to suggest a motive for lying may not be persuasive.

A police officer found to have committed perjury in a criminal trial would be exposed to loss of career and pension, and probably to extreme penalties. There would always be a risk of detection, e g, if the truth were to emerge later.

Malice against the accused personally might be one defence suggestion, but it meets the difficulty of exploring past relations between the accused and the police officer, and perhaps revealing previous convictions.

It might be suggested that police witnesses, who genuinely believed in the defendant's guilt, had exaggerated the weight of certain incriminating evidence in some way. This could happen where one police witness identified the defendant, sincerely, and, another, insincerely after discussion with the first.

In making the extreme allegation of deliberate perjury with the risks involved, a defence cross-examiner might find it difficult to elicit evidence of facts which point to such conduct, even where the allegation is true. Many police officers with court experience are more or less professional witnesses, and if they are indeed launched on a false story, they would persist in it.

Also defence imputations against police witnesses may deprive an accused of statutory protection against cross-examination as to bad character.

The state of the evidence at the time of the alleged confession has a bearing on whether or not the police would lie, as well as on whether or not the defendant would confess. If the evidence against the defendant is strong anyway, police who might have lied to secure a conviction would have no reason to incur the risks of doing so. If the incriminating evidence was weak, a confession might be crucial, and more likely to be fabricated. This is yet another reason for the prosecution or the defence, where they may gain from it, to explore the state of evidence as known to the police and to the suspect at that stage.

Apart from the motivations of the accused and the police, the defence cross-examination can apply other tests to evidence of a confession.

Probing various aspects of the alleged confession other than what it means, may be productive if it has a purpose, e g, by asking whether the accused was cautioned before he made the statement, whether it was voluntary, whether the officers who noted it were also involved in the enquiry, who was there, who wrote it, if it was not the accused, then whether it was read over to the accused or he read it over himself, whether he was told that he could alter anything in it, whether it contains any corrections and if so, how these came about, whether his signature is genuine, whether the confession was dictated by the accused and recorded verbatim or obtained by question and answer, whether the accused was interrogated, whether the language is natural to the accused or contains police jargon, whether the spelling gives any clues, how long it all took, or whether it was hurried.

Such questions put to any single witness to the confession may create some opening for suggesting that the confession is not genuine, provided that anything put to the police witness is based on the cross-examiner's information, and will be confirmed by the defendant if he gives evidence.

If the evidence of the confession is false, comparison of the answers to such questions by two or more police witnesses may yield significant inconsistencies which can be exploited.

However well prepared liars are, it is impossible for them to foresee every possible question. Having no memory of reality to fall back on, they must invent answers to unforeseen questions. If these are put rapidly in unpredictable sequence, lying witnesses may be led into self-contradiction or inconsistency with each other. This is true of cross-examining lying witnesses generally about collateral matters. Where a confession in a police station is the subject matter, the surrounding circumstances are restricted, but the secondary details of the taking of the confession referred to above offer various facts for use in testing whether a confession is genuine. The effect of tape recording of confessions, which is under contemplation, has yet to emerge.

Apart from testing evidence of confessions by reference to the motivations of the accused and the police, and the secondary features of the situation as described, the content of the alleged confession could be the subject of defence challenge in which it was related to all the other evidence about the issues. Objective features of the alleged confession would be assessed with regard to all the evidence in the trial and the tests of inconsistency, improbability and contradiction by other evidence would be applied. A defendant's denial of the confession, in evidence, may at least raise a reasonable doubt about it, and thus lead to its rejection.

## 4 Alibi evidence

It is to be expected that an accused who is insisting on his alibi will testify in support of it.

An alibi witness could, by mistake, identify the accused at some place other than the scene of the crime when it was committed, or be wrong about the date of an accurate identification. But prosecutors do not challenge alibi evidence very often as mistaken; they usually allege that the accused and alibi witnesses are lying, as they know the facts.

When alibi evidence is given, a prosecutor might at first explore the character and motivation of each witness, where something is to be gained by this. He should ensure that the witness's link with the accused is made explicit. The closer this is, the more vulnerable the evidence may be.

Standard tactics, then, are to probe the story in detail, to explore collateral facts, to seek both minor and material inconsistencies between alibi witnesses and to exploit any improbabilities.

Probing the story in detail involves questions of the 'What was on the television?' type for which lying witnesses have probably prepared. But it is noticeable that the motivation of lying alibi witnesses varies in strength; some may be word-perfect in their stories, whereas others may have prepared with less care. Moreover, lying alibi witnesses are not always conspicuous for their intelligence. So such probing may be productive.

Exploring collateral facts generally uncovers some area for which lying alibi witnesses are unprepared, viz the circumstances which preceded, accompanied or followed the alibi situation. Rapid and unpredictable questioning in a random sequence, may defeat the witness's capacity to invent facts for which he has no basis in memory. While such a witness might be hesitant or claim amnesia for some essential detail in the alibi situation, if he feels threatened by questions, he may be less concerned about points which seem remote from the central facts. This lowering of defences may be exploited with a number of witnesses so as to build up a network of surrounding facts which are in conflict with the alibi situation as described and with each other.

By such methods, a prosecutor would try to lead or drive false alibi witnesses into inconsistencies. These too, may be developed further. One witness might be asked about unexpected facts to which another spoke. His hesitation or reluctance to commit himself may be transparent. If he does make a definite statement he should be led into asserting it as dogmatically as possible. This will intensify the effect of inconsistency. Alternatively, after leading various witnesses to commit themselves in different directions, the prosecutor may simply leave this mixture of statements for a forceful closing speech so that it is beyond correction by the defence.

Since a false alibi must often be constructed within the parameters of certain facts which cannot be disputed, or has other limits, it may seem to be strained and improbable. A prosecutor would, again, exploit any such improbability by expanding it to the point of absurdity, where he could.

Some recurrent patterns of alibi evidence and how they may be dealt with, require to be mentioned.

Where it seems that an alibi has been memorized in detail, a prosecutor might start by asking the witnesses to repeat their evidence-in-chief. An identity of phrase or wording might show collusion.

To ask alibi witnesses if they have ever discussed their evidence often yields improbable denials which tend to discredit them. Since even honest witnesses are sensitive about the subject, lying witnesses may well respond in a way which makes them suspect.

Lying witnesses to an alibi, under pressure, may take refuge in 'amnesia' claiming that the event happened so long ago that they cannot recall the facts about which they are asked. Here, the prosecutor might note the facts said to be forgotten, how often this occurs, and may compare this 'amnesia' with the claimed sharpness of recollection for other facts.

Some false alibis are real events on a date other than the date of the crime. To break these, which is difficult, the surrounding elements relating to date may be probed. Also, the Crown evidence will contradict them by implicating the accused.

Any challenge to alibi evidence as false, assuming that it is in fact not genuine, should not, realistically, be expected to lead to retraction by the witnesses or immediate destruction. The aim is so to weaken the alibi evidence that it succumbs to positive and contradictory evidence led by the prosecutor to the effect that the accused was the offender.

Destruction of an alibi does not per se place the defendant at the scene of the crime or establish his guilt, e g, an innocent person may resort to this in lieu of a weak defence. But in some circumstances, an alibi shown to be false may have an adverse effect on the defence.

## II PROBLEMS WITH WITNESSES

Typical problems arise in cross-examining various kinds of prosecution and defence witnesses.

### A Prosecution witnesses

#### 1 Police

Police evidence has been discussed in various contexts, but a reminder of some salient points may be helpful for cross-examiners. Police witnesses testify in most criminal trials, and are often very important. They have no special status as witnesses. Their evidence may be challenged as mistaken, unreliable or untruthful like that of any witness.

Errors of observation or memory of the kind which can affect the testimony of any witness are also attributed to police witnesses, quite commonly, by the defence. Two features related to mistaken evidence, are of special interest to defence cross-examiners, viz discussion of evidence, and the possibility of occupational bias.

Teamwork and pooling of information are typical in police enquiries. Many written records must be kept, e g, notes of interviews, or reports which may be circulated or made available to colleagues and senior officers.

The duties of police officers oblige them to discuss their cases, and they often work in pairs. Sometimes, such discussion may be capable of influencing and modifying their eyewitness evidence by suggestion, although the witness sincerely believes that he is reporting his original observations accurately and independently.

An illustration is the risk of error where police witnesses see a group of youths in a riot, and, influenced by later discussion, albeit in good faith, implicate an uninvolved person who was merely present.

As has been pointed out, to ask witnesses if they have discussed their evidence is an excellent test of their sincerity. Generally, they are reluctant to admit it, or if they do, to admit that it has influenced their testimony in any way. Sometimes this reluctance leads to manifestly insincere statements.

The defence often fail to grasp the opportunities for cross-examination which arise from the routine discussion of the case and the evidence by police witnesses, which might lead to mistakes or unreliability.

The evidence which would be most vulnerable to such causes of error would be that relating to intangible crimes or elements in crimes, and visual identification.

Any occupation may create typical attitudes and there is no reason why police should be an exception. Indeed, some habits of mind are desirable in their work, e g, curiosity, alertness to possible wrongdoing, suspicion, scepticism, determination in tracing and apprehending offenders and, when they assist the prosecution, the expectation that the suspect, if guilty, will be convicted. Of course, police officers are expected to carry out their duties with impartiality and fairness, especially when they testify, but human nature may be moulded in various ways of which people are not always aware.

At times, a defence cross-examiner might suggest that bias has led to mistaken police evidence or has contributed to mistakes in the evidence of lay witnesses with whom police witnesses came into contact. Such mischief may seem more likely in evidence of a marginal kind, e g, reports of ambiguous or obscure situations, such as the actions of a person suspected of acting as a lookout. If the cross-examination is carried out diplomatically, showing that the witness's sincerity is accepted, a fair-minded police officer who has not committed himself irrevocably to some stark statement, might make concessions, e g, that he would naturally be suspicious about youths lurking about in the darkness of a car park and that perhaps the accused was just holding the door handle to steady himself as he was drunk.

Biased police officers, without intending it, may influence the evidence of lay witnesses with whom they come in contact during their enquiries. Visual identification of the accused would be particularly vulnerable to this in the range of pre-trial identification procedures, e g, giving descriptions, confronting suspects, being shown photographs, or taking part in identification parades.

If a defence advocate has ground for arguing in his closing speech that the bias of a police witness is so extreme as to amount to partisanship, he can meet the evidence head-on by open and direct challenge, in cross-examination, to the effect that it is inaccurate because of bias and partiality.

Alternatively, he may conceal his doubts and encourage the witness to become more and more one-sided and dogmatic until he discredits himself by showing how untrustworthy he is.

Any formal irregularities which are suspected, should certainly be brought out in cross-examination, as well as any other expressions of bias which did not come up to that level, but which may still have influenced the witness. In view of the burden of proof on the Crown, an identification may be rejected if the cross-examination can persuade the court that the identification is tainted or unreliable, even if it cannot show that it is wrong.

The credibility of police evidence has been discussed, e g, in relation to confessions. A few reminders will suffice here. The defence are free to attack the veracity of police witnesses, but should only do so on responsible information, which will normally be supported by the accused's evidence; otherwise the challenge may be open to criticism. Defence advocates often seem to shrink from such confrontations by suggesting that police witnesses are mistaken about facts which they clearly know, so that they must be either truthful or untruthful.

If the accused has a criminal record, the defence advocate should consider whether such a challenge may amount to an imputation against police witnesses which exposes the accused to cross-examination on his record. If the accused has no criminal record or it is insignificant, it may help to obtain confirmation of that from a police witness.

Common weaknesses in any attack on the truthfulness of police witnesses are the suspect motivations and, perhaps, poor character of the accused, the exemplary record of the police officers, the serious consequences of such misconduct, and the lack of explanation for it.

The defence advocate must be prepared for such difficulties and should try to meet them where he can, in the course of cross-examination and, where possible, by leading other supporting evidence, in addition to that of the defendant.

## 2   Complainants

The evidence of complainants is normally led to support the proof that the crime was committed or the identification of the offender, or both. Since only one of these matters is normally in dispute, it alone will be the subject of defence cross-examination, even where the complainant saw the whole incident. But a complainant who was not an eyewitness, may sometimes be cross-examined on some relevant point, e g, to challenge a householder's identification of a stolen television.

Cross-examination about the crime may be considered first, distinguishing between challenges to evidence as mistaken or as untruthful.

If the complainant was an eyewitness to the whole crime, to attack his evidence as mistaken may only seem reasonable if it refers to obscure or ambiguous facts, e g, whether or not a tresspasser in his garden at night, was trying to force the french windows. If the facts were stark, e g, in a charge of menacing the householder with a hammer in the house, he could hardly be mistaken about that.

But where lying about the crime is the basis of cross-examining a complainant, some motive for inventing the crime should be shown or suggested. Typical motives are hostility or malice arising from prior relationship, or the event itself, or the complainant's attempt to exonerate himself from blame in the event, or to gain from it.

Hostility arising from prior relationship is the issue where a rejected wife's evidence that her husband attacked her is said to be false. The parties' relationship and the wife's motives would be relevant subjects for cross-examination.

In sexual offences not involving intercourse, the intangible nature of the evidence may open the door to false accusations, inspired by malice, e g, where schoolgirls make a false complaint of indecency against a male physical instructor who reported them to the headmaster for smoking in school.

Hostility arising from the event itself is shown where the complainant and defendant, although they did not know each other before, become hostile in or as a result of the incident, as where an argument is followed by a fight, and only one party is charged with assault.

The challenges to the complainant may range all the way from suggesting that he was the real offender, e g, where self-defence is pleaded, to accusations that he is exaggerating the crime maliciously, e g, where a victim of an assault attributes his head injuries to an attack with a brick, whereas the defence is that he slipped and struck his head on the pavement in a minor struggle.

In a charge of rape, it may be alleged that the complainant consented to intercourse but decided to lie about this because of the circumstances arising from the event, e g, discovery by her husband or parents.

A complainant may be said to be lying about the crime with which the defendant is charged, in order to exonerate himself from a criminal charge, e g, motorists in accidents often blame each other for the careless driving which caused them. (Similar situations which often arise with accomplices or co-defendants, will be considered separately.)

A cross-examiner may suggest that a complainant is lying for gain, e g, that a householder is inflating the list of unrecovered stolen goods falsely with a view to augmenting his insurance claim.

Apart from the types of challenge mentioned, another form is not uncommon, where a police officer is alleged to be lying about a non-existent crime out of malice alone, which led him to arrest the defendant and charge him with the crime, without any grounds at all. Often this refers to some form of disorderly conduct.

In cross-examining the complainant in all such situations on the basis that he or she is lying about the crime, a central line of enquiry is to expose and lay bare his or her motive, e g, malice, hostility, self-exoneration or gain—which may not be exhaustive. It cannot be expected that the complainant will admit to lying. A successful cross-examination will need to establish facts and circumstances from which this can be inferred, at least to the extent of creating a reasonable doubt about whether the crime was committed.

This may involve some probing of the past relationship of the parties, or the collateral circumstances of the incident, which would always, of course, have to be within reasonable bounds on pain of exclusion as irrelevant or remote.

It should also be stressed that however important the evidence relating to the complainant's motive may be, this is only one element in the whole picture. A cross-examiner would also tackle other objective defects in the complainant's evidence such as inconsistency or improbability. His immediate aim would be so to weaken that evidence that his own contradictory evidence would overcome it.

The question of whether or not the crime was committed will be settled in the light of the whole of the evidence given by all witnesses, perhaps including the defendant. This may include other eyewitness evidence or circumstantial evidence.

Where the real issue is the identification of the accused, complainants who were eyewitnesses are most commonly challenged as being mistaken.

This possibility must always be taken seriously, especially where witnesses are not familiar with the offender or the accused. Where a complainant's visual identification is crucial, if the defence can sow reasonable doubt about its reliability, that should be sufficient for their purpose, even if they cannot establish misidentification firmly. The cross-examination would follow lines already discussed.

It is uncommon for cross-examiners to accuse complainants of lying about the identification of the accused as the offender: to lie in this way a complainant would have to be so strongly motivated as to be both prepared to commit perjury and to be responsible for convicting an innocent person.

But such an attack is sometimes made on police eyewitnesses, e g, by suggesting that in a riot at a football match, they decided, improperly, to incriminate all the members of a group, without knowing what the defendant was doing personally.

Occasionally, defence allegations go further, even to the extreme of a police conspiracy to convict the accused, including the 'planting' of exhibits so as to incriminate him, perhaps as a cover-up for a crime committed by the officers themselves. Evidence is to be expected in support of such grave and substantial charges, since the defence is unlikely to succeed by cross-examination alone.

In attacking the evidence of police complainants as untruthful, defence cross-examination would consist of techniques discussed already. The character of the witnesses is unlikely to be blemished or attacked, but evidence of facts may be drawn out from which their improper motives could be inferred. Any self-contradiction in the evidence of any such witness, and any inconsistencies when the evidence of several is compared, would be exploited. Any improbabilities in their evidence would be intensified in relation to collateral circumstances.

If the accused has a criminal record, such imputations against police witnesses would deprive him of his shield against cross-examination as to his character by the prosecutor, which may be expected, together with an attack on the character of other defence witnesses who also have a record. Otherwise, the prosecutor's cross-examination would follow similar lines to that of the defence, in which he sought to reverse anything which the defence had achieved.

Where two groups of youths are involved in violence, and some are charged with assault, the defence may contend that a complainant is casting his net too widely by implicating an uninvolved accused from the opposite group. But while a victim might include someone as an assailant, wrongly and out of animosity, he would be unlikely to omit the real culprit towards whom he had good reason to feel hostile. Thus, if there is only one defendant, it might seem odd that a victim would exonerate the real culprit who attacked him, and incriminate an innocent person who did him no harm.

The distinction between alleging mistakes and alleging lies is not absolute in practice. Less stark forms of deception than outright perjury were discussed, i e, reluctance and evasiveness, omissions and false qualifications. The last category is important here.

Obviously, a witness's doubtful identification may be influenced by suggestion and the pressure of circumstances until it becomes more positive than it really should be. If, as is often the case, the witness is really unaware that he is bending his evidence, and he firmly identifies the wrong person, this would be classed as a mistake.

But to the extent that the witness is aware that he is yielding to any form of influence and he colours his degree of confidence in his identification intentionally, this is a false qualification which belongs rather to the realm of half-truths and deception than that of mistakes. Such an identification would contain both a genuine element, i e, the witness's belief that he was identifying the proper person, and a false element, i e, the witness's assertion that he is sure, when in fact he is not.

Complainants are often in a position where they may be vulnerable to influence, e g, the elderly lady whose house was burgled, and who appreciates all the consideration and trouble of the police in recovering her valuables and in catching a suspect. She thinks that the man whom she picked out at the identification parade, with some hesitation, and who is in the dock, is the man she saw climbing out of her window. From gratitude, the feeling that the police know what they are doing, and reluctance to cause any trouble, she confirms her identification firmly in court.

Such motivational patterns are often not far from intentional mis-statements, which can matter greatly. Degrees of confidence in identifications can range from certainty at one extreme to no more than thinking that there is some resemblance at the other. Because of the subjectivity of visual identification and its role in the criminal process, doubts like this which would not matter in describing a galloping horse, may be crucial to a verdict. Defence cross-examination of complainants as to identification should be thorough and should cover this twilight zone of half-intentional denial of doubts.

As always, when private psychological processes are in issue, direct questions about them may be unproductive—although they have to be asked, if only to inform the court of the cross-examiner's contentions. However, he should seek to elicit facts from which doubts about the identification or influences on it may be inferred.

## 3  Accomplices

The class of prosecution witnesses, denoted by 'accomplice' and when warnings or corroboration are required, are governed by rules of evidence. Here, since the concern is with tactics, the term 'accomplice' is used in the general sense of the word and not in that legal sense.

The testimony of accomplices has always been viewed with

caution. Their characters and motives are usually suspect. The witness may be a self-confessed offender, willing to betray the defendant, who testifies to get immunity or a lighter sentence. Often, he has an interest in the evidence or the verdict. For his own purposes, he might incriminate the defendant falsely, e g, to exonerate a friend, or he may minimize his own role in a crime, and exaggerate that of the defendant.

As the witness is an accomplice, this implies that it is not the crime, but rather the defendant's implication in it which is the issue.

Defence cross-examination of an accomplice usually has a flying start: his involvement, and perhaps his criminal record would be revealed in his evidence-in-chief. The cross-examiner will emphasize his motivations, aiming to discredit him and make his protestations of truthfulness sound hollow and unconvincing. Hesitancy, reluctance, inconsistency or improbability are often seen in such evidence as a result of the dilemma of choosing the expected gain from giving the evidence, and unwillingness to incriminate the accused, perhaps combined with fear of reprisals. A competent cross-examiner should be able to show that such evidence per se is too unreliable as a basis for conviction or even to support it, although of course there may be other trustworthy evidence to implicate the defendant.

## 4 Children

Children are often called as witnesses for the prosecution and typically in cases involving indecency. This section refers to those who are competent witnesses.

Psychological research has yielded no established body of knowledge to help cross-examiners in testing the reliability or credibility of children's evidence. This has to be said because of the current public debate on this subject. In any event, where a witness is accepted as competent, it is inappropriate that any such general findings should have any significance. It is the quality of the evidence given by a particular child in a particular case which must be evaluated by a particular court.

Current public opinion about the evidence of children is so intense that cross-examiners ought to have regard to its possible effect on the views of jurors or lay magistrates. Mounting concern about the incidence of child abuse and the need to prosecute it is off-set by widespread anxiety about the psychological effects of the trial process on child witnesses. The need to protect an accused's right to a fair trial is another recognized factor. These considerations do not coincide, and may lead in different directions. Proposals and counter-proposals for taking the evidence of children abound, and procedural changes are in contemplation.

For advocates, the immediate difficulty with child witnesses is neither the reliability nor the credibility of their evidence: such problems arise and are dealt with constantly in adult witnesses. The real obstacle is that child witnesses are so often inarticulate and tongue-tied, especially in the sensitive areas of their testimony.

Despite all the steps taken by the court and advocates to put children at their ease, and the presence of a parent, they are often subdued, their speech is often inaudible, and they may even not answer some questions at all. This can only be met by encouragement and sometimes by a little harmless humour, but not by threats or anything which makes them even more anxious.

In examination-in-chief, unless a certain amount of leading is allowed with defence consent, it might often be impossible to obtain any coherent account at all. But the quality of the evidence given by a child in response to leading gives a court very little guidance, since the evidence is often limited to 'Yes' or 'No' answers.

The defence have to conduct a cross-examination in these difficult conditions, and usually in an atmosphere which is unsympathetic to any possibility of harassing or upsetting the child. Above all, patience, tact and consideration are necessary. This is not an ideal forum in which the art of cross-examination can flourish.

Accordingly, while the defence advocate is entitled to and must often cross-examine on some topics in the interests of the accused, he should make the most of any measures other than forceful cross-examination which are open to him. It may upset a child, and may be unnecessary, to drive a point home in cross-examination such as inconsistency or improbability. Moreover any harassment may invite the intervention of the bench, or have an unpredictable effect on a jury's verdict. The point can usually be made in the speech.

If as much as possible is left for a forceful argument in the closing speech, the court is likely to appreciate this and to take the defence advocate's tact and restraint into account. He should certainly emphasize the burden of proof borne by the Crown, the exacting standard of proof beyond reasonable doubt, and the grave danger of basing a conviction on the testimony of a relatively inarticulate child witness.

Other courses open to the defence are, of course, to cross-examine prosecution witnesses other than children, as forcefully as may be necessary, and to lead evidence, including, if so advised, that of the defendant.

Having set up the framework within which cross-examination of child witnesses generally occurs, some comments on the process may be helpful. The cross-examiner's task may vary greatly according to what exactly is in issue.

If the question is whether the crime was committed, medical evidence of physical signs, such as of intercourse, may reduce the evidence required from the victim, but may not be conclusive by itself, e g, where physical signs on a mature female child could have been caused by intercourse or by using a tampon. Here again the child's evidence may be vital, although sometimes a mother can give relevant and admissible information.

But where the disputed crime consists of alleged acts of indecency, which left no physical traces that expert evidence can support, it is generally very difficult to take a child's evidence in the form of an exact description of such acts, and even more difficult to cross-examine about it.

Resort may be had to diagrams, gestures, anatomical dolls, and euphemisms or popular terms for sexual parts or acts.

In such intangible conduct-crimes, which leave no physical signs on the victim to confirm what was done, the direct evidence is crucial and often stands alone more or less, with no eyewitnesses to what took place between the complainant and the defendant. Unfortunately, here, where the child's evidence has great importance, both the prosecutor and the defence advocate may face difficulties in extracting testimony.

The situation may sometimes be less tense for the child where the issue is one of identification, but again, difficulties could arise if the defendant is a close relative towards whom the child has mixed feelings, or perhaps a stranger of whom the child is still afraid.

Whether the commission of the crime or the defendant's implication is the issue, in cases involving children, a cross-examiner should strive to obtain whatever help he can from collateral facts, e g, the absence of an immediate complaint by the child, although he or she had opportunities for this, or the facts concerning the defendant's normal relationship to the child, if any, or how he came to have access to the child otherwise.

A final qualification to everything said on this subject would not be amiss. The age and individuality of a child witness can make a vast difference to performance in court. A few may sail through the proceedings with the aplomb of adult witnesses, in which case the cross-examiner may not encounter the difficulties mentioned, to such a great extent or at all.

## 5    Expert witnesses

An expert witness is one whom the court recognizes as having special knowledge of a subject through qualification, training or experience so that he is allowed to state opinions on matters outwith the knowledge or experience of the ordinary lay person. With the advance of science, increasing use is being made of expert witnesses, mainly by the prosecution who are better able to bear the expense. They have been included here as prosecution witnesses, but substantially this section also refers to cross-examination of expert witnesses called for the defence.

Expert evidence may support proof of the crime, e g, if given by experts in fire-raising or explosions. Medical evidence of a victim's injuries is common.

Expert evidence may help in the identification of the offender, e g, if given by fingerprint experts. Forensic science is developing rapidly and can often establish traces of the offender at a locus or on a victim, or traces on the offender or his clothing, of the victim or the locus.

An advocate should prepare for any technical cross-examination of an expert witness by such study of the subject as is necessary. He should master the contents of reports provided by expert witnesses on either side.

Questions of the admissibility of expert opinion evidence belong to texts on the law of evidence. It is assumed here that the witness is accepted as an expert, but that does not necessarily end the matter. He should not be asked for an opinion on a point which is outwith his field. He may be an expert on some aspects of the facts in issue, but not on others, e g, a neurophysiologist should not give a psychiatric opinion. Objection should be taken if boundaries are overstepped.

An expert's qualifications may affect the weight of his opinion, especially if other experts disagree. The qualifications are usually excellent in themselves, but sometimes a witness's status in relation to the fact in issue may be undermined. A cross-examiner may explore some aspects of his qualifications, e g, degrees, training, positions held, membership of professional associations, or the special field of expertise and how it was gained, with apparent approval, not to enhance the witness's status, but to build up a picture of his experience, in order to show that it does not equip him to give the opinion which he has stated.

To do this well can be impressive, but the cross-examiner should be sure of his ground and of the demarcation lines between fields of expertise. He should consult any expert witness about this, whom he intends to call himself.

A similar type of question, which may be risky unless a favourable answer is reasonably predictable, is to ask the witness how many times he has had actual experience of an identical situation. A pointer to doing this is that the technical question is something very exceptional.

Such cross-examination which suggests that the expert witness is stepping out of line, need not go as far as raising a belated objection to the admissibility of the opinion which he has stated, especially if he may be marginally entitled to give it. But it may weaken its effect.

It would be exceptional to attack expert evidence as untruthful, although such a possibility cannot be excluded. The usual grounds of challenge are that the expert has based his opinion on facts which are incorrect, or has drawn the wrong inference from them. In support of the criticism of his inference, facts suggesting one-sidedness or bias may be suggested tactfully. Of course if the opinion is correct, a cross-examiner should not expect to destroy it, but that is for the court to decide. Moreover, even if the opinion is wrong, as is the case with all evidence it may be weakened but not destroyed at the time, and could then be defeated by contradictory evidence. But if the expert evidence is crucial to the Crown case, this may be defeated by cross-examination alone, which raises a reasonable doubt about some essential fact.

Apart from challenging an expert's evidence in the ways stated, a cross-examiner would incur a risk in opposing technical points in the expert's field and which the witness has prepared himself to deal with in the trial. Here, an experienced expert witness could intensify the damage to the defence case.

But it could help a cross-examiner to ask the witness to explain technical terms and concepts, or jargon, in plain language. Once the mystique and fog of terminology are removed, ordinary facts may be revealed which a jury can assess on a common-sense basis, with less reliance on the expert.

Before embarking on any form of destructive cross-examination, it would generally be best for the defence advocate to cross-examine constructively, viz by emphasizing helpful facts, or eliciting new facts which could assist his case. It is best to do this at the outset when the witness, not yet having been challenged, is likely to be at his most co-operative.

The constructive technique discussed above of seeking to elicit new meanings, when applied to an expert's opinion, can hardly be separated from destroying the meanings which he attaches to the facts, so that both constructive and destructive tactics might be interwoven in this situation.

Expert witnesses may give evidence of both facts and opinions. They may report facts which are inaccessible to lay witnesses, e g, the alcohol content of the deceased's stomach in a post-mortem examination. But cross-examination is usually aimed at inferences drawn from facts to which the expert has applied his special knowledge.

In the examination-in-chief, the prosecutor should have caused the expert witness to state the facts on which he based his opinion, and which must be proved by admissible evidence given by the expert or other witnesses. The court can then evaluate the expert's opinion. Neither information given to an expert witness out of court, nor hypotheses put to him in the trial, are evidence.

In cross-examining an expert witness, either the factual basis of an inference, or the inference may be challenged.

To challenge the factual basis, a first step is to establish what it is, if this was not brought out properly in the evidence-in-chief. This having been done, any such facts in dispute which depend on the expert's observation, would be dealt with in the ordinary way, in cross-examining him, or where they depend on the observation of other witnesses, these too would be cross-examined about them.

The cross-examiner could ask the expert to accept that his opinion is based on facts which are in dispute, and that he cannot personally deny that they may be otherwise, or be as the cross-examiner asserts. If so, a key question is whether he agrees that on the basis of the alternative facts, his conclusions would be different, and, if so, what they would be. To resist this reasonable line of questioning might suggest bias.

Cross-examination should expose any inadmissible factual basis for an expert's evidence, viz, hearsay or facts put to him hypothetically in court. Any confusion should be eliminated which might give a jury the impression that facts in dispute, or which are not the subject of admissible evidence, are somehow validated by the expert's opinion, e g, where the prosecutor's hypothetical questions led the expert to agree that his findings were consistent with some version of non-technical facts in issue.

The expert could be brought to confirm that 'consistency' here only means that the prosecution version of the facts could co-exist with his findings, but that this did not tend, in any way, to prove those facts.

In cross-examining as to the inference from the facts, new meanings may be suggested. The witness's response may range from accepting them to outright rejection.

But however the witness responds, the cross-examiner will usually gain in some way. Merely putting the questions suggests the alternative interpretations to the court. If the witness accepts them, or responds to them favourably, good progress has been made. If the suggestions are reasonable, but he rejects them dogmatically, he may discredit himself as biased. The evidence would only be harmful if the cross-examiner suggested an unreasonable inference from the facts.

Although it would be exceptional to suggest that an expert witness was lying, questions of bias and partiality do arise. As a background to cross-examination, the following considerations may be kept in mind.

Expert witnesses are expected to comply with the oath which they take, like any witnesses. Many must conform to the standards of the professions to which they belong. Indeed, expert witnesses are often eminent in their fields. They are also independent witnesses in the sense of having no direct connection with the case. They are generally treated by advocates as persons of integrity.

But on the other hand, expert witnesses are not independent assessors appointed by the court. They have entered the arena. They are instructed and paid by one of the parties in an adversarial conflict. An expert may appear in court regularly for the Crown, or for a particular firm of solicitors to the extent that he becomes a professional witness with a continuous relationship with his client. Experts may be consulted during the preparation of the case. Sometimes they remain in court to hear other evidence before testifying. Their time is expensive, and lawyers may try to derive the greatest benefit from this by consulting them during the trial. This places the expert in the dilemma of being, on the one hand, a partisan adviser in an adversarial contest, and on the other, an impartial witness.

Also, an expert may have committed himself to certain views in a written report provided to the party who instructed him, and perhaps produced in court, on the basis of which he was called as a witness. He might, understandably, be reluctant to change those views under cross-examination and there may be a risk that he might present information selectively for persuasive effect to support a mistaken opinion.

That this can happen is suggested by the fact that equally well-qualified expert witnesses on opposite sides often disagree completely, particularly in interpretative fields like psychiatry.

Where expert evidence is influenced in such ways, unintentionally, battles of experts may occur and a few may be open to attack in cross-examination as guns for hire.

A cross-examiner's duty is to the party whom he represents, and to the court. He need assume nothing. If he has reason to test or challenge expert evidence on grounds which imply partiality, e g, as mistaken, one-sided, biased, unreasonable or dogmatic, he should not hesitate to do so—especially if he does it on the advice of his own expert. It would, however, be proper to do this without hostility, and within the bounds of good taste, courtesy and respect.

Even where no substantial challenge of expert evidence is made, it is often a good tactic to ask just one or two questions to prevent the evidence seeming to be beyond criticism.

# B   Defence witnesses

In cross-examining, a prosecutor's overall aim is to destroy any defence evidence which may leave a reasonable doubt about the essentials of his case, whereas the defence need only raise a reasonable doubt to succeed. But a prosecutor not only has a more exacting task than a defence advocate; he is restricted by his role as a public official who merely presents a case to the court for decision. He must be fair, and be seen to be so. He must not cross-examine oppressively, or go all out for victory at all costs. Indeed, if defence evidence is strong enough, he may even not seek conviction.

## 1   Defendant

The prosecutor's reasonable attitude should be seen most obviously, in his cross-examination of the defendant.

The defendant, in evidence, will contend either that the crime was not committed or that he was not the offender. Some techniques of cross-examination have little application here.

Constructive techniques whereby favourable concessions are obtained from a witness, are rarely of use here. A defendant cannot be expected to concede anything. But the constructive technique in which a party puts his whole alternative case to a witness who knows the facts, must of course be employed by the prosecutor. This is usually done at the end of the cross-examination—often by a brief and comprehensive question containing the essential elements, viz to the effect that the defendant committed the crime charged, which only permits of a simple denial, whether he is innocent or guilty.

To put all the incidental facts to the acused, *seriatim*, will just elicit detailed denials. This may sometimes be done for emphasis by repetition, but this is usually unnecessary where the facts have been gone over again and again.

In cross-examining a defendant, the destructive techniques will normally be limited to those which are applied to a lying witness. It is not inconceivable that an accused person could be mistaken about his innocence. Scenarios could be imagined in which he had amnesia after a blow to the head in a fight, or in which he was genuinely unaware that the pedestrian was killed by the motor car which he was driving, and not by another. But such situations would be exceptional. Normally, the prosecutor proceeds on the basis that the defendant must know the truth, and that since he denies it, he must be lying. If the defendant is in fact innocent, that line of cross-examination should fail.

It is often advisable for a prosecutor to start his cross-examination of the defendant mildly, giving him every chance to reply, and without undue pressure. If the defendant is being obstructive, evasive, inconsistent, or becomes a difficult witness in any way, the need for firm or forceful cross-examination will emerge by itself, and it can then be undertaken with the tacit approval of the jury.

Among the destructive tactics for cross-examining a liar, some are unsuitable with an accused. Indirect tactics to lead him into a trap are less likely to succeed with the defendant who, truthful or not, distrusts the cross-examiner completely.

Direct tactics remain, as the method of choice, but even here, there is a major exclusion. A prosecutor may only attack a defendant's character in circumstances which are strictly defined by statute and which do not arise in the majority of trials. This refers only to evidence of bad character in relation to credit, and not as evidence of guilt by showing a prior disposition to act in the way charged; similar fact evidence is not considered here.

As a result of all these restrictions, to which, of course there may be exceptions a prosecutor's typical method of cross-examining a defendant is usually an open and direct challenge to his truthfulness, which focuses on any inconsistencies or improbabilities which can be found in his evidence, or on comparing it with other defence evidence, as well as the contradictory evidence of Crown witnesses.

Where, as is usual, character cannot be attacked in the sense of eliciting evidence of previous convictions, unimpressive features of the personality and motives of an accused who is lying, often emerge while the evidence is being probed objectively.

The defendant's response to inconsistencies in his own or other defence evidence is often significant. An improbable story may be made worse by amplification and exploration of collateral circumstances. The lack of realism in his evidence, on the lines discussed earlier, may become manifest. The ineffectuality of his denial of contradictory facts spoken to by Crown witnesses, with which he is confronted, may be obvious. But however damaging his cross-examination may be, a prosecutor should not expect it to destroy the accused's evidence there and then, in the sense that he will break down and confess. The realistic aim should be to weaken it as much as possible, so that it succumbs, after final arguments, to prosecution evidence which is accepted and leaves no reasonable doubt about guilt.

Where the crime is in issue, what is in question is likely to be some intangible element, e g, the accused's intention, or some intangible form of crime, e g, a threat with a knife. The cross-examination of the accused, and his response to it may be crucial to the verdict.

Where the issue is whether the accused was responsible for the crime, he may concede that he was at the scene but took no part in it, or he may deny that he was present, with or without the added defence of alibi.

In the first situation, the accused's identity is not in doubt, but he may have to explain why he was at the locus and what he was doing there. It is one thing to be at a football match where a riot occurred, and another to be seen at or near a broken shop window at 3 a m far from home.

The question in this kind of situation is that of relating admitted identity to observed actions, or to inference, not one of visual identification. Eyewitness evidence might have been led for the prosecution, which related the accused to what was done, and which he denies. The accused might be confronted with descriptions of his conduct derived from that eyewitness evidence. If the eyewitnesses were police officers, he might claim that they were lying. If the eyewitnesses were independent lay persons, to suggest that they were lying, may be so improbable as to shatter the defence. Finally, if the accused, says that lay eyewitnesses must be mistaken, the outcome may depend on their number, lack of connection or discussion with each other, and the effect of ordinary obstacles to observation which have been considered.

Special features may be found in such situations, where the accused is charged along with others as co-defendants, depending on whether they incriminate or support each other in evidence.

Apart from this, where presence at that place at that time is, per se, suspicious, there is scope for destructive cross-examination applied to the explanation for this which the accused gives. Often this raises questions of improbability, e g, the accused claims that when the police car arrived he was simply passing the broken shop window with a girl whom he met at a disco and who hid in a lane. He is not helped by the facts that she is not a witness, and that he does not recall her surname or address.

Where an accused simply denies that he was at the locus of the crime when it occurred, without specifying where he was at that time, this may raise typical problems of visual identification, circumstantial evidence, or confession, of the types already discussed.

This is also the case where the accused speaks to an alibi. If it is genuine, it should prevail. If it is false, the accused and his supporting witnesses will be exposed to the range of tactics which can destroy an invented story spoken to by several witnesses as well as contradictory evidence from Crown witnesses. This has already been discussed.

A prosecutor should not fail to cross-examine a defendant about any confessions or admissions spoken to by police witnesses, and which the defendant denies.

An accused can seldom claim, convincingly, that a report by a police witness that he admitted his guilt is mistaken, where this has been noted in the witness's notebook, and is also spoken to by another officer. If such a report is inaccurate, it must proceed from lying in collusion. Here, again, a defendant may have difficulty in persuading the court of this.

## 2   *Special classes of defence witness*

Some witnesses, linked in some way with the accused, fall into special classes under the rules of evidence, viz the defendant's spouse, co-defendants and the spouses of co-defendants. Provisions, which are not the subject of this book, govern the competence and compellability of such persons as defence or prosecution witnesses, rights of cross-examination, the need for warnings or corroboration, and the extent of judicial discretion.

Their evidence is often highly motivated. Spouses may become reluctant to give incriminating evidence, and often depart from previous inconsistent statements. Co-defendants may support each other but a court may be critical of the weight of such evidence. Co-defendants may also blame each other in a 'cut-throat defence' which, again, may be suspect. Cross-examination by a prosecutor is assisted by the fact that such motives are obvious, although what this means in relation to the facts will depend on the context of the whole of the evidence.

## 3   *Other defence witnesses*

With regard to cross-examination of defence witnesses other than those in the above special classes, a practical division of importance to the prosecutor is into witnesses who are connected with the defendant in any way, and those who are independent.

A prosecutor may probe possible links between the witness and the accused, e g, those which may arise from family relationship, friendship, or being neighbours or fellow-employees. If there is some relationship which was not brought out in evidence-in-chief, this may not enhance the court's view of the witness's credit nor the defence advocate's candour.

The existence of a connection between the witness and the defendant may have a bearing on the credibility of the evidence, and on the prosecutor's approach. He is more likely to treat such witnesses as untruthful than to suggest untruthfulness in regard to independent witnesses.

The evidence led for the defence may be eyewitness testimony about the incident under enquiry.

If such evidence is given by witnesses who are closely associated with the accused, the prosecutor is likely to attack it as untruthful since it may be motivated, e g, where a man denies that his brother assaulted a police officer at a football match. But a jury might think that such witnesses could be motivated to support an innocent as well as a guilty accused.

In view of the prudence of maintaining rapport with a jury, and his own role, it might be counter-productive for a prosecutor to start the cross-examination of such witnesses in a hostile and obviously sceptical way. It may be better to begin in a neutral way, perhaps with indirect tactics, allowing the need for direct and forceful attack on the witness's veracity to emerge from his obviously unsatisfactory evidence, as the jury will then understand.

If the eyewitnesses are accepted as independent and sincere, but mistaken, the prosecutor should show this by his way of cross-examining them. After probing how mistakes could have arisen, and suggesting this, he might lead witnesses who are impartial to concede doubts, or by means of constructive tactics, to give favourable evidence, although unrealized partisanship and loyalty to the defence who called them may be an impediment.

Circumstantial evidence from which a fact in issue may be inferred, is most common in prosecution cases but such evidence may also be led for the defence. Sometimes it is true, and sometimes it is simply an elaborate invention to off-set incriminating circumstantial or direct evidence.

If the inference could be material, and the prosecutor disputes the factual basis, he will again tend to cross-examine defence witnesses who are closely associated with the accused, as untruthful, and independent witnesses as mistaken. On the other hand without disputing the facts, he might attack the inference when it forms part of direct evidence given by the defendant, as well as in his closing speech.

Defence witnesses who give alibi evidence tend, mostly, to be persons associated with the defendant—which, of course, need have no sinister significance per se. These are the people in whose company he might be expected to be. There is generally little chance of a mistake in a detailed alibi which has been worked out, checked, and discussed by the witnesses, unless about dates. Usually, a prosecutor will cross-examine alibi witnesses associated with the accused on the basis that he and they are lying.

An independent witness to an alibi is likely to be challenged as mistaken in his identification of the accused, or about the date or time of the incident.

If witnesses associated with the accused give untruthful eyewitness evidence, circumstantial evidence or alibi evidence, as the prosecutor will contend, they must have planned it before the trial, and will try to monitor evidence given in the course of the trial so far as they can.

Such witnesses know each other and have the opportunity to meet easily and frequently. Their original motives, to help the accused, may have been weaker than his, but once these witnesses are involved in the criminal project of committing perjury, their motives must be intensified by concern to protect themselves. They cannot afford to treat the risks casually.

Monitoring and reporting prosecution or defence evidence to defence witnesses, so they can adjust false stories for consistency, or to meet some difficulty, can only be excluded totally in a short summary trial, not interrupted by lunch, and where witnesses who have yet to testify, are completely secluded. Informants among the public, including witnesses who have already testified, may contrive to contact witnesses waiting to be called. In any summary trial which lasts for more than a day, and in jury trials, to prevent improper discussion of evidence is impossible.

For the prosecution, discussion of evidence by defence witnesses may be either a problem or an opportunity.

The problem is that it is by discussion that false evidence is planned or modified; the opportunity is that the evidence may be discredited if collusion is detected.

A good approach to probing pre-trial discussion is to establish the extent of mutual contact between witnesses: how, when, and for how long it happens. Even here, a collusive witness who sees the point, may start to become evasive, thus initiating the process of discrediting the defence story.

The witness may then be asked if he has discussed his evidence with other witnesses. Often, he will deny it, thus opening the door for the cross-examiner to show how improbable this is, especially if he has just established frequency of contact. The witness might be asked if some dramatic event in issue, is a commonplace happening or trifle in his experience, not worth talking about, or why he cared so little about the outcome of prosecution of his associate, yet was willing to testify on his behalf. He might be asked if he had deliberately avoided discussion, and if so, why.

If the witness admits discussion, he may be asked with whom, where, when, how often, and what it was about. This gives a basis for cross-examining other witnesses to the same effect, and comparing the answers. If one admits and the other denies discussion, something has been achieved. Similarly, there may be benefit in asking whether the witness was affected by or learned anything from, the discussion, and if so, what.

Possible contacts between witnesses in the course of a trial are often worth probing, e g, where they had lunch, where they were overnight, with whom they talked and what was talked about. In so many situations, to deny discussion is unreal, but to admit it is to become vulnerable.

The aim in cross-examining lying witnesses about whether they have discussed their evidence, is not the expectation that they will admit it; the aim is to demonstrate their bad faith by their denials, which lead to inconsistencies and improbabilities in their evidence. This can go some way towards discrediting them and tainting their evidence when it is challenged on objective grounds.

# CHAPTER 10

# Re-examination

## I   INTRODUCTION

Cross-examination occurs in a context which includes the limited potential of re-examination to restore the effect of the evidence-in-chief.

Re-examination is a method of repair. Its general aim is to counter any material harm caused by cross-examination. The specific approach will depend on the type of harm and how it arose.

Re-examination consists, mainly, of giving the witness a chance to add to or to qualify his testimony, by explaining what he said in cross-examination. Explanations can often reduce the effect of seemingly damaging admissions, or clarify something left in doubt, or which gave a wrong impression.

The right to re-examine a witness is governed by two main rules of evidence, viz it is confined to matters arising out of cross-examination, and leading questions are not permitted.

## II   MATTERS ARISING OUT OF CROSS-EXAMINATION

The restriction of re-examination to matters arising from cross-examination, allows witnesses to explain or expand the answers which they gave at that stage, but no new matter may be introduced.

The advocate who cross-examined the witness should object to any questions asked by his opponent which contravene this rule. An issue may then arise as to whether or not a topic was raised in cross-examination. This will present no difficulty if the topic was raised

expressly, but problems arise about lines of cross-examination
which only imply something, without bringing it out explicitly.

Generally, any testimony in cross-examination, being relevant to
the issues, would have some meaningful connection with other
topics which were also relevant to the issues, even if they were not
mentioned expressly. The distinction between matters raised in
cross-examination and other such matters, may not be absolute.
The scope of re-examination may depend on whether the rule is
interpreted narrowly or liberally.

In exceptional circumstances, re-examination might be allowed
on a new topic, with a further opportunity of cross-examination.

## III   NO LEADING QUESTIONS

In re-examination, the general rule excludes leading questions.
Objection should be taken to breach of this rule on material points.
Some advocates let this pass, hoping for similar indulgence, or to
avoid giving a bad impression to a jury.

The rule excluding leading questions refers only to disputed
matters. On uncontested facts, leading questions are allowed even
in examination-in-chief. In re-examination, then, to some extent,
an opponent's objection, or lack of it, may settle the admissibility of
a leading question.

What is, and what is not, in dispute will generally have been
defined, expressly or by implication, in the course of the cross-
examination. As was seen in chapter 2, in nearly every case, either
the issue of commission of the crime, or the identity of the offender,
becomes non-contentious sooner or later.

By the time any witness has reached the stage of re-examination,
and particularly if he is one of a party's later witnesses, the area of
uncontested facts is likely to have become defined and to have been
considerably expanded. Thus, despite the general rule, re-examination may offer the greatest scope for leading questions on
undisputed facts. But why should there be any need to ask further
questions about such points?

In re-examination, a leading question about undisputed matters
is an efficient way of directing a witness's attention rapidly to the
real point, and avoids a long series of non-leading questions to cover
complications introduced in cross-examination.

## IV   DECISION TO RE-EXAMINE

Judgment is needed in deciding whether to re-examine at all, or on what topics, and how. It should only be undertaken with a clear purpose and a reasonable prospect of success.

Re-examination is not a routine practice in criminal trials. Generally, it is the least important stage of taking evidence. It is often omitted, or is undertaken very briefly. When carried out, its main function is explanatory, rather than argumentative.

An advocate should not re-examine if cross-examination did not affect the evidence-in-chief materially, and left its main points undisturbed, or caused only slight, remote or potential harm. Unnecessary or bad re-examination only draws attention to the weakest points of the case and suggests that they are important, whereas ignoring them reduces attention and suggests that they do not count. To re-examine here is to help the opponent.

However, if material harm was caused, it is often of little or no help to re-examine. Saving the case may depend on other acceptable evidence.

Re-examination should not be carried out to explain every point where the main facts are clear or to emphasize anything in the evidence-in-chief, or to alter the case previously put forward.

If something material was omitted from both evidence-in-chief and cross-examination, from oversight or intentional tactics, it is too late to rectify this by re-examination.

While an advocate may re-examine on topics arising from cross-examination, he should not do so merely to emphasize any helpful evidence which his witness gave then. He can do this in his final speech.

There are other risks in re-examining on matters arising from cross-examination.

A line of cross-examination may have been curtailed because of uncertainty about possible answers, or else as a trap leading to unexpected material for the re-examiner. If, for some good reason, he thinks it necessary to follow this up, caution is advisable.

The above emphasis on the negative aspects of re-examination, explains its relative infrequency. However, it can help at times. Its form will then depend on the nature of the damage caused by cross-examination, and by what technique.

# V   COUNTERING CONSTRUCTIVE CROSS-EXAMINATION

Despite the problems connected with re-examination, it should sometimes be undertaken in response to either of two forms of constructive cross-examination, viz suggesting new meanings for undisputed facts, or introducing new facts.

In re-examination, an advocate should try to reverse new meanings which the cross-examiner insinuated for undisputed facts. He should use the same method, i e adjusting the evidence here and there in favour of the original interpretation as presented in the evidence-in-chief.

This may not be wholly successful. Once alternative possibilities have been realised, both are likely to remain in mind during the court's deliberations. However, the aim of re-examination here is to tilt the scales in favour of the desired meaning, rather than to eliminate the alternative.

If a cross-examiner elicits new and material facts in his favour, which must have been known to, and must be accepted by, the opponent, this will create a bad impression. The omission from the examination-in-chief will seem like concealment.

The legal duties of the prosecutor and defence advocate with regard to the omission of facts, and the tactical aspects, have already been discussed.

Difficulties of law and tactics, would face an advocate who tried to contest new facts brought out from his witness in cross-examination. He can only challenge his own witness in extreme circumstances where the court allows him to be treated as hostile. That does not follow simply because the evidence of a witness is damaging to the case of the party who called him.

Moreover, in re-examining to that effect, an advocate would be in the dilemma of opposing his own witness about some facts, while relying on him for others.

Thus, if new facts emerge in cross-examination which are adverse to the advocate who called the witness, some damage may be inevitable, no matter how he re-examines.

If an advocate has allowed himself to be caught in such a situation, the only point of re-examining, and all that he can hope to gain, if anything, is to elicit some explanation to colour his omission of the evidence from the examination-in-chief, i e to save face.

# VI  COUNTERING DESTRUCTIVE CROSS-EXAMINATION

Whether, and if so, how, to re-examine, to offset destructive cross-examination, depends on the extent of the damage. This may be graded as minimal, moderate, or severe, for the purpose of discussion.

If the damage was minimal with only a slight bearing on the issue, it is usually better to let it pass. To re-examine will focus attention on a potential weakness and may give it a significance which it would otherwise lack.

On the other hand, the damage may be severe, e g if a witness is exposed as a liar, or a story is shown to be absurd. If so, it would be extremely difficult or impossible, by re-examination, to restore evidence which has been virtually destroyed by cross-examination. Generally an advocate should not expect this to succeed, and to attempt it may only make matters worse. Unless he accepts defeat, he can only rely on other witnesses and argument.

Where cross-examination causes moderate harm, i e which is not conclusive, there may be some prospect that good re-examination can restore the position.

The best way to re-examine here would depend on what damage was done and how, whether mistake or lying is in issue, and whether the question for decision is the commission of the crime, or the identification of the accused as the offender.

To enumerate the exact methods of counteracting every type of destructive cross-examination would duplicate and invert much of the previous text. For practical purposes, a bold statement of a few principles should enable specific applications to be worked out for particular situations.

Confidence in the accuracy of evidence may have been put at risk by a challenge to the witness as mistaken or untruthful, or by criticism of the quality of his evidence, or both. One line implies the other. The witness's cognitive state, i e being mistaken or untruthful, must be reflected in inaccurate evidence, and vice versa. But one approach or the other is usually emphasized.

Where the witness was the main target, a key to the line and prospects of re-examination is how far this may have impaired the court's trust in him.

It is difficult to restore trust once it is lost, but it will not be extinguished merely by exposing an honest mistake in an isolated part of the witness's evidence, which leaves the rest, and his integrity, intact. Here, the remedial aim of re-examination would be to underline the witness's sincerity, and the objective grounds for holding that this part of his evidence is accurate.

If, point by point, a general challenge to the reliability of the witness's observation or memory was built up, any disputed part of his evidence may be suspect. Re-examination will then be more difficult, and may fail to restore confidence in him. All is not necessarily lost, however. It may be contended that while the witness may not merit reliance, he is not necessarily wrong. Other witnesses could then provide the needed evidence.

However, the worst prospect for re-examination is where cross-examination raises such doubts about whether a witness is lying, that the whole of his disputed evidence is tainted with distrust.

The grounds of attack may have been the witness's attributes, e g bad character, motives for lying, or striking defects in the evidence, e g inconsistency or improbability. In combination, such factors may be devastating.

Re-examination about bad character or motivation seldom helps. If such facts emerge in cross-examination, they are probably beyond dispute. The inference to be drawn from them about veracity is what counts. The witness, may be expected, in re-examination, to deny perjury, but this repetition is unlikely to play a major role in the verdict. It is better to re-examine on such topics, only formally and briefly, if at all, and to leave the significance of character or motives for final argument, in the context of all the evidence.

It could be worthwhile to re-examine in order to refute alleged self-contradiction, as the basis for a claim that the witness is lying. The advocate may try to clarify, explain, or reconcile statements to show that even if they were vague, ambiguous or seemed incompatible, they were not really inconsistent. If this cannot be done, to re-examine may be pointless or may make matters worse.

Perhaps the attempt to discredit the witness was based on the improbability of his evidence, on matters ranging from single facts to his whole story. A skilful advocate can exploit this in cross-examination, especially with a weak witness, but on the other hand a skilful advocate may also be able to remedy it in re-examination. Improbable does not mean impossible, and what is unlikely may still be true.

Gross exaggeration of the improbability and how this was brought about, may be obvious to the court, and this can offer an opportunity for correcting the cross-examination, which should be taken in suitable situations. There is often a reasonable prospect of restoring the balance, by means of patient reconstruction in the desired direction.

Of course if the evidence has been exposed as patently absurd and ridiculous, re-examination should not be expected to defeat this.

If the real issue in the trial is whether or not the crime was committed, it is likely to be an intangible conduct-crime, or to depend on some intangible element. The reasons were explained in chapter 2, viz. that result-crimes are usually proved, uncontested, by overwhelming physical evidence, whereas intangible criminal situations are often in dispute, and proof depends on eyewitness evidence of the main incident.

If it was claimed in cross-examination that various obstacles to observation and memory, had led the witness into error about the commission of the crime, such a contention is often exaggerated and debatable. Difficulties of observation, forgetting, and suggestive influences often cause inaccuracy about the peripheral details, but do not lead inevitably to reporting the essential facts of a crime wrongly.

Where this kind of cross-examination may have done any damage, there is generally scope for restorative re-examination. Apart from such further evidence about the facts as may be needed, the witness may be guided into confirming his adherence to his account. If he is trusted, his confidence, and assurance that the facts are as he states, is likely to be more persuasive than the impediments to observation or recollection. Both in his examination-in-chief and in re-examination, the advocate who called the witness should be careful to maintain this trust by eliciting the evidence in a reasonable way, conceding difficulties if they are appropriate.

Intangible crimes or questions of fact, easily lend themselves to lying. Nothing is left after the incident to point one way or another. It is largely the word of one set of witnesses against another set, or even of one against another. The scope for re-examination to offset a challenge to the truthfulness of a witness has been discussed above.

Where the real issue in the trial is the visual identification of the accused as the offender by Crown witnesses, any doubt created about such evidence by cross-examination may be beyond the power of re-examination to remedy—particularly in view of the heavy burden of proof on the prosecution concerning this crucial fact. While trust in the witness, and a witness's self-assessment are important tests of accuracy as distinct from error, correct visual identification is not guaranteed by a witness's confidence alone. A sincere witness, who was quite sure of this, might still be mistaken.

Even if a re-examined witness reaffirms his certainty in a visual identification, that alone may not remove doubts which arose from cross-examination. It might be necessary for a prosecutor to support the identification by other witnesses or in other ways, e g, by circumstantial or forensic evidence, or admissions by the accused.

It has been seen that there are few opportunities for effective re-examination. The evidence obtained in examination-in-chief or in cross-examination, is more important. But where re-examination is in fact undertaken, it should be kept as short as possible.

# CHAPTER 11

# Cross-examination: speeches

In the closing speech, the case for the prosecution or defence should be crystallized. Having ensured that the issue is in sharp focus, an advocate should, as persuasively as possible, present his total view of the essential evidence, facts and law in support of his case, with concentrated impact, emphasizing what is important and meeting opponent's criticisms, or the court's possible doubts. Evidence should be summarized holistically, showing how it is interrelated, and contradictions should be highlighted.

This chapter does not set out to explore all these or other aspects of a closing speech. Limited by the theme of the book, it simply notes some salient points of closing speeches which are directly connected with cross-examination.

## I  SPEECH AS GUIDE TO CROSS-EXAMINATION

The format of a closing speech, drafted when preparing for trial and when there is time to think, towards which everything will converge, is the best overall guide to the aims of cross-examination and to swift tactical decisions.

Thus, the advocate is always ready for his final presentation, without hasty improvisation under pressure. Naturally this outline must be provisional and flexible enough to take account of what actually happens.

# II  COMPLETING CROSS-EXAMINATION

The process initiated by cross-examination is often completed in closing speeches.

This is most obvious where a cross-examiner has desisted from asking a final explicit question in order to avoid an unwanted answer. In his closing speech he can invite the court to reach the desired conclusion by inference.

A different, but related, situation is where the cross-examiner, having obtained a helpful answer, dropped that line of enquiry at once, to prevent the witness from retracting or qualifying it. A cross-examiner may also have wished to obscure the significance of the concession from the opponent who could otherwise have tried to rectify it in re-examination or by leading further evidence. Those dangers having passed, the advocate is then free to develop the favourable implications of the answer in his closing speech.

A further opportunity to complete cross-examination arises from the advocate's ability to show that what seem like molehills are really mountains.

In the closing speech the advocate may combine and build up seemingly unimportant elements taken from his cross-examination of single witnesses or several witnesses, to striking effect.

Whether cross-examination elicits helpful testimony or weakens harmful testimony, it is not completed if it is isolated, and not integrated somehow into the cross-examiner's case.

The importance of presenting a version of the facts in the form of a coherent story has been stressed earlier. An advocate's closing speech should ensure that important evidence which he obtained in cross-examination is integrated into the account which he presents, or is shown to be in conflict with the story which his opponent presents.

If a witness contradicts himself, a cross-examiner may either tackle him about it at that stage, or else leave the inconsistency to be exploited in his closing speech. Dealing with the inconsistency at the time is best where the witness cannot escape from his dilemma, and if his plight can be made worse. But if it is thought that he may extricate himself or change his evidence, it may be best to leave the coup de grâce until the final speech. So this is yet another form of completing the cross-examination in the closing speech.

If a cross-examiner draws two or more of the opponent's witnesses into conflicts of evidence, he has a similar choice.

To ask one witness, about facts spoken to by another may elicit inconsistencies, but a cross-examiner should not ask one witness to comment on another's evidence; his opinion is irrelevant.

In any event, whether or not inconsistencies were put to a

witness, a cross-examiner can bring them out and emphasize them in his closing speech. This is very common.

## III  MISTAKEN EVIDENCE

In a substantial amount of defence cross-examination, the evidence of Crown eyewitnesses as to a crime or to the identification of the accused is challenged by the defence as mistaken.

Where the commission of the crime is in issue, the defence argument that the evidence is mistaken, or too unreliable to prove guilt beyond reasonable doubt, will often be based on inconsistency, as a prominent part of their closing speech.

It is generally a weak and unsuccessful argument to exaggerate minor discrepancies which arise from the universal fallibility of observation and memory. Inaccuracy about secondary or peripheral facts is usually the result of what the witnesses were focusing their attention on, and does not mean that they cannot be trusted to report the main facts properly. It is common for witnesses to give an account which is accurate about the essentials although not accurate about details.

But other inconsistencies may be regarded as material or significant, i e as a sound reason for doubting the accuracy of some of the evidence in question. Such a contention will certainly be an important aspect of the closing speech for the defence, whether or not the points were made during the cross-examination.

Where eyewitness evidence is in conflict, and questions arise as to whether difficulties of observation or memory are responsible, a conclusive argument about this, one way or another, is seldom possible on that basis alone.

What is likely to prevail is the overall degree of trust or distrust which the court feels in the sincerity of the witness and the reliability of his self-assessment. Therefore, closing speeches should exploit any evidence which suggests flaws in the witness which could reduce confidence in him, e g, bias or irresponsibility.

Courts are now more receptive than ever to defence contentions that Crown witnesses may have misidentified the accused in error. Defence cross-examination will try to expose sources of error in observation or memory which could have led to mistaken identification, or which make it too unreliable to prove guilt beyond reasonable doubt.

Argument based on factors adverse to visual identification, may not be conclusive in itself, apart from extreme situations, in which event a judge might withdraw the case from a jury.

If the evidence incriminating the defendant is confined to visual identification, the court's view of the witnesses' state of mind and the trust placed in them and in their self-assessment, will be crucial. In this situation, the speech may emphasize everything which could affect the court's impression of any witness in these respects. Vital points may be the exact words used in making the identification at a parade or in court, the slightest hint of doubt as compared with assertions of certainty, questions of bias or sincerity and so on. A recurrent possibility of confusion is the distinction between recognition and resemblance, as expressed in the words 'It looks like him'.

Related questions may be the effects of delay, discussion between witnesses, or pre-trial police procedure, which could have affected the visual identification. This is material both for cross-examination and for emphasis in the closing speech.

There may also be incriminating evidence in the form of alleged admissions by the accused to the police. It is uphill work for the defence in cross-examination, to challenge officers, each of whom has noted a full confession in his notebook, as being mistaken, or to argue this in the final speech. If the objection has merit, it would suggest a joint hallucination.

Frequently, visual identification evidence is supported by, or even replaced by, circumstantial evidence from which an inference as to the accused's implication may be drawn.

Some circumstantial evidence is powerful, insofar as the factual basis is indisputable, and the inference to be drawn from it may be strong. Here, although the facts themselves were not challenged in cross-examination, the inference to be drawn from them is the subject of the closing speech for the defence.

In other cases, the factual basis may have been challenged in cross-examination, and there could be argument about that, as well as about the inference to be drawn, in the closing speech.

However, the closing speech for the defence will not simply carry forward the defence cross-examination. It will emphasize defence evidence, e g the accused's denial of guilt, and possibly alibi evidence. Major emphasis in the defence speech will also, probably, be placed on the Crown's burden of proof and the right to acquittal if there is any reasonable doubt about guilt.

# IV  LYING EVIDENCE

Cross-examination of witnesses who are treated as untruthful generally combines an attack on their credit with a challenge to their evidence as being inconsistent or improbable. To create distrust and expose implausibility are the cross-examiner's aims.

Sometimes, for reasons which were discussed, an advocate may be reluctant to charge a witness with lying, while he is actually under cross-examination. An advocate may lack confidence in the challenge; a defence advocate may fear that the defendant will lose his shield if imputations are made against Crown witnesses; or there may be good tactical reasons for not disclosing one's position.

If so, the closing speech is the time to specify that the allegation is that the witness was lying and not just mistaken.

Reference in closing speeches to inconsistency in evidence has already been discussed in regard to mistakes in testimony. The position is similar in relation to allegations of lying. However, both the cross-examination and the speech may go further by spreading the attack. Inconsistency due to lying may taint the evidence of one or more witnesses more widely than the immediate subject of inaccuracy. An able cross-examiner will often be able to show that the evidence of a witness as a whole should be regarded as unacceptable for this reason.

When evidence is challenged in cross-examination as being improbable, this is an excellent subject for development in the closing speech. The improbability may range from a single element in the opponent's case, to his whole story. The test is ordinary experience, and there is scope for extending initial improbability to the point of absurdity and ridicule, thus destroying credibility.

# V  CIRCUMSTANTIAL EVIDENCE

Circumstantial evidence may be challenged by disputing either the underlying facts or the inference to be drawn from them, and sometimes both.

Sometimes the underlying facts are virtually beyond dispute, e g a number of details of little importance in themselves, and which are only significant when they are considered together. Such minor facts are often spoken to by independent lay witnesses who have no connection with the case or each other. Their evidence is unlikely to be challenged in cross-examination, or disputed in speeches. If so, it may be better to concede it.

It is usually difficult to challenge the factual basis of circumstantial evidence of a medical, scientific or technical kind, spoken to by expert witnesses. Also, the status of such witnesses may lend weight to their views. However, expert evidence of this kind is regularly challenged, and this is likely to form an important part of a closing speech which reinforces cross-examination.

However, speeches in which circumstantial evidence is challenged, may be based not only on destructive cross-examination, but also on the constructive forms discussed earlier, which involved shifting of emphasis, creating new meanings, and eliciting new facts.

# VI   CONCESSIONS IN CLOSING SPEECHES

So far, the discussion in this chapter has focused on how an advocate can enhance his cross-examination in his closing speech. In suitable circumstances, he can also strengthen his speech by conceding points which were obviously made in his opponent's cross-examination.

Even where a closing speech is not compelling, it should at least have the overall quality of reasonableness. A court is always impressed by reasonable concessions; they tend to gain respect for the advocate and to place him on the judicial level of thinking, rather than giving the impression of blinkered partiality and unreasonable dogmatism.

One type of concession which is nearly always open to the defence, without harm, is to admit a main branch of the Crown case which is not really in dispute, viz either that the crime was committed, or that the defendant is the person who was involved in the situation under enquiry. This arises from the considerations discussed earlier to the effect that the real dispute is normally only about one of these issues. Where it is obvious that the Crown have proved the undisputed issue, to concede this gracefully may make a good impression.

Even with regard to the issue which remains, some facts may be beyond challenge, if they were the subject of compelling evidence which the opponent led, or admissions which he obtained in cross-examination.

Where the opponent exposed weaknesses by his cross-examination, which did or obviously will form part of his final argument, it is unimpressive to pretend that they do not exist. It is better to face up to, and make the best of, them.

This type of approach is in accordance with the best traditions, but regrettably, not with the universal practice, of advocacy. It is a question of bringing both intellectual honesty and the will to win into focus so that they coincide.

# Index